Separated

Separated

*Family and Community in the Aftermath
of an Immigration Raid*

William D. Lopez

Johns Hopkins University Press
Baltimore

© 2019 Johns Hopkins University Press
All rights reserved. Published 2019
Printed in the United States of America on acid-free paper
9 8 7 6 5 4 3 2 1

Johns Hopkins University Press
2715 North Charles Street
Baltimore, Maryland 21218-4363
www.press.jhu.edu

Cataloging-in-Publication Data is available from the Library of
Congress.

A catalog record for this book is available from the British Library.

ISBN-13: 978-1-4214-3331-8 (hardcover : alk. paper)
ISBN-10: 1-4214-3331-1 (hardcover : alk. paper)
ISBN-13: 978-1-4214-3332-5 (electronic)
ISBN-10: 1-4214-3332-X (electronic)

*Special discounts are available for bulk purchases of this book. For more
information, please contact Special Sales at 410-516-6936 or specialsales
@press.jhu.edu.*

Johns Hopkins University Press uses environmentally friendly book
materials, including recycled text paper that is composed of at least 30
percent post-consumer waste, whenever possible.

For Mia and Migs,
Never stop crossing borders. Never stop breaking down walls.
Never stop building bridges. Arriba y Adelante.

Anthropology that doesn't break your heart just isn't worth doing anymore.

—Ruth Behar, *The Vulnerable Observer*

Contents

Foreword

Ruth Behar

Victor Haim Perera Collegiate Professor of Anthropology,
University of Michigan

The stories in this book are so powerful and so powerfully told that I
suggest you sit down and start reading them right away. This is the first
book to address with compassion, eloquence, and profound firsthand
knowledge the immigration home raids taking place in the United States
at this very moment. This book will open your mind and your heart.

Honestly, I didn't think this book needed a foreword. But William was
my student, and he thought the book would benefit from a few words
about his work from his former teacher. What I can say is this: William
took my Ethnographic Writing graduate seminar at the University of
Michigan, and he ran with it. He has made ethnography the center of
his work and the result is a stunning book that offers unforgettable and
crucial insights about our era of deportations.

Ethnography is a relatively new genre in the history of writing. It
is a form of scholarship and self-expression based on slow, careful, and
intensive listening to the stories of others. Our aim is to understand
how people think about and talk about what is meaningful and what
is painful in their lives. In this storytelling and story-listening process,
those telling their stories open up to ethnographers, feeling an urgency
to share their stories and give us the gift of their lived experience. We, in
turn, the ethnographers, must carry those stories forward with integrity
and respect, so they can be heard by the world. We need stories. They
are what make us human. Stories move us, unsettle us, change us, help
us to find clarity in times of darkness.

The best ethnographers, and William is surely one of them, are those
who can tell the stories of others while making it clear to the reader where
they are positioned and how they are affected by what they're hearing.
Many years ago, I wrote about how the ethnographer ultimately needs to

become a "vulnerable observer" to be fully present throughout this emotional journey. William is an inspiring vulnerable observer in this book in several ways—as a Latino man, as a parent, and as a male researcher who chooses to focus on the stories of women and children, those who are most vulnerable in our society. The result is a book that brings us into the lives of Latinas and Latinos who are experiencing trauma, fear, racial profiling, and brutal forms of immigration law enforcement, showing us how this situation is causing extreme pain to many innocent working families, dehumanizing them, and in the process dehumanizing all of us who are sitting by and not doing enough to end this suffering.

One quite compelling aspect of this book is that William didn't move to an "exotic" part of the world to conduct his research. He writes about the actual community in which he lives, in Michigan. The immigration home raids he presents in this book are happening at home, in his home, not in a distant borderland in the desert. It seems the borderlands are everywhere now, in our America. The borderlands are in the streets we walk each day, in the houses we drive past. What is clear is that some of us live busy, unconcerned lives while others live a precarious existence, fearing that wrenching moment of violence, of exclusion, of exile.

But it need not be this way. Read this timely and beautifully written ethnography. It will teach you why we must move beyond this era of deportations if we are to build a more just, loving world for all those generations still to come.

Ruth Behar is the author of *Translated Woman: Crossing the Border with Esperanza's Story* (1993) and *The Vulnerable Observer: Anthropology That Breaks Your Heart* (1996).

Separated

Introduction

I was ready to go.

I was ready to get on the plane, fly to Mexico City, take a bus to his small pueblo on the coast of the Gulf of Mexico, and interview Santiago, face-to-face, *cara-a-cara*. It would be the perfect culmination for the final chapter of a book that I would write about Santiago's arrest, detention, deportation, and return to the very poverty and danger he had attempted to flee with his family in the first place. I envisioned myself sitting across from him, sharing a cup of coffee as we both lamented the violence of the deportation machine that rips men from their day-to-day lives and thrusts them back across the border. It would certainly be a fitting end to the story of a man who had worked in a small automobile shop nine miles away from the university at which I was writing my dissertation. The peaceful image of a friendly host welcoming me into his home would contrast strongly with the villain whom Immigration and Customs Enforcement was so determined to arrest and deport that it leveraged a county SWAT (Special Weapons and Tactics) team with their bulletproof vests and automatic weapons to kick in his door and gather evidence of the illegal drugs he was accused of selling.

But I never went to Mexico. I never shook Santiago's hand. I never hugged him. I never shared so much as a *mucho gusto cara-a-cara* with the man whose life has largely become the focal point of mine for five years and counting. Simply, the invitation never materialized. The family in Mexico didn't think it was safe for me to come to an area where violence had coaxed them into leaving in the first place.

However, not meeting Santiago was perhaps the best possible outcome at the time, as it forced me to expand my naïve and limited understanding of the impacts of immigration law enforcement. See, it's easy to focus on the acute trauma of deportation, on the violence of the arrest, the detainment, and the removal, to see each individual deportation as a story in itself and each individual deportee as the lone character in a one-act tragedy. It's easy to be drawn into the story of the man removed and to miss the women, families, and community left behind.

The US Immigration and Customs Enforcement Agency, or ICE, began to gather evidence against Santiago a week before the raid. They arrested Santiago at about nine o'clock in the morning on a Thursday in November of 2013. But, in the hours following his arrest, ICE and local law enforcement officers continued arresting Latino men who drove out of Santiago's property throughout the day. One woman, Hilda, watched through her car window as ICE cuffed and shackled her husband and searched his brown body for tattoos while he stood surrounded by law enforcement *patrullas* on the side of the road. Hilda then called a local community-based organization, which used its text messaging service to spread the word that any Latino driving down Huron Avenue was marked for arrest.

Then, at about 6:30 p.m., ICE and a SWAT unit raided Santiago's first-floor automobile workshop, or *taller*, and the apartment above it in which he lived with his sister, wife, 18-year-old son, and five children under the age of 6. Kicking in the door, pointing weapons at women and children, detaining and deporting the Latino men they found, they left mothers depressed and suicidal, families broken and homeless, a community terrified of the police who swore to protect and serve it, and a community of color wary that brown skin marked them for legal violence dispensed at the whim of racist law enforcement.

So, no, Santiago's arrest was not the beginning. His deportation was not the end. And the story was not nearly so simple.

■ ■ ■

I never took a red-eye flight to Mexico. I didn't ride a bus from Mexico City to a small town off the map, hike the hills to a tiny house with a dirt floor, and have coffee poured for me as I sat across from Santiago.

Instead, I went to Dunkin Donuts in a small, everyday Midwestern town in southeast Michigan, picked up two coffees and fifteen doughnut holes, and went to visit Santiago's sister, Guadalupe, a Mexican woman with dark black hair and glasses who was 26 years old at the time of the raid. Guadalupe and I ate in her tiny kitchen as her youngest daughter, Fatima, ran around us, occasionally stopping for her mother to wipe her *moco*-y nose from a cold she just couldn't shake.

Guadalupe shares with me that Fatima's cold was just one of many: her three children's health had all deteriorated after the raid. She wasn't sure whether their illnesses were the result of the gas that had been *echado* into the room as it was being raided, the *frio* in the November air that enveloped Fatima's 2-month-old skin after agents had kicked in the door, or the *pavor* of military-grade assault weapons pointed at their heads. But Guadalupe confesses that the children's erratic health and changing behaviors further complicated the near impossibility of finding jobs and childcare in the absence of Santiago, who was also her economic provider.

When Guadalupe and I finish talking, she plugs her cell phone into the speaker system she has mounted in the ceiling. She dials in a calling card number she has memorized. Then she calls the small town in Mexico that I will never visit, and Santiago talks openly to me about the raid and his deportation.

When he is done, Santiago passes the phone to his wife, Fernanda.

Fernanda was 22 years old when Santiago was arrested. She lived with Guadalupe in the apartment above the *taller* with her two kids, 3-month-old Ignacio and 1½-year-old Lena. Fernanda, depressed, suicidal, broke, and with kids whose health similarly fell apart, took a bus from Michigan to Texas and walked across the border to Mexico to be with her deported husband. As Fernanda divulges her story, I can hear her stifle her tears. Her daughter, Lena, doesn't stifle anything and cries in the background as the Mexican police drive by her house. Even a country away, she fears that law enforcement officers want to beat her.

Fernanda and I speak, and then the phone is passed yet again. Santiagito, Santiago's son from a previous marriage who was 18 years old at the time of his father's arrest, was also in the apartment when it was raided. Like Fernanda and Guadalupe, Santiagito had questioned whether that Thursday in November was the day he was going to die. Then, like his father, he was cuffed, detained, and deported while his girlfriend, Jessica, watched.

After more than an hour, Guadalupe tells me that she needs to leave to pick up her older daughter, Sofía, and starts to bundle up Fatima in her winter jacket to take her along. All three of them leave, so there is no one—physically—in the apartment except me. But Santiago's, Santiagito's, and Fernanda's voices continue to fill the room. It's haunting, hearing their voices, and hearing their children in the background.

Haunting, but appropriate. The citizen, comfortable, warm. The family, scattered, scared. Cold.

■ ■ ■

Not going to Mexico forced me to think deeply about a vastly different side of immigration violence. I was made to reckon with an aspect of immigration law enforcement too often overlooked: those left behind, who are not the targets of immigration enforcement actions, who may not even be undocumented themselves, must nonetheless deal with a militarized, traumatic, and profoundly violent deportation machine, the repercussions of which are both gendered and painfully familial. These stories—the stories of Guadalupe, Fernanda, Hilda, and others like them, the stories so frequently made invisible—form the crux of this book.

There are other stories—and, consequently, other heated immigration debates—that I do not take on here. I do not ask why Guadalupe, Fernanda, Hilda, Santiago, or others in their community or throughout the United States crossed the border in the first place. I do not assume that, because of their initial illegal border crossing, their entire lives become wrapped in "illegality" and that they therefore deserve the trauma and assaults to their health they encounter.[1] Instead, I take at face value that anyone—regardless of immigration status—has a right to be happy, healthy, and with their family.

I am the author of this book, a book that has a beginning and an end. But I am not the author of this story. This is Guadalupe's story. This is Fernanda's story. This is Hilda's story. And the book you hold in your hands is only a glimpse into a life of targeted surveillance and violence that began before I started writing and has yet to come to an end. It is a violence that destroys lives, destroys families, and can happen any day of the year. I only hope to do the story justice.

Collecting the Stories in This Book

This book emerged from the dissertation research I conducted for a PhD in public health. At the time of the raid, I was a public health student and a volunteer with the Washtenaw Interfaith Coalition for Immigrant Rights, or WICIR (pronounced "wicker"). I wanted to use the research to allow those most directly affected by the event to paint a vivid picture—what anthropologists call a "thick description"[2]—of what it felt like to be in an apartment when it was raided, swept up in the enforcement that preceded it, or forced to put your life back together after it. To do this, I engaged in one year of fieldwork beginning in 2015, about a year after the raid occurred. When I began the fieldwork, I had already lived in Washtenaw County, Michigan, for about six years, and had been volunteering with WICIR for many of those years, so I was building on established relationships with people and organizations as well as a level of trust and rapport that had grown throughout the preceding years. I was volunteering and engaging in advocacy during the time of the raid and directly participated in organizing after; formal data collection started about a year later.

I conducted twenty-four interviews with twenty-one individuals associated with the raid and the immigration enforcement actions that preceded it. Among these individuals were those who directly interacted with law enforcement agents on that day, such as Guadalupe, Fernanda, Santiago, Santiagito, and Arturo; their families and friends, such as Hilda; and members of organizations that generally supported them. This allowed me to get perspectives from those in the raided apartment, those arrested as they drove away from the *taller*, the families and friends of each, and the lawyers, advocates, and WICIR urgent responders who provided support after the event.

While many organizations were gracious enough to allow me to work with and advocate alongside them, I primarily collaborated with WICIR. WICIR was originally founded in response to an immigration raid in a mobile home complex that bore many resemblances to the raid on Guadalupe's apartment.³ Part of WICIR's work is to organize a team of urgent responders. One urgent responder carries an urgent response phone that community members call during immigration-related emergencies. WICIR also mobilizes urgent responders to react to immigration raids; three urgent responders arrived at Guadalupe's apartment as the raid was concluding and contributed greatly to this project. I served as a WICIR urgent responder for the period of fieldwork, and, for a portion of that time, I carried the urgent response phone.

While some of this fieldwork was conducted in the county in which the raid occurred, much was not. Immigration law enforcement—and the stigma of being a target of that enforcement—often forces individuals to leave their communities when they no longer feel safe or adequately connected to friends and resources. Some community members left the county after the raid. Others simply moved away to follow work and family opportunities. Some returned to their countries of birth. And many were deported. I did what I could to collect these stories in person regardless of the state to which individuals had relocated and spoke with individuals in Arizona, California, Ohio, Texas, and elsewhere in the United States. I engaged with the advocacy communities in these locations whenever possible. I also collected fliers, photos, and other materials to supplement the pages of field notes taken before and after most interactions.

I honor the language and experiences of participants in explaining and detailing the events they describe. For example, while the enforcement actions involved law enforcement and ICE and began early that morning, I did not hear community members refer to the event as anything other than "the raid," or "*la redada*," even though the literal kicking in of the door did not occur until the end of the day. While I often describe the raid as "collaborative," because law enforcement worked alongside immigration enforcement agents, and other times I refer to the days' events using the collective "enforcement actions," I frequently use "the raid" as well, to honor the community's language and the prioritization of the home invasion aspect of those actions. Similarly, I describe the space above Santiago's automobile workshop as "an apartment," even though the space was not zoned for residential use, as this is how community members referenced it generally, regardless of the original builder's intention for the space. I refer to the apartment sometimes as "Guadalupe's apartment" and other times as "Santiago's" or "Fernanda's apartment," as all were residents and shared the space equally. I also honor community members' descriptions of their relationships. For example, if participants used "husband" or "wife" to describe someone, I do as well, whether they were legally married, married in the United States or elsewhere, or use the term to denote the significance of a relationship unacknowledged by the law.

Similarly, I call the community a "Latino" community, aware of the well-established criticisms that gendered words tend to devalue women's contribution to the group and reinforce a dichotomous notion of gender. There are many useful alternatives, such as "Latino/a" or "Latinx," but I maintain "Latino," as this was the label that community members used when they spoke collectively. Individual women would sometimes use "Latina" to talk about themselves, and many community members often identified by their countries of birth, calling themselves, for example, *"Mexicana"* or *"Colombiano."* I use these labels throughout this book as well, but maintain "Latino" to describe the community as a whole. I also use the term "brown" to describe Latinos, a word that gestures toward the criminalization of the color of our skin, an experience shared, to some extent, with Black communities.

This project occurred in both Spanish and English. I am responsible for the translated text presented here; though when I needed a second opinion for Spanish phrasing with which I was not familiar, I relied on the assistance of a professional translator with whom I had worked previously. Because Spanish words are often used in English sentences to preserve mood and nuances of the interaction[4] (for example, the Spanish word *"taller,"* or "automobile workshop"), I italicize Spanish words and phrases to make sentences easier to read. If a Spanish word or phrase lost meaning in the translation, I explain and use the Spanish word throughout the book. Indeed, it is the words that defy translation that can provide the most insight into the lives of mixed-status community members and the damage of immigration enforcement. Often, individuals whose first language is Spanish would speak to me in English. When this occurred, no matter how fluent in English they were, small errors in language became apparent when these interviews were transcribed. Much of this is simply a factor of converting spoken language to written language; that is, simple errors become more apparent when written. I maintain these errors in interview text instead of removing or editing them in order to honor the bilingual nature of the work and community.

All quotations in this book were directly spoken by study participants during interviews or reflect words directly spoken and noted during participant observation, with a few exceptions. Two individuals (Jaime, a former Immigration and Naturalization Service agent, and Lisbeth, a cofounder of WICIR), spoke with me at length and allowed me to record these discussions. I describe both these interactions in notes in the corresponding sections. All quotations contained in this retelling of the raid (that is, the sections titled "The Raid") come from audio recordings of participant interviews and, thus, reflect either participants' descriptions of what they and others said or general phrases used in standard situations described by a participant (for example, an officer's saying, "Put your hands on your head.").

I changed many details throughout this book for the sake of anonymity. Names of people, organizations, and locations—with very few exceptions—are pseudonyms, and descriptions of each have been altered. At times, I changed countries of birth, ages, family organization, or time in the United States or in Washtenaw County. Some individuals are composites of multiple others, and some dates, times, and locations may be changed or details altered for anonymization. Even though it pains me not to highlight the law enforcement departments whose officers were exemplary (or, on the contrary, racist), I do not distinguish one department from another.

While it was ICE—a federal agency—that ultimately deported the men arrested in and around Santiago's *taller*, it was a SWAT team from a local law enforcement department that kicked in Guadalupe's door. And while many deportations happen because of arrests made by ICE, in our county, as in counties throughout the country that are not located near international borders, we do not have ICE or Border Patrol regularly patrolling our roads. Consequently, many arrests that lead to deportation occur because of interactions with the police.

Throughout the study period, I made every effort to engage with the department that collaborated with ICE. This included attending a workshop on community and police relationships, attending meetings of the Law Enforcement Citizens Advisory Board (LE-CAB,[5] which served as a liaison between law enforcement and the community), and meeting personally with representatives and officers from the department. Through these events, I sometimes connected with other law enforcement officers, who invited me to be involved in other ways.

Because law enforcement events to which the community was invited were likely to present a strategic face to the public, I also attempted to observe a number of behind-the-scenes, day-to-day law enforcement activities. Most of these observations occurred through ride-alongs with four different law enforcement departments in our county. Throughout the course of these ride-alongs, I was generally able to meet and talk with many other officers, mostly men, mostly white, with important exceptions I detail later.

I used the Freedom of Information Act (FOIA) to request any information generated from the enforcement actions on Santiago's *taller* in 2013. I received the police report of the event from the department involved in the arrests and the raid but did not receive any records from ICE, as this required Santiago's signature. While it was possible to fax Santiago the FOIA request for him to sign while he was in Mexico, I refrained from doing so for two reasons. First, even though Santiago had been deported, much of his network remained in the United States, and we were collectively hesitant about signing ICE documents so soon after his deportation. Second, I did not want to remind Santiago and Fernanda of the triggering event any more than was absolutely necessary.

It is important to clarify that the fieldwork with law enforcement I discuss here is not intended to provide an equal and alternative perspective to the stories shared by the Latino mixed-status community. Comprehensive ethnographic work focused on law enforcement already exists.[6] Rather, law enforcement agents and the ways in which they enforce the law cannot be extricated from the lives of members of communities of color, as it is these agents who patrol the streets and enforce the law at their discretion. Information gathered from these interactions is meant to be interpreted in combination with other fieldwork that together creates a more holistic picture of the context that shapes the lives of a mixed-status Latino community in the county in which the raid occurred.

Much of my work with officers occurred during the growth of the Black Lives Matter movement.[7] This movement began in February 2012, when a Black teenager, Trayvon Martin, was gunned down and killed by a 28-year-old man in Sanford, Florida. Even though 17-year-old Martin was carrying only a bag of Skittles and iced tea when he was killed,[8] George Zimmerman claimed that he shot Martin in self-defense.[9] A jury of Zimmerman's peers agreed with him, and Zimmerman was acquitted of murder charges about a year-and-a-half after he killed Martin.

Then, in July 2014, about eight months after Guadalupe's door was kicked in, a white male New York Police Department officer wrapped his arm around the neck of Eric Garner, a Black man, and, despite Garner's "I can't breathe" protests, the officer choked Garner to death after accusing him of selling cigarettes without a permit. Even though the use of this chokehold is against NYPD regulations, Officer Daniel Pantaleo was not indicted for the killing.[10]

The killings of Trayvon Martin and Eric Garner and the inability of the court system to convict either of their killers were followed by a seemingly endless stream of videos capturing images of Black men (and one boy) shot and killed by police. The videos—sometimes from cell phones, other times from officers' body or dash cams—ignited a firestorm of racial tension throughout the United States, as the country witnessed what Black communities had always argued: being Black in public can be deadly.

I have three reasons for writing about the killings of Black men, women, and boys and the growth of the Black Lives Matter movement in a book about immigration violence. First, stories are shaped by the context in which they are told. And the stories about immigration violence told here emerged during a time of national tension between police officers and multiple communities of color. This tension tinged most every interaction I had with law enforcement, as officers constantly shared with me their thoughts on the most recent killings of Black men, the effect these killings had on police departments, or the role the media played in shaping public perception of the police. That is, the deaths of Black community members and the growth of the Black Lives Matter movement were simply what everyone in uniform was talking about.

Second, while this book aims to cast a spotlight on the real-life effects of immigration enforcement violence, I also intend to be fully authentic to the ways in which that violence occurs. Undocumented individuals live and work alongside individuals of all immigration statuses. Black and brown communities intertwine; the structures that affect one community also affect the other. In the same moments in which brown people are deported by ICE, Black people are shot by the police. And, of course, brown people also experience police violence, as do undocumented Black immigrants who are arrested and removed from the United States.[11] To write about the stories of immigration enforcement while ignoring the influence of local police would amount to an erasure of the lives of minority community members caught in intersecting webs of law enforcement violence from multiple arms of the state.

Last, research on police violence in Black communities and immigration violence in Latino communities has, for too long, existed in separate tracts. I show that oftentimes the logic for one informs the logic of the other. That is, many of the arguments used to justify the killing of Black community members are also used to justify the arrests and deportation of undocumented Latinos.

In sum, I used a range of methods to bring the reader closer to the experiences of Guadalupe, Fernanda, Hilda, and others who were impacted by an immigration raid. These stories, while unique, also represent immigration violence that occurs throughout the United States on any given day of the year.

Me: A Latino, a Father, a Citizen

Feminist ethnographic tradition teaches us that who we are—both how we identify and how others identify us—is critically important to the work we do. Our identities not only influence where we focus our attention and how we engage with what we observe but also shape the relationships we are able to form, fundamentally altering what we can observe in the first place.[12] Being a Latino man and a father fundamentally shaped what I saw, what I did, and where I was able to create and nurture relationships. Throughout this project, I attempted to always be aware of the identities I held—and those that were projected on to me—to better understand aspects of the community that I was observing and address what I was missing.

As a Latino who spoke Spanish, my presence in Latino and Spanish-speaking spaces was generally accepted without any suspicion that I could perceive. I was assumed to be either part of the community or an ally attempting to be supportive. My ethnicity (or more specifically, the visible markers of it, such as my black hair, brown skin, and ability to speak Spanish) also allowed me to be seen with community members in ways that would not instantly call attention to the interaction. Often, this invisibility was necessary for community members who viewed public space as an area of potential risk.

But my ethnic identity and presentation took on an entirely different meaning when I was with law enforcement officers. One of the questions I am constantly asked, and often asked myself, is why I was allowed to observe so much police activity and spend so much time sitting in cars with police officers to begin with. It was especially surprising that these uncensored conversations were allowed during such a racially tense moment in our country's history.

But I began to sense that perhaps I was not allowed in police cars despite the killings of Black men and women by police officers but because of these killings. Police departments seemed hungry for approval from people of color, and here I was, an overeducated, light-skinned, clean-cut Latino man with no visible tattoos and no accent. I was also, as the stereotype goes, a Latino researcher who was interested in immigration research, which was perceived to be unrelated to police violence in Black communities. As far as I could tell, I was not automatically assumed to be antipolice (as experience told me other men of color, especially Black men, had been) and was generally greeted by police chiefs with a handshake, a smile, and professionalism. I felt as though most officers were unsure of how to interpret the presence of a Latino man and therefore allowed me some sort of access while hoping for the best. For once, I suppose, the invisibility of Latinos in an America divided into a Black/white binary worked to my advantage. I did not know at the start of this project how much this invisibility illustrated the contemporary (and faulty) US understanding of communities of color: Latinos worried about *la migra*. Blacks worried about cops. And each of these branches of the government was operating independently, their similarly violent enforcement tactics merely coincidental.

In addition to race, gender also powerfully shapes ethnographic work. Deborah Boehm, who writes about transnational Mexican families, describes how her gender "limited and facilitated access to particular individuals and topics."[13] Specifically, she noted, "it was culturally acceptable to visit more and converse more intimately with women, [and] there were cultural practices already in place that enabled me to do so."[14] I similarly felt that, as a man, I could easily approach men and had a readily available and shared set of culturally acceptable topics and practices in which we could discuss and engage.[15] I have been invited to play in soccer games, to hang around at automobile shops, to put in fence posts, and to clean out the pens of farm animals with Latino men from the mixed-status community. With women, however, it would be taboo for us to be alone, and the shared topics of culturally acceptable conversation were few.

But fatherhood drastically altered the gender dynamics of the relationships I formed. Because I had children, there was a range of conversations open to us. The tension of long car rides was reduced in a car filled with Cheerios, toys, and sometimes even our children. And there were endless opportunities to share resources in either direction and engage multiple times while our children just "hung out."[16] For example, I passed on clothes when my children grew out of them, and my kids received their share of clothes when they no longer fit the children of others. My children (as well as my partner, who is white) frequently joined me during community events. While I believe I was generally accepted in these spaces because of my ethnic background and Spanish fluency, watching children hit a piñata with a bat admittedly has the dramatic effect of bringing together people across class, race, and gender lines. Having my own growing family fostered relationships with those with similar families, as well as powerfully influenced the factors on which I focused.

Lastly, I strongly identify as a Latino in the mixed-status community of our county, and generally perceive that I am accepted as a part of that community. Much of the motivation for this work was simply to do something to address the legal violence directed at my friends and neighbors. But I also live a life of enormous privilege. I am a citizen, as are my children and my partner. My mother, born in Mexico, became a citizen when she was about 5 years old, and my father is a US citizen born in Texas to Mexican parents. My extended family are all US born or naturalized US citizens of Mexican heritage. I am also fairly light skinned, though not as light as my multiracial (white and Latino) children. I have spent my life comparatively insulated from the deportation of immediate family and friends, and I largely do not fear for my own safety or that of my immediate family because of the color of our skin. Further, while I am a parent who, like most parents, is willing to die or at least break the law for the sake of my children, unlike many of the parents with whom I spoke, I never actually had to do so.

In anthropological terms, I was a "nonnative native" field-worker;[17] that is, while I was a member of the community with which I was working, I differed on important aspects of identity and privilege likely to shape relationships and observations. I did what I could to address this gap by building and maintaining relationships with those who were closer to the experiences of immigration enforcement than I was, but my life of privilege—as a man, as a light-skinned and well-educated Latino, and as a citizen—was frequently front and center. Throughout this book, I frequently reflect on this privilege and encourage other researchers and advocates to reflect on their own and its impact on the work we do. Where can we go that others find inaccessible? Where can we speak when others are forced into silence?

I hope to accomplish a few things in this book. First and foremost, I hope the reader comes away with a deep sense of the brutality of our current methods of immigration enforcement, especially immigration raids. These enforcement tactics are militarized and violent, with little regard to the physical and psychological damage done to those at whom they are directed, their families, or their communities. For people who do not come from these communities, they simply may be unaware of how violent these tactics are, how much they rely on racial profiling and war-on-drugs rhetoric, how they shape the day-to-day lives of mixed-status Latino communities, and how often the same logic of law enforcement violence results in both the deportation of Latinos and the killing of Black men, women, and boys. After reading this book, it is my hope that they can no longer claim ignorance of the systemic injustice happening next door.

Second, I hope to encourage the reader to think less about individual acts of immigration law enforcement and more about a system that *marks* undocumented individuals and uses the potential for extraordinary violence to control their families and communities. Marking Santiago for arrest allowed ICE to collaborate with local law enforcement, arrest and deport individuals who had no relationships to Santiago—save for being his customers—and unleash a tremendous amount of militarized violence throughout his community, including on his wife, sister, and young children. In this way, the full force of local police and ICE can be leveraged against any Latino, not only those who are undocumented, simply because of the relationships among us. It is the everyday potential for catastrophic violence that allows for the coersion of entire marginalized communities.

Third, I write this book as a public health researcher, who believes deeply in the power of social science to improve the lives of the most marginalized. While I focus on the health impacts of immigration law enforcement throughout this book, I conceptualize health as broadly as possible, as mental and physical, as familial and communal, as belonging, worth, and meaning. And while I draw on many traditional tenets of public health—trauma-informed analyses, multilevel thinking, and social networks among them—I also hope to encourage social scientists to acknowledge that legitimate suffering is happening now. This is a suffering that should not be overmedicalized. It is a suffering that we have the tools to address. And it is a suffering that does not require researchers to come to their work with a blank slate but with the empathy and the fire that brought them to public health in the first place.

Last, I write this book from a position of vulnerability, as an overeducated researcher, a citizen, and a man, who dares to speak about the lives of undocumented Latina women who give their bodies to physical labor, cleaning the very hotels I sleep in when I talk about their suffering at academic conferences. I do this in part as an act of reparation for my position as a beneficiary of undocumented labor, as a citizen in a neoliberal system that largely maintains its existence through the overworked, underpaid, uninsured immigrants we simultaneously vilify. I do this because we, as people of privilege, owe it to the marginalized members of our communities to use our privilege to improve the quality of their day-to-day lives. I speak on behalf of Guadalupe, Fernanda, and Hilda because society has chosen not to listen to undocumented Spanish-speaking Latina mothers when they speak for themselves. When society decides it is finally time to hear them, I will promptly be silent.

Chapter 1

Guadalupe, Fernanda, and Hilda

Guadalupe Morales

Guadalupe Morales[1] came to the United States in June 2007, a hot summer made hotter by the lack of water and strong sun she faced as she walked into the United States. Guadalupe crossed the border from Mexico into the United States with the encouragement of her brother, Santiago Morales, who had lived in the United States since his first illegal border crossing in 2000. Guadalupe was a scared teenager—scared of the desert, scared of the Border Patrol, and scared of the five other men with whom she was traveling: "I come from a small pueblo where everyone respects everyone, very peaceful. But I was scared because the men kept coming by to touch you."

As Guadalupe crossed the desert—sweltering during the day—she and the others hid in places that were wet and cold at night "until you couldn't feel your hands, feel your feet." At times, she thought she was going to die: "Sometimes you'd run into gangs, or stuff lying around from people who had died on the path I was on. I didn't know if I was going to make it."

After three days of walking through the Mexican desert, Guadalupe made it to the US-Mexico border. She then moved on to Houston, Texas. In Houston, she spent the night in a stranger's house before getting in a truck to travel farther north to Michigan, where she finally met up with her brother, Santiago. It was there, in southeast Michigan, in a small town that was about 5 percent Latino, that Guadalupe would try to build a life for herself and her future children.

Despite her efforts, Guadalupe's life was filled with loss, trauma, violence, and family separation. Sometimes, the pain was simply the stuff of life, the deaths or divorces that could affect most anyone. Other times, the pain was distinctly man-made, a function of our country's efforts to surveil, arrest, and deport undocumented immigrants like her.

In 2008, Guadalupe met Eduardo, a *hondureño*, who washed dishes across from her at a local restaurant. The two became serious, and Guadalupe later gave birth to his son, whom they named Carlitos. Things weren't always good between Guadalupe and Eduardo, and, at least once, Eduardo became violent with Guadalupe, assaulting her outside of the fast-food restaurant where she worked. Then, in early 2011, Eduardo's car wrapped around a tree a few miles from their house, killing him.

Guadalupe continued to work, and Carlitos grew up without his father, at least until Guadalupe met Antonio, who was, like her, Mexican and undocumented. Guadalupe soon gave birth to her first daughter, Sofía, and Carlitos came to accept Antonio as his own father. Their family continued to grow, and Guadalupe was soon pregnant with another child.

But in 2013, Antonio was pulled over by ICE while Carlitos was in the car. Carlitos, 4 years old at the time, watched as agents pointed weapons at Antonio before handcuffing the man who had become his father and pushing him up against the side of the car. Guadalupe, who had no driver's license, drove to the site of the arrest to pick up a distraught, confused Carlitos, who had just lost the second father figure from his life before he was even 5 years old. When Guadalupe, visibly pregnant, stepped out of the car, the ICE agent told her, in English, to calm down for the sake of the baby. That baby—Fatima—would be born shortly after, with no father to meet when she arrived. Fatima would also have a much more brutal and violent encounter with ICE than her initial encounter in utero, as, a few months later, the apartment she lived in would be raided.

In the days and months that followed Antonio's arrest and deportation, Santiago, Guadalupe's brother, helped whenever he could. Santiago owned and operated a *taller*, or automobile shop, situated on Huron Avenue, the town's main drag. Other Latinos throughout the community would bring their cars to Santiago's *taller*, and plenty would just hang around there, drinking beer, chatting about the lives they have and reflecting on the lives they had.

Above the *taller* was a small warehouse space that Santiago had converted into living quarters, using deep fryers for heat during cold Michigan winters. To support his sister, nieces, and nephews, Santiago invited them to live in the makeshift apartment, sharing an already cramped space with his own wife, Fernanda, their two small children, and Santiagito, Santiago's 18-year-old son from a previous marriage who had just arrived in the United States.

The apartment and *taller* were thus frequently filled to the brim with Latino families and community members sharing space, sharing meals, sharing drinks, and, on a Thursday in November of 2013, sharing tragedy.

■ ■ ■

Guadalupe is short, with dark black hair and thick glasses. She's always talkative, despite what I sense to be a deep bone-weariness that comes from working nonstop for little pay while caring or arranging care for her three children without either of their fathers. When I went to Guadalupe's house in October 2015, about two years after the raid, her son Carlitos stood in front of me in a white polo shirt that contrasted sharply with the black hair that was as dark as his mother's. Like a proud child giving a book report to his class, he explained to me in Spanish a bit about his family tree, noting that his father had been deported back to Honduras and had since died. I paused to consider whether Carlitos was conflating the story of his birth father, who had died in a car crash, and that of his sisters' father, whom he had witnessed being handcuffed and detained before he was deported to Mexico. I looked up at Guadalupe to see if perhaps I was missing something.

But Guadalupe looked back at me through her thick glasses and silently gestured in confirmation that, yes, her son was indeed talking about two different people, was intertwining two different stories that described the means by which the men in his life had been torn away. But she let Carlitos continue with the story anyway, as if there were little reason to differentiate death from deportation for a 6-year-old boy. I was shocked by how composed Carlitos appeared to be. I could not even begin to imagine how my daughter of the same age would have responded to the constant removal of people she loved.

At the time her apartment was raided in 2013, Guadalupe was one of about 11 million undocumented immigrants in the United States, one of about 6 million undocumented Mexicans,[2] and one of about 130,000 undocumented immigrants in Michigan.[3] Her children, Carlitos, Sofía, and Fatima, were born in the United States, and hence as the US citizen children of an undocumented mother, composed a mixed-status family. *Los Morales* are therefore one of about 2.3 million families throughout the United States[4] in which family members have different immigration statuses, are provided with different resources to maintain their health and live their daily lives, and are differentially targeted for deportation.[5] Santiago's deportation was one of about 440,000 that occurred that year[6] and, given that not all arrests result in deportation, one of many more detainments and detentions that remove individuals from their families and communities. Likewise, Carlitos was one of many children who had a father figure cuffed and removed from his life.[7] And Guadalupe, along with her sister-in-law, Fernanda, were two of millions of women who struggle emotionally, psychologically, and financially after the deportation of a financial provider.[8]

Guadalupe and her family illustrate many truths about undocumented immigrants in the United States. Contrary to popular portrayals, undocumented immigrants do not live together in neighborhoods composed solely of other undocumented immigrants. Rather, undocumented immigrants are the mothers, fathers, sisters, and brothers of US citizens, visa holders, other undocumented immigrants, and those nebulously between immigration statuses.[9] In real life—on the ground—laws, policies, and surveillance that affect undocumented immigrants cannot be untangled from impacts on the families of which they are a part.

Guadalupe and her family interact every day with other mixed-status families just like hers, including Santiago, his undocumented wife, and their citizen children. That is, undocumented immigrants, such as Guadalupe, are part of mixed-status families, which in turn are part of mixed-status communities, or communities composed of individuals and families of all immigration statuses living, working, playing, fighting, arguing, loving, and sharing in one another's lives. As Guadalupe and her community show us, the effects of immigration enforcement extend far beyond the targets of deportation, beyond even their families, into the communities in which they live.

Fernanda Moreno

Unlike Guadalupe and I, Fernanda and I never met face-to-face. In a photo I've seen of her, she seemed happy, dressed in a light purple shirt with matching barrettes in her dark black, wavy hair, pulled back behind her hoop earrings. But I can't tell you much about her personality, her sense of humor, or her mannerisms. I only heard her voice, shaky and cracking through tears, as she talked over the phone to Guadalupe and me as we sat in Guadalupe's tiny new apartment. Her absence, of course, spoke volumes, another member of the mixed-status community whose life was reduced to a story about why she's gone, another mother who couldn't care for herself and her children while coping with the disappearance of the family's primary breadwinner, another immigrant back in her country of birth against her will even though she was neither arrested nor deported.[10]

While much of the trauma of deportation comes from the detainment and removal of loved ones, an unlucky few just happen to be standing near those arrested in the moments the doors are kicked in and the guns are drawn. This was certainly the case for Fernanda. A mother of two who was originally born in Mexico, Fernanda was about 22 years old at the time of the raid. Throughout her interviews, Fernanda was deeply emotionally and psychologically disturbed by the events of that Thursday in November. It was likely that she could have been diagnosed with post-traumatic stress disorder from the encounter.[11] Indeed, throughout her forty-eight minutes of interview time, Fernanda used the verb *apuntar*—to point a weapon at—ten times and some form of *matar*—to kill—three times. She talked extensively about the moment in which the agents kicked in the door and about how hard it was for her and her daughter to breathe because of the gas—likely the incendiary smell of a flash bang grenade—that agents had thrown in the room. And she lamented the impossibility of finding work—and the childcare that permitted it—when she had never worked before. But Fernanda's traumatic story, like Guadalupe's story, is not unique. Rather, her experience also shows us many truths about the ways in which immigration law enforcement takes place in mixed-status communities throughout the country.

When ICE raided Guadalupe's apartment, they weren't acting alone. Rather, they collaborated with a SWAT unit from the local police department because of accusations that Santiago had trafficked guns and drugs through his *taller.* These SWAT units—modeled after armed elite military units—were originally designed to address kidnappings or terrorism. But as you will read in detail later, the war on drugs and the anti-Black and anti-Latino rhetoric on which it was founded, created a new villain at which departments could direct their militarized violence.[12] The type of raid that Fernanda experienced—in which the SWAT officers use no-knock warrants to enter into a residence without first gaining the permission of those inside—happen thousands of times per year in the United States,[13] mostly in Black and Latino communities like Fernanda's.[14]

When the apartment was raided, Fernanda sat alongside Guadalupe, watching as the men around them were removed while they shivered, cold and terrified. That Fernanda and Guadalupe were left behind while the men were detained and deported is typical of a much larger pattern of immigration enforcement in the United States. For decades, immigration law focused on facilitating the arrival of men for their labor while restricting the migration of women, who were considered a burdensome drain on social services.[15] As a country, the United States was more worried about the shivering Fernanda and her sister-in-law Guadalupe, whose children may one day enroll in taxpayer-funded public schools or require taxpayer-funded supplemental food assistance. The men around them, however, represented a potential source of untapped labor. Only later would Santiago and his dark-skinned neighbors come to represent the dangerous threat to American ideology they do today.

Immigration law enforcement changed drastically following the events of September 11, 2001, in which nineteen individuals hijacked four airliners, flew two into the World Trade Center, one into the Pentagon, and crashed the fourth in southern Pennsylvania.[16] The Homeland Security

Act, passed in 2002, created the Department of Homeland Security (DHS), which absorbed the Immigration and Naturalization Services (INS), formerly responsible for enforcing immigration laws.

With this reorganization came a restructuring of the INS into three organizations, Immigration and Customs Enforcement (ICE), Customs and Border Protection (CBP, though colloquially referred to as "Border Patrol"), and the US Citizenship and Immigration Services (USCIS).[17] DHS described its national strategy as one meant to "ensure a homeland that is safe, secure, and resilient against terrorism and other hazards." The individual missions of each DHS component reflect this larger DHS strategy, as ICE aims to "promote homeland security and public safety,"[18] while Border Patrol's mission is to keep "terrorists and their weapons out of the U.S. while facilitating international travel and trade."[19]

Thus, following the events of 9/11, federal immigration law transformed from a means of labor control to a tool of maintaining national security and managing terrorism.[20] The effect was the conflation of criminal and immigration law, increasingly casting immigrants as violent foreign threats instead of merely people who took jobs and government resources to which they were not entitled.[21] For many, the rotating acronyms of faceless departments that enforce immigration law made no difference in their lives, but those in mixed-status communities quickly realized that how the government addressed the theft of jobs and resources differed drastically from the ways in which it addressed the threat of the next potential bomber of another World Trade Center.

As brown migrants went from cheap, exploitable labor to a "new danger that is masculine, personified by terrorist men and 'criminal aliens,'"[22] the focus of immigration enforcement also shifted from the border to the interior of the United States.[23] In 2011, the number of removals (which involve an immigration hearing or waiving one's right to do so) surpassed the number of "returns" (which occur when CBP prevent entry into the United States) for the first time since 1941, insinuating an increased focus on apprehension of those, like Santiago, who were already in the United States.[24]

While DHS no longer publishes statistics on the gender of deportees, studies from countries to which immigrants are deported continue to find that most deportees are, like Santiago, Latino men,[25] and any mixed-status family, community, or organization with which you speak could confirm the large gender disparity in deportation practices. In addition to purposefully targeting men, men are simply more likely to encounter law enforcement than women as men are generally more likely to drive, to work, and, in some cities, to solicit work in visible areas such as parking lots.[26] More time in cars and in public spaces means more opportunities for law enforcement agents to interrogate one's right to be in the country. (This does not mean that undocumented women are not deported, only that they are deported at lower rates than men.[27]) Women, however, will often remain at home to care for their children, which is not only less expensive than paying caretakers but also reduces their need to drive.[28]

This "gendered racial removal program"[29] may appear to be sympathetic to the undocumented women who are passed over as targets for deportation. Certainly, I am not advocating for a gender equality in deportation that would have seen Fernanda arrested and deported alongside Santiago. But Fernanda's story shines a light on the ostensible sympathy of the deportation machine toward undocumented women: Targets of immigration law enforcement are not the only ones who suffer the emotional and psychological repercussions of the arrest tactics used to detain undocumented immigrants. Those arrested and deported are not the only ones who have to abandon the lives they have established in the United States. Rather, violence against those in mixed-status communities takes many forms. One form, commonly portrayed in the media, is the acute trauma of arrest and deportation. But a second form of violence experienced by mixed-status communities is the slow and chronic suffering engendered by a loved one's haunting absence and the emotional and economic impacts it causes. This violence is patterned by gender, and while all outcomes can be severe and life altering, it is largely the stories of women, fighting to keep their families from slowly unraveling amid their own emotional pain, that are rendered invisible in national discussions of immigration enforcement. This emotional, psychological, and economic turmoil forces women like Fernanda—who will never appear in any official deportation statistics—to uproot their lives and leave the United States, often taking their US citizen children with them.

Hilda Del Cid

Hilda's energy was contagious. She spoke like she moved: quickly and in short, purposeful bursts. Her language was a mix of Spanish and English, peppered with colloquial phrases from her country of birth in Central America. Hilda, like Guadalupe and Fernanda, was part of a mixed-status family. But she differed from Guadalupe and Fernanda in a few notable ways. First, like two-thirds of undocumented immigrants, Hilda had been in the United States for more than ten years,[30] fifteen years altogether, compared to Guadalupe's eight years and Fernanda's two years. Hilda's husband, Arturo, had similarly been in the United States for fourteen years.

This longer time in the United States—ironically influenced by the increasing border security that prevents back-and-forth migration—has caused undocumented immigrants like Hilda to increasingly set down roots and bring their families into the United States. Many have moved from states with traditionally large numbers of Latinos and immigrants, such as Texas and California, to the Midwest,[31] settling in predominantly white, rural counties like those in southeast Michigan. And many of these families, just like Hilda and Arturo's, have spent the bulk of their incomes to build their lives in these tiny Midwestern towns, investing in homes and cars and developing extensive networks and ties with their Spanish- and English-speaking neighbors. The children of mixed-status families, such as Hilda and Arturo's two US citizen sons, have only ever known US schools. Their children join sports teams, debate clubs, and choirs all alongside peers born to US citizen parents.

And with this increasing time and attachment to the United States comes a simultaneous distance from countries of birth. Let's reframe Arturo's time in the United States as his time *away* from Mexico, where he was born. For Arturo, deportation to Mexico would mean deportation to a country he hadn't seen in fourteen years, where he likely had few formal ties, job prospects, or even recent memories.

But Hilda differs from Guadalupe and Fernanda in another critical way that illustrates the reach of immigration enforcement. Guadalupe and Fernanda, Santiago's sister and wife, respectively, had long and established relationships with Santiago and lived with him in the same apartment. Hilda, however, barely knew Santiago. To Hilda and Arturo, Santiago was simply the man who was fixing their car. Arrested after he drove away from Santiago's *taller*, Arturo was swept up in immigration enforcement procedures for which he was not the specified target. Hilda was thus left to cope and raise two children with a husband caught in a broadly cast net of immigration enforcement.

Yet the way in which Hilda's husband was arrested is not uncommon. Immigration enforcement actions frequently result in collateral arrests, or arrests of individuals who are not the target of the actions to begin with and who themselves have no criminal records.[32] Each collateral arrest is, of course, a person, too, intimately connected with a family and community that must suddenly cope with his removal. Not only are these collateral arrests common, but, to some extent, they are incentivized. Congress has mandated that 34,000 detention center beds be filled each night in exchange for funding,[33] and many Field Operation Teams—the units who conduct many of the immigration home raids on behalf of ICE—have monthly arrest quotas they are ordered to fill.[34] Evidence shows that collateral arrests increase under these quota systems.[35] Hilda's husband, then, with no criminal record and connected to Santiago only because he hoped Santiago would be able to fix his car, was one more notch toward that congressionally mandated 34,000 annual detentions.

Hilda's story is harrowing. But it's not unique. Her mixed-status family has lived in the United States for more than a decade, setting down roots and building relationships throughout their community. Hilda's husband, just like thousands of undocumented immigrants throughout the country, was swept up in immigration enforcement for whom someone else was the target. And Hilda's efforts to keep her family together mirror that of other undocumented mothers—or spouses of detained and deported fathers—throughout the United States.

■ ■ ■

Guadalupe's, Fernanda's, and Hilda's stories can be read individually, as narratives of *mujeres podersas* struggling to keep their minds and families intact against the militarized violence of immigration law enforcement.

But their stories, when taken together, teach us about the reach and brutality of an immigration system designed to destabilize Latino mixed-status communities. Together, they illustrate a militarized, violent, and gendered immigration enforcement system that collaborates with those who swore to "serve and protect" and that breaks psyches en route to separating families with deep roots planted in their Midwest communities and homes. Indeed, Guadalupe's, Fernanda's, and Hilda's power is on display not only as the mothers they are, and the resilient survivors they were forced to become, but also in the stories they chose to share. Their individual stories and collective voice illustrate what a life of targeted and racialized violence is like. It is with this knowledge that we can best dismantle this violence.

The Raid: Before

Thursday, November of 2013

About 9:00 a.m. It's cold outside. Inside, in a small makeshift apartment heated by a deep fryer, there's a little more warmth. But the children are getting hungry, and there's not enough milk in the fridge for everyone. Guadalupe asks her brother, Santiago, to pick up some milk from the grocery store. Santiago agrees. He loves Guadalupe's children—his 4-year-old nephew, Carlitos, and his 2-year-old and 2-month-old nieces, Sofía and Fatima—and the grocery store is just across the street, visible from their property. He will just have to walk down the staircase, hop in the car parked on the dirt driveway, and drive over. He shouldn't be gone for long. They could also use some onions and tomatoes for a stew, Guadalupe tells him.

Santiago walks down the stairs and passes the first floor of the warehouse, which serves as the *taller,* or automobile workshop, which is the family's primary source of income. Santiago is aware that the money generated from this *taller* is essential to keep his wife, Fernanda, and their two young children, 1½-year-old Lena and 3-month-old Ignacio, financially afloat. The pressure to make money increased two months ago when Santiago's 18-year-old son, Santiagito, arrived from Mexico. Then, about a month after that, Guadalupe and her children moved in as well, following the arrest and deportation of her daughters' father.

Santiago agrees: milk and stew would be good for everyone in the expanding family, so he and a Guatemalan friend, Julio, who was hanging around the *taller* at the time, get in their car to go to the grocery store. They turn right out of the short street in front of the property and onto

Huron Avenue, the street that would become the site of many other arrests that would happen that day.

There aren't many stores on this stretch of road. Though it's one of the city's main thoroughfares, buildings are fairly sparse, and often set in-between full blocks of trees. Some bigger companies have used the empty space wisely, a scrap metal recycling place, a lumber center, and a landscaping supply store among them. As Santiago and Julio approach the grocery store, an ICE vehicle pulls them over, and agents quickly order them out of the car.

"Put your hands on your head! Put your hands on your head or we'll shoot!"[1] the agents shout. The men do as they are told, fearing they would otherwise be shot in the head.

"Don't run!" the agents yell, pointing their weapons at Santiago and Julio. "Show us your identification!"

Santiago hands the agent his passport.

"Are you residents of the United States?" the agents ask.

"*No, nosotros somos ilegales. No tenemos papeles,*" Santiago responds.

They are "illegals." They do not have papers.

Santiago and Julio are handcuffed and taken to ICE offices.

■ ■ ■

It is Thursday morning, so Arturo and his wife Hilda do what they do every Thursday morning: they drop their children off at school. Afterward, they drive in a single car to Santiago's *taller* to pick up their other vehicle, which Santiago had agreed to repair for them. Arturo and Hilda, both in their early thirties and both undocumented, arrive at the *taller,* pick up their other car, pay the worker, and drive away in separate cars as planned.

Arturo activates his turn signal. With his blinker flashing to the left, he heads west, toward the restaurant where he works, and pulls out onto Huron Avenue. Hilda pulls out shortly after him. Moments later, an SUV from a local law enforcement department flashes its blue and red lights and forces Arturo to pull over on the side of the road. When the agent approaches Arturo's car, he does not ask for his registration, nor does he ask for Arturo's driver's license. Instead, the agent tells Arturo that he needs to speak to him.

Arturo says that until he knows why he has been pulled over, he is not going to say anything.

"You turned your blinker off too soon," the agent says.

Arturo pauses.

He knows he did not turn his blinker off too soon. He would never turn his blinker off too soon. The stakes are simply too high for a brown undocumented man to be turning his blinker off too soon. He would never give law enforcement any possible reason to pull him over.

"Well, what do you need from me?" he asks.

"I don't need anything. But someone else will."

As Arturo remembers it, he had just turned his car in the direction indicated by his blinker when, in "a matter of seconds, I had four cars surround me, pull me out of the car, and started just asking me a thousand questions. And I keep refusing to answer those questions. Until finally another SUV pull over and say, 'You know who I am?' And I'm like, 'I don't know.' He's like, 'You gotta cooperate; I work for ICE.'"

ICE searches Arturo's car, moving the seats, opening the trunk, and banging on the tires. Then they pull off Arturo's shirt to see whether he has any tattoos. "We want to know if you are in a gang," the agent tells him.

In articulate and fluent English that he has perfected after a decade in the United States and in multiple managerial jobs, Arturo responds that he currently is not, nor has he ever been, part of a gang. The agent accuses Arturo of lying.

"I've been working this job forever," the agent says, "and I know people who have been here for twenty years who don't speak as well as you do." The agent cuffs Arturo's wrists and shackles his ankles. He takes Arturo to the ICE office for processing.

Hilda, who followed Arturo onto Huron Avenue, pulls off the road and watches through her window as law enforcement agents pull over, surround, shackle, and drive her husband away. Frightened and unsure of what to do, Hilda picks up her phone and dials Graciela, a board member of Casa Latina, a community-based organization that serves Washtenaw County Latinos and with whom Hilda had worked closely.

Graciela does not hesitate to warn Hilda. "That's immigration detaining your husband. Don't go near him." Graciela then begins to alert the community. Casa Latina sends out a mass text message. Others post on Facebook. Word spreads.

About 2:30 p.m. The sheriff's office receives word that the "no-knock" search warrant has been approved, and agents assemble at Station 2, a few miles from the spot where Santiago was arrested hours before. There, agents likely ready their ballistic helmets, tactical vests, combat boots, AR15 assault rifles, sidearms, and flash bang grenades and prepare to raid Santiago's apartment and *taller* a few hours later.

Law enforcement had begun their investigation of Santiago at least a week before his arrest. ICE agents had conducted a stakeout on the Huron Avenue property to gather evidence of drug trafficking they believed was occurring in his *taller*. During their surveillance, they observed Santiago move back and forth between vehicles in and around the *taller*. They then brought this information to the sheriff's office. As the police record states, "[The agent] observed several cars enter into the complex; Santiago would then retrieve something from inside the truck and then walk back to subject and hand it to them. The vehicle would then leave the area." ICE believed that such behavior—going back and forth between cars in an automobile shop—suspiciously resembled drug trafficking. The stakeout continued on the day of the raid, on which, again, Santiago had suspiciously walked from one vehicle to another before he was arrested as he drove out of his property to pick up some milk for the kids and vegetables for the stew. He was not allowed to make any phone calls after his arrest, lest he alert his wife, sister, children, and nieces that the SWAT team would be raiding their apartment in about nine hours.

According to the police report, Santiago was not the first arrest that day. Earlier that morning, two undocumented Latino men were taken into custody "for being an alien present without permission." One of these men testified that he had seen a shotgun, cocaine, and heroin in Santiago's *taller*. Santiago also had a prior arrest and deportation that occurred about four years earlier, in 2009. When he was arrested, he reportedly had "three .22 caliber rifles and ammunition in his possession along with several crossbows and swords."

Thus, the county's SWAT unit decides to serve the search warrant on Santiago's apartment and *taller*. As the webpage describes:

> Utilization of the...SWAT and Washtenaw Crisis Negotiation Team may include anti-sniper tactics, anti-terrorist tactics, barricaded subjects, and apprehension of armed and/or dangerous persons, executions of search warrants in hazardous situations, crisis situations and hostage rescue operations, dignitary protection, and other situations which may require special training and expertise.

About 3:30 p.m. Francisco, or "Paco" to many of his friends, has a wad of money in his pocket from the seventy-plus hours he works as a dishwasher in a local restaurant. Without a driver's license, it is hard for him to get a bank account, and because he is undocumented, he has not been able to get a license since the REAL ID Act of 2005, implemented in Michigan in 2008. Thus, Paco takes the cash, *el sudor de uno*, or "one's sweat," as he calls it, to pay Santiago for the work on his car. Paco leaves work at about 3:00 p.m. and goes with his friend Esteban to Santiago's *taller*. When the pair arrive, they find the *taller* closed, the gate locked. Paco and Esteban, disappointed that they cannot pick up the car, drive off the short dirt road and onto tree-lined Huron Avenue. When they do, as with Santiago, Julio, and Arturo, agents surround them.

The agents order them out of the car. They point guns at the two men and tell them to hand over their weapons.

"*Pos no traigo armas.*" No weapons, Francisco tells the officers.

"Drugs?"

"*Tampoco.*" No drugs either.

"Car insurance?"

Francisco hands the agent his expired license and the insurance paperwork registered to Frida, Francisco's girlfriend and the current owner of the truck. He also hands the agents his wallet, in which his wad of cash totals about $500. The agent looks at the wallet curiously and asks Francisco where he acquired so much cash.

"It's more money than you could ever make in your life," the agent tells him.

The agents eventually ask Francisco for his immigration papers. He doesn't have them. Francisco is handcuffed forcefully, and the metal digs into his wristbones. He asks the agent to loosen the cuffs. "If you talk more, they are going to be even tighter," the agent says. Francisco and Esteban are both taken to the ICE office.

Despite his many requests to make a phone call, Francisco is forbidden from calling anyone, and, as he is driven away to the ICE office, Frida's truck sits on the side of the road, abandoned.

Thus, between about eight o'clock in the morning and four o'clock in the afternoon, Santiago and Julio, Arturo, Francisco and Esteban, and at least one other man arrested before Santiago left his apartment for the grocery store, all of whom are Latino, none of whom have weapons or drugs in their possession or in their cars, are taken into custody as they drive away from Santiago's *taller*. Word spreads in the community of anti-Latino enforcement. Huron Avenue has been marked: if you are Latino, stay away.

About 4:00 p.m. Guadalupe and Fernanda are getting anxious. Sometimes Santiago would be gone for long stretches at a time, meeting and talking to folks about work. But hours had passed since he left to get milk, onions, and tomatoes from the grocery store, and he still has not returned. Guadalupe's youngest daughter, Fatima, had just been born in August 2013, the same month in which her father was arrested and deported. Guadalupe is perpetually thankful that Santiago has allowed her and Fatima, as well as her two other children, Sofía and Carlitos, to live in the warehouse-cum-apartment with Santiago and his wife. Pooling resources is helpful for everyone, even if the family keeps getting bigger.

Without Santiago, Guadalupe and Fernanda know their lives will change considerably. Who will pay the rent? Who will buy the food and diapers for the five children under the age of 5 living in the apartment?

They need to find out where he is, and they need to find out whether he is okay.

Fernanda decides that she needs help from an English speaker who can better navigate the formal US institutions into which Santiago may have disappeared, so she calls Diane. Diane is a white US citizen and mother to Jessica, who frequently babysits Fernanda's and Guadalupe's children. Sixteen-year-old Jessica also happens to be dating Santiagito. Diane comes over to the apartment and calls the hospital, but Santiago is not there. Eventually, she calls law enforcement, who tells her that Santiago had been arrested and is currently detained.

It is now about 4:00 p.m., so Guadalupe's 4-year-old son, Carlitos, has left school and is at the house of his *madrina*, his godmother. Guadalupe is hesitant to leave the apartment to pick up Carlitos and wonders whether she, too, will be yet one more Latino arrested on Huron Avenue. But she wants to be close to her son again, so she leaves the apartment with an acquaintance, Roberto, who offers to drive her.

Not long after driving off the property, Guadalupe glances in her rear-view mirror, looking past her 2-year-old daughter buckled in the booster seat behind her and sees the blue and red lights of an approaching vehicle.

As with Santiago, Julio, Arturo, Francisco, and Esteban, Guadalupe and Roberto are pulled over, and the agents ask Roberto whether he has his immigration papers. He does not. Again, as with Santiago, Julio, Arturo, Francisco, and Esteban, Roberto is quickly handcuffed, put in a vehicle, and taken away.

The agent turns to Guadalupe.

He pauses to lock eyes with her and then glances to the back seat. "And you? Is this your daughter?" The agent gestures toward 2-year-old Sofía.

"Yes, that's my daughter, and I have another in the house. But I still need to pick up my son." The agent tells Guadalupe that she needs to go back to her apartment right away, without Carlitos. Then the agent leaves. Guadalupe drives back to the apartment as instructed.

About 5:00 p.m. Elena Maria, a former urgent responder with the Washtenaw Interfaith Coalition for Immigrant Rights (WICIR), leaves work. A few hours before, a friend had told her that something was going down on Huron Avenue, and after posting a few questions on social media, Elena Maria was directed to a property across the street from the grocery store.

She drives over and parks her car in the parking lot of Fresh Fish N Chickn, a restaurant adjacent to the string of warehouses in which sits Santiago's *taller*. Elena Maria can feel the tension in the air and calls other urgent responders to find someone to join her. Ofelia, also a social worker, and Amalia, a pastor at a local church, meet Elena Maria at the parking lot. A few moments later, the urgent responders watch as law enforcement vehicles start piling up outside of Santiago's *taller*.

Chapter 2

Un Día Común y Corriente

We sat on folding metal chairs under the shade of a tall pine tree in her yard. It was sunny but not hot, and Hilda would periodically take a break from our Spanish interview to negotiate in English with the customers who paced her front yard in search of clothing and appliances to purchase from her garage sale. I had learned about Hilda's garage sale from a post on Instagram and drove by to see whether her kids, about 11 and 8 years old, had grown out of any clothes that would fit my kids, about 6 and 3. I also wanted to talk to her about the day her husband, Arturo, was arrested on the road outside of Santiago's *taller*, the day that, I imagined, was unlike any other she had ever experienced.

Hilda's house was situated on a moderate-sized plot of land, with both a front yard and a backyard. Two cars and a camper were parked in her driveway in front of a two-car garage. A typical midsized Midwestern home, the lawn was well manicured, with wood chips and gravel placed at strategic intervals to add personality to the front of the house. The nice lawn, however, did nothing to stop Hilda's sons, Sebastián and Alejandro, from chasing each other around on their bicycles all over the grass. Every so often, they would even bump into the table where Hilda and I sat, under the tall pine, discussing what it was like to be an undocumented Central American woman with two US citizen children married to an undocumented Mexican man who was swept up in the most intense immigration enforcement actions anyone in the area could remember. Nearly two years after the raid, the impacts still affected everyone deeply.

I turned on the recorder, and Hilda began to speak rapidly, looking back and forth between her children, her potential customers, and me: *"Fíjate, fue un día común y corriente."* "Listen, it was a day just like any other day." Then, in the same breath, Hilda launched into the story of

Arturo's arrest and detention, and her struggles to keep her family together amid her own mounting depression, to lie to her children about her
husband's whereabouts, and to raise the money required to keep him in
the United States.

But, as important as the story Hilda shared about her husband's arrest
is the way in which she started the story—"Listen, it was a day just like
any other." Hilda and Arturo were doing what they and every other family
in the county did every morning: dropping kids at school, picking up cars
from the shop, driving to work—the general stuff of daily life. Sometimes,
unpredictably and arbitrarily it seemed, these ordinary average days
were interrupted by encounters with law enforcement. These encounters
could end in a wide variety of ways, ranging from verbal warnings or
firm lectures about driver responsibility to being surrounded by five ICE
vehicles while your car is searched for drugs and your body is inspected
for tattoos, or, as I show later, being choked to death on the sidewalk or
shot and killed in your car in front of a 4-year-old child. And no matter
how one acted during the interaction, the end result seemed to be simply
a function of officer discretion.

Indeed, while Hilda spent much of the conversation discussing how
her husband was pulled over, interrogated, and detained in the winter
of 2013, she didn't just discuss that encounter with law enforcement.
Rather, she, like nearly everyone in the mixed-status Latino community
of Washtenaw County, could detail an encounter with law enforcement
officers that *almost* resulted in deportation. Life was simply filled with
close calls and near-deportations: with deportations that almost were,
could have been, and just might be next time.

For Hilda and Arturo, these interactions began with law enforcement;
for other community members, they extended to a range of formal institutions, such as clinics and other government offices, throughout the
county. No matter where these interactions took place and regardless of
the outcome or the extent of the violence, the same basic formula was
followed. First, an official attempts to establish that you are undocumented and, therefore, deportable. When he has done so, he may then coerce
you into obedience through the threat—whether actual or implied—of

deportation. Cues to investigate your immigration status often come from a combination of the documents you have and your physical presentation, including your skin color, accent, language ability, and a host of other factors that together have been described as "symbols of deportability."[1] To put it as simply as possible, when an official thinks you are undocumented, your world can quickly be reduced to two choices: compliance or deportation.

Hilda and Arturo show us the various ways in which undocumented status is used to coerce compliance through the possibility of deportation. Yolanda, another community member, illustrates the ways in which this coercion can extend to interactions with a range of institutions. Finally, through a ride-along with Officer Lisa Flynn, we see that the control exerted over undocumented community members can also be used to control the citizens and visa holders with whom they live and work. Through each interaction, we witness the enormous range of discretion available to officials, who can interpret symbols of deportability in any way they choose. Taken together, the everyday endeavors in which Hilda, Arturo, Yolanda, and others are nearly deported also remind us of one additional fundamental truth of life for undocumented Latinos in mixed-status communities: the stuff of every day is simultaneously necessary and exceptionally risky.

"You Can't Even Make Licenses in Your Country"

Hearing the sirens behind her, Hilda slows down her car and pulls over to the side of the road. She's scared, and more than a little nervous. Her Michigan driver's license has been expired for four years, but, she notes to herself, she is not driving illegally. While she knows this to be true, however, she is going to have to convince the officer. Her mind flashes to her children and her husband, and she hopes she is able to make it back home to them later.

Certainly, many citizens are unfamiliar with the fear Hilda was experiencing at that moment. But to millions of undocumented immigrants throughout the United States, who, like Hilda, are unable to get driver's licenses, that fear is all too familiar. Thanks to information-sharing programs such as Secure Communities, anytime someone is booked into a county jail, her biometric data are sent to a number of other law enforcement agencies, including ICE. If the person is undocumented, ICE can request a detainer, commonly called an "immigration hold," in which the individual is held for forty-eight hours past the time of her release so that ICE may place her in immigration proceedings.[2] So, every time Hilda steps behind the wheel, she must ask herself whether the drive is worth the risk of being pulled over and the catastrophic potential for deportation that could follow.

But this wasn't always the case. The change in driver's license accessibility can be traced back to the sweeping policy changes that constituted part of the US "Global War on Terror." The 9/11 Commission, which formed in the aftermath of the events of September 11, 2001, recommended that the federal government set uniform standards of identification across all states to prevent "terrorists from obtaining state-issued identification documents" in order to "secur[e] America against terrorism."[3] This recommendation came to fruition with Public Law 109-13, also called the REAL ID Act of 2005, which made it impossible for a range of immigrants to obtain driver's licenses.[4]

The REAL ID Act is complicated, and its patchwork implementation across states only adds to its complexity. Officially, the REAL ID Act created two different types of driver's licenses, with different individuals eligible to apply for each. US citizens and some categories of lawfully present immigrants are able to apply for licenses that can be used for "official purposes," including boarding aircraft and entering federal buildings and nuclear power plants. The remaining lawfully present immigrants and all undocumented immigrants could only apply for licenses that cannot be used for federal purposes.

Theoretically, anyone in the United States could access a driver's license regardless of their immigration status, but providing these licenses would require states to commit to creating and maintaining the bureaucratic infrastructure to produce, screen for, and regulate two different types of licenses. While about twelve states and the District of Columbia opted to comply with this two-tiered system—thus permitting undocumented immigrants to apply for and renew driver's licenses—undocumented immigrants in most of the United States were suddenly unable to drive legally. Michigan numbered among these states. Those with licenses issued before implementation of the REAL ID Act watched as looming expiration dates signaled the day in which yet another aspect of their *días comúnes y corrientes* would take on exceptionally more risk. Many undocumented minors who grew up in the United States lost yet one more traditional American rite of passage.[5] For those entering the country after 2005, driving legally would never be a part of their lives.

Thanks in large part to US efforts to restrict terrorism after 9/11, Hilda sits in her car without a Michigan license to show the approaching officer, who now peers at her through her rolled-down car window.

He asks Hilda to show him her driver's license.

But Hilda doesn't hand the officer an expired Michigan license. Instead, she hands the officer the driver's license from her country of birth in Central America, along with an English translation of it.

That's when he begins to get angry.

Hilda: Yeah. And then he tells me, "What is this?" I tell him, "It's a license from my country."... [He tells me] "I don't know what this is." I told him, "I think you can read English because here it is translated into English [handing him the translation], so what is the problem?" So he tells me, "You can't even make licenses in your country." And I tell him, "And you, how do you know if you aren't from my country?"... [He says], "This doesn't mean anything to me," and I tell him, "Well for you no, but for me, yes." And he got so angry...

Hilda was correct. Her license, along with the English translation, did "mean something." Specifically, it meant Hilda was driving legally. Given the potential for police interaction, it is no surprise that driving is a source of constant stress, not only for undocumented drivers but for all members of their families, who fear that when someone drives away—to the grocery store, to the doctor, to pick their kids up from school, or, perhaps, to pick their car up from the shop—they may never return.[6] So, since the implementation of the REAL ID Act, undocumented drivers without access to state driver's licenses began using a number of strategies to reduce the time they spent behind the wheel. Some relied increasingly on public transportation or bicycles to get to their destinations. Other times, they asked for rides from those in the mixed-status community who had driver's licenses—either because their licenses had yet to expire or because they were citizens or visa holders who could validly apply for or renew a driver's license. Sometimes, they reached out to organizations, such as the Washtenaw Interfaith Coalition for Immigrant Rights, whose volunteers often had licenses.

But all of these risk-reduction strategies have their limits. In northern states, such as Michigan, climate can make it impossible to bike consistently throughout the year, and public transportation outside of major cities can be unreliable or have inconvenient operating hours that limit the ability to schedule around it. Manual labor jobs, such as roofing or landscaping—common jobs for many members of mixed-status communities—often require vehicles to transport tools to and from the job site. Volunteers are simply not always available or are available inconsistently. And, for many, the demands of family life, such as taking one's children to school, to church, or to a doctor's appointment, require an available caregiver to drive them there. No matter how mixed-status communities rearranged themselves and changed their behaviors, it was—and is—virtually impossible for all undocumented community members to refrain from ever driving at all. So, like Hilda and Arturo, they choose to drive.

Undocumented drivers without licenses use at least one more strategy to reduce the risk of driving without a state driver's license: they drive with driver's licenses from their countries of birth. The 1943 Convention on the Regulation of Inter-American Automotive Traffic lists a number of treaty countries whose licenses are accepted throughout the United States, including in Michigan per the Michigan Vehicle Code Act 300 of 1949, Section 257.302a. Among these treaty countries is Hilda's country of birth in Central America, along with others like Mexico or Guatemala, from which members of the mixed-status community in Washtenaw County originate. But licenses from treaty countries alone do not always automatically replace state driver's licenses. Because they are often written in the dominant language of the country in which they are produced, in many states, an English translation of the foreign license is also required. These translated driver's licenses are marketed as "international driver's licenses," a confusing label, the relevance of which will be clear shortly. To add to the complexity, law enforcement departments—often individual officers like the one now peering through Hilda's window—tend to have their own standards in regards to traffic stops and foreign licenses.[7]

Unable to convince Hilda that she is driving illegally, the officer tries another tactic to assert his control in the interaction.[8]

Hilda: ... But listen, he got angry with me, so he asked me, "Why are you talking to me like this?" I told him, "I am not talking to you without respect; I am responding how I should." And you know what? He had the nerve to tell me that in my country we can't even make driver's licenses. I told him, "Well in my country it is not a license like the one in the US, but let me tell you, in my country we were at least free to express ourselves ... That's just how it is." And he got very upset, and he threw my license and told me, "You know what, I don't even know what to do with you." I told him, "It's cause I haven't done anything." ...

With admirable presence of mind, Hilda asks why he had pulled her over in the first place.

Hilda: Yes, and after [he threw my license at me], he told me, "You know what, it's better if you just go. It's better to go before I change my mind," he told me. Just because he stopped me doesn't mean I had broken a law ...

William: And were you scared?

Hilda: Well, yes, I was scared, but I wasn't going to show it. Because like I said, I hadn't done anything.

William: Mm-hmm.

Hilda: So I asked him why he stopped me, and he said, "Because your license is expired" [referring to Michigan driver's license, which expired about four years prior]. ... But I told him "here is the license from my country. I know that I can drive with it. So?" ... Yeah, so he told me "for me this is worthless." I said, "Well it's what I have. At least I have it." He got so mad, and he let me go. He said he didn't know what to do with me.

Hilda's interaction with the officer was not unique; instead, it typified countless other descriptions of interactions between undocumented Latino community members and police officers in which laws, ostensibly unrelated to immigration status, have the potential to disrupt their lives and result in their removal. The REAL ID Act did not simply create another opportunity to break a law and suffer the associated penalty. Rather, it manufactured additional circumstances in which the world of the undocumented immigrant could be reduced into two opposing choices: compliance or deportation. This opened up enormous opportunity for officers' discretion whenever they pulled over and knocked on the windows of people like Hilda and Arturo.

These interactions—*comúnes y corrientes* that they are—often appear to be regular traffic stops, with no mention of immigration, deportation, or documentation status by either the officer or the individual he has pulled over. In Hilda's description, she never says how she came to the United States or why she doesn't have a US driver's license, and the officer doesn't ask (though plenty of officers do). But the entire conversation is filled with attempts on the part of the officer to reveal Hilda's undocumented status and that, if he wanted, he could have her deported. Each of his efforts is met with a countermove by Hilda, and each of these countermoves is filled with risk: Will this question, this argument, this rebuttal, allow me to stay with family, or will it push the officer to deport or kill me? Should I stand up for myself and resist the unjust accusations, or take the penalty and move on? And what will the penalty be?

I do not detail the regulations around licenses and driving so that the reader may become an expert on these regulations. Rather, it is important to acknowledge the enormity and complexity of the web of policies and required items that shape everyday activities—in this case, driving—of a significant portion of the mixed-status community. Each shift in driving policy, each nuance in licensing regulation, each conditional requirement creates the space for law enforcement officers to exercise their discretion in the face-to-face interactions with undocumented drivers on the road. What do they choose to do with this discretion? Often, as Hilda and Arturo now show us, they coerce compliance through the threat—whether implicit or explicit—of deportation.

Hilda, of course, understands well the undertones of the interaction between her and the officer, though she doesn't use the words "coercion" to describe it. She simply calls it "racism."

Hilda began her description of the interaction with the officer by saying, "Just a bit ago, a police officer stopped me. So racist." I asked Hilda what she meant when she described the officer as racist.

Hilda: Well, "racist" because they [police officers] see you and they stop you, just because we look Hispanic... Later, they ask, "Don't you speak English?" and you are trying to communicate with as little or as much English as you can. But they still say, "I don't understand you" and start to *indagar mas* (further investigate, look into). When you [are not] able to communicate, you give them a chance to start investigating where they shouldn't. And I know they don't have any reason to ask you about your [immigration] status. But they do it.

To Hilda, the attempts to invalidate her right to drive are rooted in the fact that she "looks Hispanic," a presumable reference to her skin color and, likely, a number of other physical features like her hair color, stature, and clothing. Hilda also immediately connects her appearance to her language ability. That is, "looking Hispanic" provides both the motive for the stop and the first clues into how the officer can begin to invalidate the defenses of the person driving the car. Pull them over. See whether they can speak English. If not, *indaga un poco mas*, dig a little deeper. In the description of racism Hilda gave, lack of English fluency was sufficient motive for the hypothetical officer to turn a traffic stop into an immigration interaction. In Hilda's case, because of her skill in English and knowledge of the law, this did not happen to her, but the officer no less attempted to find a crack in her story that he could use to investigate her immigration status or at least imply that he knew she was driving illegally. His attempts were equally rooted in anti-Latino immigrant stereotypes: documents in the "wrong" language from bureaucratically nonfunctional home countries are inherently invalid.

Hilda's scenario illustrates one possible way in which these interactions can end, as she is able to drive off without being detained or ticketed despite the officer's frustration with her. Her husband's traffic stop, however, illustrates how drastically different these interactions can conclude, depending on the whims and ulterior motives of officers. Further, Arturo's interaction with the police during a traffic stop embodies the result of driving that many undocumented drivers fear most: threat, humiliation, and long, expensive detentions away from family and community. Yet, despite the many ways in which the outcome of his interaction differed from his wife's, the strategies the officers use to coerce Arturo into compliance mirror those seen in their interaction with Hilda: delegitimize one's right to be in the United States until the only alternative to deportation is compliance. Also, like Hilda's situation, the encounter begins with the everyday act of driving and interactions with the local police, not with immigration authorities.

"You Turned Off Your Blinker Too Soon"

I sip on the Diet Coke in a large Styrofoam cup that Arturo hands me when I visit him at his second job. He smiles as I greet him. After much encouragement from Hilda, Arturo has agreed to talk to me about his arrest and detention. Arturo is jovial with me, just as he is with the hungry, predominantly white students of a local Midwestern university who periodically order burritos from him.

In between customers, Arturo walks over to my table, waits for me to turn the recorder back on, and then continues his story exactly where he left off, alternating between following my prompts and guiding the interview to where he really believes it should go anyway. Hilda told stories rapidly and had the habit of telling the same story multiple times, recapping and reviewing, adding new details at each retelling, and starting at different points each time. Arturo's style was different: linear, lyrical, and almost always following a narrative arc with protagonists, antagonists, and a clear climax to each story. He's funny at times, dark at times, and, always, thoroughly engaging. Most impressive, at least to me, is that he manages to be all of these things in two different languages.

But Arturo and Hilda both shared a storytelling habit that I love: the scenes they created were filled with dialogue, and, at times, they each served as both omnipotent narrators and characters in their own vignettes.

Arturo serves another burrito and then sits back down at our table. I unpause the recorder, and he begins to tell me about the moments after he picked up his car from Santiago's *taller* and drove back onto Huron Avenue.

Arturo: So that day, Hilda and I, my wife, we went to the shop…It was right after we drop our kids in school…I get back in my car ready to, headed to downtown for other stuff plus my meeting, and she was gonna do her normal activities. You know, go back home. You know, clean and whatever.

But before he is able to drive even "an eighth of a mile," the sirens go off behind him, and he pulls over to the side of the road. Shortly thereafter, an officer from a local law enforcement department approaches him. The officer tells Arturo that he turned his blinker off too soon after changing lanes.

Moments later, Arturo is surrounded by five law enforcement vehicles, at least two are from ICE. An ICE agent approaches him:

Arturo: [The ICE agent is] like, "You gotta cooperate. I work for ICE. You know what that means?" I'm like, "I do know what it is." He's like, "So are you legal?" I'm like, "Why do I have to answer those questions? I'm pretty sure if you work for ICE you should know."

[A higher-ranking ICE officer says], "You better cooperate because I can make your life miserable or I can make your life really easy. What do you wanna do?"…So at that point, he just put handcuffs tight from my hands, my ankles, and my wrists, and I was like, "[You] need to do all this for who knows what?"

The agent wastes no time reminding Arturo of his discretionary power, telling him that, depending on what Arturo does next, his life can be "miserable" or "really easy." Just like in Hilda's interaction with the officer, there is no explicit threat of deportation. In this case, however, especially when immediately following the agent's inquiry as to whether Arturo is "legal," the implication is clear.

His wrists are cuffed, his ankles shackled, and agents begin to search his car. Then, as they did to his wife, they begin to delegitimize Arturo's right to be in the United States:

> **Arturo:** So they flip my car upside down, literally. They move the seats, they opened the trunk, they banging on the tires, the whole body of the car, and they pull my shirt off and they say if I have any tattoos. I say, "No, I do not."

I am not surprised they search Arturo's body for tattoos. The Department of Homeland Security often interprets tattoos on Latino skin as a sign of gang involvement.[9] But when the shackled, bare-torsoed brown man on the side of the road does not have any visible tattoos, officers try a second tactic to delegitimize his presence in the United States.

> **Arturo:** And I was like "Why [are you asking about tattoos]?" He's like, "[Are] you part of the gang?" I'm like "No." "You know what it [a gang] is?" "Of course I know what it is, but I never been part of it. And I never will be." He's like, "Are you sure you have no tattoos at all?" I'm like, "I guarantee you that."

As with his wife, officers are having more trouble delegitimizing this fluent English-speaking immigrant than they had likely anticipated. They first search for visible clues of gang involvement: in this case tattoos, but only because they are on Latino skin. But they find none. Then they imply that "gang" may be one of those English words Latino immigrants just don't understand and ask him whether he knows what a gang is. Arturo responds not only by confirming that, yes, he does know the meaning of the word "gang" but also by "guaranteeing" that he is not in one, and then by using the present perfect and future tense conjugations to describe that he has never "been" nor ever "will be" part of a gang. This level of English fluency seems to frustrate the agent.

So the agent tries a different strategy. Maybe the issue is not that Arturo speaks English poorly. Maybe the issue is that Arturo speaks English *too* well:

Arturo: And then he start criticizing me and questioning me of why. He's like, "Can you write, read, and speak English?" And I'm like, "Yeah." "How long you been in United States?" [I told him] "I been for eleven plus years." He's like, "So how do you learn?" I'm like, "Just jobs and school and I just pick it up on the street, with friends, and you know, coworkers and stuff." He's like, "It's not normal. I've been doing this for decades, and I know. Write this for me."

Arturo stands there befuddled. How has his English fluency—an ability the United States continually demands of immigrants—turned criminal so quickly? First, it was implied that he didn't know English well enough to recognize the word "gang" and therefore couldn't be expected to say whether he was part of one. Then, it was suggested that his English was so good that he must be involved in some high-level illegal activity. Arturo realizes the trap set for him, that, somehow, if he takes the pen from the agent's hand, he is—however little sense it makes—incriminating himself by confirming his now-criminal level of English fluency. But, at the same time, the agent has already laid out the only two options Arturo has: disobey the officer and experience something "miserable" or comply and enjoy the "really easy" route of the benevolent agent who favorably exercises his discretion.

Arturo, cornered between deportation and compliance, takes the pen from the agent's hand and begins to write:

Arturo: So I write it down. At that point I was with the mentality that if I cooperate and if I show that I can be a person who can earn the spot with the society in United States, and I've been doing everything that I should, he would be easy and probably, you know help me out. It was the other way around.

Indeed, it was "the other way around" for Arturo. Arturo is placed in the back seat of the ICE cruiser, where he drives around with officers for five hours, witnessing the arrest of others who look like him. When he finally arrives at the detention center he finds himself among, according to his estimate, about seventy other brown bodies rounded up by ICE agents.[10] The agents, who recall that Arturo is so fluent in English that he can speak *and* write, then exercise the full range of their discretion and ask Arturo to use his nefariously acquired language skills to translate for the others they have detained. Arturo agrees, hoping ICE will make his life easier in exchange.

They don't.

And his life is about to get a lot worse.

■ ■ ■

Immigration enforcement is not simply the occasional deportation of undocumented immigrants who are removed from their homes in the United States and transferred to their countries of birth. Rather, deportation is the traumatic end result of a day-to-day life clouded by the aura of possible deportation. Every day has the potential to be life altering and financially ruinous, leaving one's children motherless or fatherless. A number of similarities between Hilda's and Arturo's encounters with law enforcement illustrate the pervasiveness of the everyday threat of deportation.

First, while it is ultimately agents from ICE who remove undocumented immigrants from the United States, immigration agents do not necessarily initiate the interactions that lead to these deportations. In both Hilda's and Arturo's cases, it was local police officers who initiated the interactions. Second, these interactions were initiated because Hilda and Arturo had (allegedly) broken laws unrelated to immigration status. For Hilda, it was driving without a license. For Arturo, it was turning his blinker off too soon. Notably, even though ICE and the local law enforcement had already agreed to collaborate to pull over and question Arturo, the initial excuse was still just a broken traffic law.

Third, in each interaction officers did not explicitly threaten deportation. Yet, through insinuation, selective questioning, and context, it was clearly the backdrop against which all negotiations took place. Once officers establish that they can deport you if they want, they are able to coerce you into compliance.

Fourth, as Hilda had implied, officers interpret a range of documents, symbols, and aspects of presentation as sufficient reason to begin to *indagar mas*—to look more deeply—into immigration status. It is not a simple matter of which ID is handed to the officer, but the color of the hand that holds it and the accent of the voice that describes it. In Hilda's case, the officer claimed that he pulled her over because of her expired Michigan license. Clearly, unlike Hilda's skin color, an expired license is not visible through a car window.[11]

How do these factors play out in interactions with institutions other than law enforcement? Some of these institutions—unlike law enforcement—may not have a direct way in which they can get you deported. Can undocumented status still be used for coercion? Can this coercion extend to the citizens who themselves cannot be deported? And last, if so many documents and aspects of presentation can be read to mean one is deportable, can those symbols be manipulated to hide that one is undocumented?

ID Roulette

Yolanda, a 30-something-year-old Mexican woman, stops her car at a red light on a regular day in September 2015. Pausing briefly, she takes her foot off the brake, turns the wheel right, and eases onto the gas, turning right on red. That's when she hears the sirens behind her and pulls over to the side of the road.

The officer approaches the car, tells Yolanda that it was illegal to turn right on red at that particular intersection, and asks to see Yolanda's driver's license. Because Yolanda has no Michigan license to show the officer, the officer gives Yolanda a ticket for driving without a license and has her car towed.

In the days that follow, Yolanda calls Rodrigo, a cofounder of WICIR, to assist her in getting her car out of the impoundment lot. Rodrigo asks me to join them, and together we drive in my car to pick up Yolanda.

While Yolanda did not have a valid driver's license, neither from Michigan nor from her country of birth, she had a number of other means of identifying herself in her purse. None of these allowed her to drive. And each was interpreted in different ways in different places by different people with different incentives to accept or reject Yolanda's attempts to prove that she belonged in the United States.

One of the identification cards in Yolanda's purse had been causing headaches in Washtenaw County for some time. Known as an international driver's license, these documents are English translations of one's driver's license from her country of birth.[12] Both the original license and the international driver's license are necessary when using a non-English driver's license from a treaty country, as described earlier. Hilda had both the license from her country of birth and the translation of it, and thus could drive without a Michigan license. But only having one of the two documents often does not suffice.[13] For Yolanda, because she no longer had her original Mexican driver's license, she was functionally driving without a license.

Now, was it necessary for the officer to impound her car? Here, as with many aspects of law enforcement, the answer depends on officer discretion. In regards to driving without a license, Michigan Vehicle Code Act 300 of 1949, Section 257.904, is silent about towing but does state that a first offense is punishable "by imprisonment for not more than 93 days or a fine of not more than $500.00, or both." Advocates in our county have seen cases in which officers ticket undocumented drivers and allow them to drive on, perhaps after lecturing them on attaining a driver's license (which is impossible); we have also seen cases like Yolanda's, in which the vehicle is towed. But given that "imprisonment for not more than 93 days" could very well lead to Yolanda's removal from the country, perhaps the towed car was preferable to the alternative, even if it was not necessary.

On the one hand, Yolanda is not taken to jail, where her information would likely have been shared with ICE; ICE might have asked the jail to hold her so they could detain her so they could, if they saw fit, deport her. On the other hand, Yolanda now had to remove her car from impound—not a simple procedure. Removing a car from the impoundment lot in Washtenaw County requires providing (1) proof of vehicle insurance; (2) proof of ownership of the vehicle, such as title or registration; and (3) a valid driver's license. There is also the fee for both the towing service and vehicle storage. If one does not have a driver's license, one must bring someone who possesses a valid license so that the pair can recover the impounded car.

Buying car insurance generally requires having a driver's license. So Yolanda, like millions of other undocumented immigrants without licenses, also lacked car insurance. Thus, acquiring car insurance was the first step of getting Yolanda's car out of impound. We first stop at a house-cum-office that Rodrigo heard about from a friend to see what Yolanda's insurance options might be. As Rodrigo, Yolanda, and I enter the house, we see a front desk covered in placards and certificates that grant what had once been a residential space an aura of professional legitimacy. A white woman, likely in her fifties, invites the three of us into her office, located just to the left of the front counter at the entrance. I follow Rodrigo and Yolanda into the office and wonder how the woman perceives the three of us. While we are all Latinos, our presentations, including our accents as we spoke Spanish and English, our clothes, and the variations in tones of our brown skin, were likely to be read individually in a variety of ways. Together, I was unsure what others would make of us and whether their interpretations could affect our interactions with formal institutions. If we (or one of us) are interpreted to be undocumented, would we be opening the whole group up to coercion?

Rodrigo, who has navigated this scenario with other community members, begins the conversation by telling the woman behind the desk that we are looking for car insurance for Yolanda, who has an international driver's license. The woman behind the desk tells us immediately that she spoke with someone about international driver's licenses just the other day, and, unfortunately, she does not provide car insurance to those with international licenses. It is unclear whether she means that she will not sell car insurance to Yolanda if Yolanda has an international driver's license only (that is, with no foreign license to match), that she will not insure foreign drivers without US driver's licenses generally, or that she understands the difference between driver's licenses from a foreign country and international driver's licenses used to translate them. Rodrigo and Yolanda do not push the interaction further, allowing the unasked question as to why Yolanda does not have a Michigan driver's license to dissipate in the air, and we drive to another insurance office.

This insurance office is located in a storefront not far from where

Yolanda's car has been impounded. I recognize the logo on the front of the office from the commercials of this large multinational, top-ten-in-the-US insurance corporation. We enter through glass doors and approach a set of three or four desks surrounded by cubicle walls staffed by young salespeople wearing headsets. A young white man, in his early twenties at most, invites us to sit across from him in his cubicle and tells us immediately that the policy of the company is to insure only those who have had a minimum of six months of insurance coverage. So Yolanda is turned away, not because of her international driver's license, but because she does not have six months of previous insurance coverage.

The young white man slowly glances from Rodrigo to Yolanda to me and back again, and asks if any of us have had six months of coverage, probably giving us the opportunity to change the storyline about who is applying, why, and with what documents and insurance history. We all let the pause linger between glances, everyone waiting for everyone else to decide what the next step is. Somewhere in the exchange we mention the international driver's license, which seems to be irrelevant because Yolanda does not have six months of continuous coverage anyway.

It seems clear this salesman is unsure of the relationships among the three of us and unsure of how to proceed, so he continues with the same corporate line: without a minimum of six months of previous insurance coverage, he cannot sell auto insurance to Yolanda. It is also clear to me that he is not really turning us away either. He's not really being firm, just letting the corporate line drift out there to see whether anyone comes up with something better.

A few moments later, someone does come up with something better.

A white woman in the cubicle next to him overhears the conversation, and tells us that, because we are using an international driver's license, her boss could find cheaper auto insurance for Yolanda. Further, because Yolanda is a foreign driver (inasmuch as she has an international driver's license), she does not have to have six months of continual coverage as was previously stated multiple times as the reason she could not buy insurance from this company. The international driver's license that was the original reason that Yolanda could not buy insurance at the first location was the only reason she was able to purchase car insurance without six months of continuous insurance at the second location.

The woman ushers the three of us into the office of a short Middle Eastern man who immediately scrolls through a few screens on his computer, and, in less than five minutes, gives us a quote of $263 for the first month of car insurance and $270 for every month after from an insurance company whose sign is not on the front door.

Yolanda agrees to the offer and pulls out an envelope full of twenty-dollar bills to pay for the insurance. The man who sold Yolanda the insurance pulls out an even bigger wad of bills, sandwiched by a hundred-dollar bill on the outside, and mentions that he doesn't know if he has change for the fourteen twenty-dollar bills that Yolanda is about to give him. Rodrigo and I pull out our wallets and try to piece together three dollars so the salesman won't further price gouge Yolanda by keeping the extra seventeen dollars for which he is unable to make change from his fat sandwich of twenties. We all know that this is our best chance for Yolanda to get car insurance, so we accept that the seventeen dollars that will end up in the man's pocket is a minor intrusion, given how powerless we actually are anyway. But we manage to find the three extra singles, Yolanda hands the man the cash, signs the paperwork, and is instructed to come back again next month to pay the newly acquired monthly insurance she was eligible for as a "foreign" driver with an international driver's license with no matching driver's license from her home country.

Thus, step one—provide car insurance—is complete. Luckily, step two—provide proof of ownership of the vehicle—is also complete, as Yolanda has the title to the car. The only remaining steps are to show a driver's license and pay for the car.

We drive away and head over to the impound facility to retrieve Yolanda's vehicle. When we arrive, Rodrigo begins to talk with one of three white women seated behind a glass window. The woman requests the proper paperwork from Yolanda, and Yolanda hands her (1) the freshly minted insurance policy, (2) registration for the car, and (3) Rodrigo's Michigan driver's license.

The woman accepts the documents Yolanda hands her.

However, because the only piece of identification with a photo is the Michigan driver's license that belongs to Rodrigo, there is no evidence that the "Yolanda" on the insurance paperwork is the Yolanda in front of the woman at that moment, and thus Yolanda is asked to produce a photo ID to prove she is the Yolanda on the insurance (which does not have a photo). Yolanda opens her wallet and hands the clerk her Washtenaw ID, a form of photo identification available to all residents of Washtenaw County.[14]

I recognize that this story is already exceptionally convoluted, but it is important to pause and give a brief history of the Washtenaw ID. The Washtenaw ID is part of a growing movement across the country to create forms of identification accessible to all members of the community. Essentially, public health researchers and advocates understand ID restrictions are yet one more means by which marginalized communities are prevented from accessing the health-promoting resources to which they are entitled.[15] The Washtenaw ID is available to all residents of the county who can meet a given set of criteria, none of which require a Social Security number, permanent address, or gender distinction that matches your gender presentation (as do most government forms of ID). I had been part of the evaluation team of the Washtenaw ID Project for a few months before it became publicly available in June 2015. Here we were, three months later, and I doubted that the ID had fully saturated the community and the myriad organizations that might encounter it. Indeed, it was possible the administrator behind the glass had never seen one before. Frankly, I feared that if the administrators wanted to reject a form of ID, the Washtenaw ID (despite being a valid form of government issued ID) would be the one they'd choose. And they likely had the discretion to do so.

Perhaps sensing the same tension, Rodrigo looks at me and, in a neutral tone just loud enough for others to overhear, tells me, in English, that he is glad to see that the Washtenaw ID is used so widely in Washtenaw County. I smile and try to subtly reinforce what I believe he is doing by emphasizing that this is a legitimate government document (which it is) used widely throughout our county. I also interpret Rodrigo's quick engagement with me about the Washtenaw ID as a strategy contrary to what we had been doing throughout the day. That is, we avoided the awkward silence so that the clerks could not think of a way to reject Yolanda and would just move along with the interaction as if it were any other interaction with someone who was not an undocumented Latino.

But there is another critical piece of the interaction that deserves analysis. Rodrigo actively called attention to the ID, but when he did so, he highlighted that the Washtenaw ID was not identification from another country but from Washtenaw County, where we, they, and all these other US citizens live, work, and play on a daily basis. Whereas Yolanda was initially rejected from buying insurance because she was read as a foreigner, here we both believed we needed to highlight her non-foreignness for the ID to be accepted.

The woman behind the glass looks at the Washtenaw ID. She does not compare the ID to a list of acceptable IDs but simply looks at it, accepts it, and hands it back to Yolanda.

The administrator had now accepted Yolanda's vehicle registration, Yolanda's car insurance that we were only able to purchase because of Yolanda's international license, Rodrigo's Michigan driver's license, Yolanda's Washtenaw ID, and Yolanda's $230, and hands us the keys to the car that was ticketed due to Yolanda's lack of a Mexican driver's license to match the international driver's license she carried with her. Rodrigo and Yolanda pause to calculate where the $230 charge comes from and agree that they are being charged for an extra day of impounding. Rodrigo points this out to the clerk, stating that he called the impound facility and was explicitly told that he would not pay for the extra day of storage if he picked the car up in the morning. He asks the clerk whether he was given the wrong information. The clerk says, yes, he was given the wrong information. But if we argue for the fair fee we were promised, would it bother the administrator? And if it bothered her, would she, like the ICE agent who confronted Arturo, decide to make our lives "miserable" instead of "really easy"? No one pursues the issue further, and Yolanda takes out her envelope of rapidly diminishing cash and pays for the extra day.

As we walk into the lot, Yolanda hands the keys to her car to Rodrigo so he can drive her home. She doesn't have a driver's license, after all.

■ ■ ■

What are we to take from Yolanda's experience? How does it compare to those of Hilda and Arturo? And what does it tell us about the daily experiences of undocumented members of mixed-status Latino communities?

In the previous two discussions, law enforcement officers attempted to leverage Hilda's and Arturo's undocumented statuses—their deportability—to reduce their world into two dichotomous choices: compliance or deportation. While Hilda was largely able to combat the officer's attempts to do so, Arturo was stuck and eventually complied, only to be detained anyway and taken to the ICE office where he was coerced, yet again, into translating for the understaffed agency. Yolanda's experience illustrates the way in which a range of institutional and organizational representatives may similarly leverage their discretion to use her undocumented status to exploit her. While Yolanda's world was not reduced necessarily to compliance or deportation, it was still similarly reduced, this time to compliance or rejection. She could choose to pay monthly, in cash, for a significantly more expensive insurance policy or not have car insurance at all, which would result in her car remaining impounded. With virtually no negotiating power, we had all even accepted that, should Yolanda not be able to find three dollars in cash, the insurance salesmen would simply keep the seventeen dollars change he owed her, unable to break his twenty-dollar bill. When Yolanda was at the towing company, though she was promised not to have to pay for an extra day of impounding, there was nothing she could do to argue with the clerk for her money. She simply had no other choice than to comply with any requests she came across in order to get her car back.

Did any of these organizations have the ability to deport Yolanda? Not directly. But the examples show that, nonetheless, one's deportability can be used for coercion in a range of interactions. For many of the mixed-status families in the community, life without a car is simply impossible. Without her car, Yolanda would not have been able to drive her children to school or to their doctor appointments, important for the 2-year-old whose car seat remained in the impounded car. She herself would not be able to clean the houses of middle- to upper-income Washtenaw County residents. So she's stuck: to live her life, she must continue to break the law and drive without a license. Everything else—losing money, unjustly expensive insurance, extra charges—is comparatively inconsequential.

Yolanda's experience also highlights that the documents and symbols of belonging that are required of undocumented Latinos are never clear-cut. Rather, having the "right" documents is a complicated moving target that varies from one institution to the next and depends largely on the discretion of administrators and officials, many of whom may have their own agendas. Further, often the same signs of belonging are interpreted differently at different times. This was most clear in the absurd number of ways that Yolanda's foreign driver's license shaped the entire experience, peaking when it was both the reason she could not apply for car insurance and, then, an hour later, the only reason she could. Perhaps Arturo provides an even more absurd example, as the agent first attempted to prove his deportability by establishing his lack of English fluency, and then, when he eloquently argued that he was not a part of a gang, established his deportability because he was fluent in English.

Undocumented Latinos must not only discern what documents and other signs of belonging are needed but also determine when each document should be made salient or hidden away. While the international license was not sufficient for Yolanda to drive, it was the document that enabled her to get car insurance. It was specifically because the woman overheard our situation (or perhaps judged us by appearance as soon as we walked in the door. Most likely it was a combination of both.) that Yolanda was taken into the manager's office and offered an array of comparatively expensive insurance options from different companies that did not require six months of continual insurance coverage. Most illustrative was Yolanda's selection of the Washtenaw ID and Rodrigo's subtle reinforcement of its validity to finally convince the clerk to hand Rodrigo the keys to Yolanda's car. Given our situation in which three

Latinos stood on the other side of the glass window from three white women listening to our collectively accented English, I presume Rodrigo understood the importance of emphasizing that this particular ID card was common and accepted in Washtenaw County (if not the country). I question what would have happened had Yolanda shown a Mexican ID or the international driver's license.

Last, though the demands were comparatively minor, Rodrigo had to take time off of work, and we both used our own vehicles to help Yolanda get her car back. Certainly, Yolanda's connection to someone like Rodrigo, who was a permanent resident with a Michigan driver's license, spoke fluent English, and had both a flexible job and an available vehicle, at least partially contributed to her ability to get her car back. Yolanda's deportability did not affect her alone but began to involve, however minimally, others of other immigration statuses, in this case, me, a citizen, and Rodrigo, a permanent resident. But is this the limit to which community members of other immigration statuses—those who are citizens or permanent residents—become involved in the lives of undocumented community members? Does deportability affect only the undocumented members of communities, or are others affected as well?

"Can I See Your ID?"

It's November 2015, about two years after the raid on Guadalupe's apartment and Arturo's lengthy and expensive detention, and I'm riding along with officers to better understand how local police enforce immigration law. Forty minutes after I arrive at my fourth ride-along, I accompany Officer Lisa Flynn to a 911 call placed from a storefront slightly removed from a main thoroughfare. The dispatcher informs us that nine calls were placed from that location, but the reason for the calls is unclear. When we arrive, Lisa knocks on the door and, peering past the six-foot-something white man who opens it, observes another man sitting near broken furniture strewn across the room. Lisa immediately asks the man at the door for identification, and then asks if she can come inside, as it's approaching midnight and getting cold. Through the microphone on her vest, I hear the man decline her request to come in with something vague like "that's okay." Lisa does not question his dissent and remains outside.

The man hands Lisa his ID and tells her his name and birthday, and Lisa comes back to the car to check for any outstanding warrants. He has none, so Lisa returns to firmly plant her booted feet a few inches away from the doorframe. Lisa smells alcohol on his breath. The man explains to Lisa that the nine 911 calls he made were an accident, as he just kept pushing redial on the phone and did not remember that he had dialed 911 the first time. He says that everything is fine now, that he and his friend had gotten into it, but now there is nothing left to worry about. The other man in the room agrees. Lisa gets ready to leave, but before she does, she tells the man at the door that he needs to get a ride home, and points to the taxicabs sitting yards away. If he drives himself home, she promises that he will get arrested for driving while intoxicated. Shortly after, Lisa and I drive away.

This was the second time within the first hour of the ride-along that I had observed Lisa ask for identification. Earlier that night, about five minutes after I arrived at the station, I accompanied Lisa to a house situated well off of the main street. As we arrived, the dark and secluded front yard was alternatingly cut with the red and blue lights of multiple police cars, and the situation felt tense and urgent. Lisa parked the cruiser in front of the house and immediately went inside while I waited in the car. At that point, I knew how to work the dashboard camera, which also recorded the audio from a microphone on Lisa's uniform shirt and was thus able to hear everything that occurred inside the house.

Though there were multiple other officers inside, when Lisa entered she immediately engaged with a frantic woman whose rising and falling voice communicated an escalating standoff with her roommate over a cigarette.[16] Lisa engaged with a soft, neutral tone, and I could easily imagine her getting down on one knee and looking the woman in the eye. Lisa told the woman she would work on getting her a cigarette and asked what kind she smoked. Calmly, Lisa asked the woman for her ID because, she says, she didn't know her yet. Eventually, the officers decided the woman needed to go to the hospital to see her counselor. Lisa escorted her to the ambulance waiting outside and told her it was nice to meet her.

In the few hours I spent with her, I saw Lisa calmly approach situations that could have turned violent and engage the individuals involved, often using personal favors and always using direct and humanizing eye contact, body language, and tone to de-escalate the situation. In the first example, Lisa did not insist on entering the storefront when the man denied her entrance, even though, as she pointed out, she could interpret the damaged property as sign of an altercation and insist that she be let in.[17] In the second example, Lisa entered the house and immediately attended to the woman who appeared to be the most distressed and, seeing that the cigarettes had come to represent the center of the argument between the woman and her roommate, asked the personally validating question of what kind of cigarette the woman smokes before offering to try and find her one.

But in addition to Lisa's skill at de-escalation, she had a habit of asking everyone with whom she interacted for identification. Perhaps most notably, in the opening vignette, Lisa requested the ID of the man who opened the door for her, who was also likely the one who had dialed 911. What would have happened had the man who dialed 911 not had an ID to show Lisa?

When I asked Lisa about this habit of requesting IDs, she explained to me that she requests IDs every time, from everyone, not just the caller or, in the case of a pulled-over vehicle, the driver.[18] If someone refused to share his ID, Lisa tells me that there can generally be a legal reason to compel someone to do so, for example, if a driver is pulled over and a passenger does not have on a seat belt.

Lisa's request for identification, though viewed as innocuous by officers, was seen by undocumented Latinos as an opportunity for officers to collect clues about immigration status in order to, as Hilda said, *indagar mas*, dig just a little bit deeper. Arturo described community perceptions of officer requests for identification at length during his interview.

Arturo: We have the mentality that they [police officers] are there to help us, to support us, not to smack it across our face and turn their back around when we need them. 'cause I feel like when you call 911, it shouldn't be like, "Who's calling? Where you from? Are you status [referring to immigration status]?" It should be like, "What do you need? Where are you at? I [will] dispatch this car right now." That's it. That should be a 911 call. But even if they try to do it, what do they do? "Who are you?" "Well, this is my name." "Well, okay." Well, first they can't speak English. Number two they don't have any type of ID so if you see something wrong like robbery or things like that you're not even going to think to even call the police because it could completely go the other way around: "Oh yeah, who called?" "Oh, I did." "Show me your ID. I just wanna see who you are." "Oh, I don't have one." "Okay, you know what, come in [to the station]." So no.

Because officers like Lisa may request identification from the person who dialed 911 as well as anyone else at the location, Latinos in mixed-status communities are forced to consider whether anyone in the vicinity lacks the documentation that will permit him to remain in the United States. If I call the cops, is everyone in the house, in the car, or on the street going to be okay? Does everyone have the necessary combination of paperwork, language skills, and presentation to prevent the officer from digging into their immigration status? As we saw in Yolanda's and Arturo's situations, will the documents and signs of belonging that worked last time also work this time?

Thus, contact between Latino citizens and local officers is limited by the possibility of repercussions for their undocumented peers, a finding beginning to emerge elsewhere.[19] As Theodore summarizes, "Fear of police contact is not confined to immigrants. For example, 28 percent of US-born Latinos said they are less likely to contact police officers if they have been the victim of a crime because they fear that police officers will use this interaction as an opportunity to inquire into their immigration status or that of people they know." Barrick[20] finds that Latino confidence that the police could fairly do their job is affected by previous encounters in which their immigration status had been questioned, even after taking citizenship into account. One's perception of police was affected by whether the officers inquired into one's immigration status, regardless of whether they were undocumented. This finding certainly makes sense in light of Arturo's comments. If an officer asked me, a citizen, about my immigration status, I would certainly assume he would ask other Latinos, and unless I were sure about the statuses of everyone in the room, I would hesitate to call the police, even in an emergency.

When I saw Lisa continually requesting IDs, I knew the habit would inevitably build a wall between her and Latino community members.[21] I sensed that Lisa had considered this, so I asked her what she would do if someone did not have an ID because he was undocumented. She responded that she usually just asks directly if the individuals are legally in the United States and is willing to use anything to prove identity, even a check stub.[22] She then said that if there was no reason to be concerned about immigration status, she would ignore it.

Here, Lisa highlights the individual discretion of local police officers when enforcing immigration law, as they choose whether to request IDs, what to accept as valid forms of ID, what repercussions follow, and under what circumstances. Complicating this discretion is the arbitrariness of the criteria for enforcing immigration law. It is not completely clear what constitutes a reason to be "concerned" about immigration status anyway.

Later that night, Lisa gives some clues as to the criteria she uses in enforcing immigration law. A portion of my field notes illustrates this conversation. After I describe to Lisa what happened in the raid of Guadalupe's apartment:

> *Lisa shakes her head in a gesture of disappointment. She says that she knows that many cops don't see things the same way as her. She tells me that if there are people here that are working and taking care of their family she doesn't see any reason to deport them. Then she follows up with that if you are undocumented and cause trouble, you "lose privileges," implying that there are large repercussions even for small crimes.*

> —*Adapted from field notes, November 2015*

What does "cause trouble" look like? When you cause it, what "privileges" can be lost? Is driving without a license causing trouble? Is your right to be in the country the privilege that is lost? When calling the police, members of mixed-status Latino communities must ask themselves: How bad is this? Is it worth risking deportation if I call the cops? Does everyone around me have identification? What kind of identification do they have? How will the police interpret this identification? If they interpret us as undocumented, do we work hard enough for it not to matter? Will they let us go or change their mind? Will they even know what to do with us?

■ ■ ■

The interviews and experiences reported here suggest that, once undocumented immigrants are standing face-to-face with officers, their deportability reduces their lives to two choices: compliance or deportation. As Yolanda and Rodrigo show, this position of vulnerability also influences interactions with institutions across the community, not just law enforcement. Throughout each encounter, undocumented Latinos must consider which aspects of the documents they carry, combined with which aspects of their presentation—the "symbols of deportability"—reveal their undocumented status. But this threat of deportation does not merely affect undocumented immigrants. Rodrigo and I stood by as Yolanda was continually overcharged and incorrectly charged, but the three of us ultimately had no negotiating power. We could not risk offending the administrators who could, at their discretion, deny any of Yolanda's requests. And, as my ride-along with Officer Lisa Flynn illustrates, officers may request identification from anyone in the premises of a 911 call, including the caller herself. Thus, those in mixed-status communities must assess whether anyone in the vicinity of the call is possibly undocumented and will be asked to show ID.

Immigration enforcement shapes the lives not only of undocumented Latinos but also of the mixed-status communities to which they belong. Much of the power of immigration enforcement stems not just from the deportations that happen but also from those that almost happen, those that nearly occur, those that form the *días comúnes y corrientes* of Latino mixed-status community members. It is through the threat of deportation that coercion is able to take place and that, ultimately, attempts can be made to silence entire communities.

However, threat only works if, every now and then, the threat is acted upon. That is, someone actually needs to be deported to remind community members that the near-deportations they experience all the time do not exist in the abstract but are real, painful, and deserve to be feared. De Genova and Peutz describe such purposefully visible immigration law enforcement as a "grim spectacle," a dark expression of power that reminds undocumented immigrants of what they call their "enduring everyday deportability," their vulnerability, every day, on the most *comúnes y corrientes* of days, to being removed from their families and communities.[23]

If deportations can shape behaviors by serving as reminders of deportability, what happens when the lead up to the deportation includes kicking in your door; raiding your home and job site; threatening your wife, sister, and children; and arresting everyone of matching skin tone? Is there a spectacle grimmer than a raid on your home?

The Raid

About 6:00 p.m. After her failed attempt to pick up her son, Guadalupe drives back to the *taller*. With Julio detained, the car now has an additional empty seat. But at least Guadalupe was able to keep her daughter in the car seat behind her. Guadalupe parks the car at the *taller* and climbs the stairs to the apartment, Sofía clinging tightly to her mother's body. She sits down with her sister-in-law, Fernanda, and together they try to make sense of the immigration enforcement that is taking more and more men out of their lives. With Guadalupe and Fernanda sit their four US citizen children (Guadalupe's daughters, Sofía and Fatima, and Fernanda's children, Lena and Ignacio), Santiagito (Santiago's 18-year-old son from a previous marriage), Jessica (a white US citizen who was dating Santiagito at the time), and Diane (Jessica's mother, who was helping to locate Santiago).

Sergio, another Latino man, arrives at the apartment. Sergio was in one of the cars that had been pulled over earlier in the day, but he was not detained because he is a permanent resident.

"They took [Santiago]. And they are detaining all the men that are leaving from [the *taller*]," he tells the women. There are now ten individuals in the apartment. It is unclear how many men are in the *taller* below them. It's November, and it's cold as the sun goes down. The group discusses what they can do, or if this, whatever "this" is, is even over.

As they speak, the SWAT team gathers outside their door.

As Guadalupe remembers it, "I was talking with my sister-in-law; that's when the soldiers arrived."

■ ■ ■

"Open the door!" Agents yell from the outside. Then, taking advantage of their no-knock warrant, an agent kicks in the door, breaks the lock, and the agents rush inside.

Guadalupe: The soldiers came in the house. They knocked down doors. They threw gas. They had guns. We were two women with small children. My nephew was 18 years old. Yes, it was absolutely terrible, to be honest. The kids terrified; the kids screaming. And, well, from there they started hand-cuffing. We were ordered to the carpet. To the carpet. And from there immigration came in. So many groups of people arrived, and since my nephew was a man, they handcuffed him and took him.

Immediately, on the other side of the door stood Fernanda, who was holding her 3-month-old son, Ignacio, in her arms.

Fernanda: Yes, they hit me with the door they broke. So, what I did, I didn't drop the 3-month-old baby boy that I had in my arms, and [Guadalupe], they already had her behind me. They were pointing guns at her...

[T]hey pushed me and I fell over all the toys. Then that is where they had me, pointing their weapons at me, at [Guadalupe], and at an American [woman] who was underage also.

Fernanda's fall—either after being hit by the door or after tripping over her children's toys—may partially account for the bruises on her body she presented at a community meeting held the following Sunday.

Fatima is lying in a cradle as agents enter the room. Guadalupe recalls, "I threw myself on the rug with the baby girl, and I remember I was filled with *coraje*[1] because my other daughter was in the cradle and [the agent] told me to take her out. When I took her out, one of the soldiers threw it."

An ICE agent looks at Fernanda and Guadalupe.

"You have to speak English," he says. "If you are here you have to speak English. What is your name, because I'm going to look for you later. I'm going to look for you and take your kids."

Another agent tries to refocus his attention on the purpose of the raid.

"Stop. Stop. We are not here for the women. We are here for Santiago."

Guadalupe recalls that there are six agents in the room at this time, two with "ICE" on their helmets and vests. The ICE agents are white, as far as she can tell. All six are men.

Agents round everyone up and sit them in the living room. One agent tries to talk to Guadalupe in Spanish. "*No tengan miedo.* Don't be scared. *Solo venimos por una persona.* We just came for one person. *Encontramos más. Es mi trabajo llevarlo.* We found more. It's my job to take him/them. *Ustedes pueden quedar aquí. Nosotros nos vamos.* You can stay here. We are leaving."

The door is broken and the breeze is blowing. While the agents are warmed by adrenaline and body armor, Guadalupe is worried about her children. "They told us to go to the living room," she says. "They put us all together, but like I told you, the door was open. The cold wind was coming in and our kids didn't have jackets. And my baby was just a month-and-a-half."

■ ■ ■

Jessica, a 16-year-old white US citizen who was dating Santiagito, recalls the moment the SWAT team arrives in the same way that almost everyone else did: an abrupt entrance punctuated dramatically by firearms.

Jessica: We were all upstairs, so they kicked in the front door, and they climbed up the stairs on the side...They held guns to everybody's head and just ordered all of us, we had to get out of the room because we were all in the room sitting down. I was changing the baby, and we all had to go in and sit on the couch that was in their living room. They were all just yelling at them like, "If you are here you need to speak English. Why are you going to come here if you are going to speak your fucking language?" and shit like that. And I'm like, "Well, why do you have this job if you can't speak their language?" And they're like, "If you are going to have an attitude, then why don't you tell them what we are saying?" And I'm like, "I don't speak their language, I help them with their kids and that's it, you done took everybody that spoke my language."

But Jessica's perceived sarcasm is not met with tightened handcuffs, as was Francisco's about three hours before. Her English fluency is not seen as involvement in illegal activity, as it was for Arturo about ten hours before. And no one threatens to take the child whose diaper she changes, threats Guadalupe received at that very moment.

An agent begins to question Santiagito. "Shouldn't you be at school? How old are you?"

He answers honestly. "Eighteen."

"Eighteen? Okay, you are old enough." The agent cuffs him a few feet in front of Jessica. Jessica slips her phone number and address in Santiagito's pocket. Maybe he can call her from the immigration office. Or Mexico.

■ ■ ■

From Fresh Fish N Chickn across the street, the three urgent responders, Elena Maria, Amalia, and Ofelia, watch as cars pile up outside of Santiago's *taller*. "You know what, fuck this. I'm gonna go see what's going on back there," Elena Maria decides. Nervously, the women walk toward the police activity and begin to take notes.

"What's going on here?" Elena Maria asks an officer.

"What do you mean, 'What's going on here?' Who are you? Who are you with?"

Elena Maria doesn't back down. "I'm a legal observer with WICIR, the immigrant rights organization, and I need to know what's going on here."

The agent pauses, then responds, "Well, you can talk to the sheriff when the sheriff gets here. We can call the sheriff for you."

Elena Maria gets angry. She had advocated for less collaboration between the sheriff's office and ICE, and the sheriff's office had been extremely receptive, agreeing that blending local law enforcement and immigration enforcement weakens relationships with the Latino community.

"How could this be a sheriff raid? We work with the sheriff and the sheriff wouldn't do this," Elena Maria tells them.

"Well this is a sheriff raid. They called *us*," the ICE agent says, failing to mention that the sheriff's office only called ICE after ICE had staked out the property a week prior to gather the evidence against Santiago.

Then a sheriff's agent arrives. He says, "Oh, well, this is a drug raid."

Elena Maria convinces the officers to let her, Ofelia, and Amalia go up to the apartment as the SWAT and ICE officers make their way out. On her way, she passes a police van. "Then I saw the van, and inside the van there were all these men getting put in handcuffs, like all kinds of men."

■ ■ ■

Once in the apartment, Ofelia notes that Guadalupe, Fernanda, and their children are scattered and distracted.

Ofelia: You could tell that they were just really charged by what had happened and their experience. And one of the toddlers, the older one, she must have been like two or so, she was just walking around—kind of like with a shocked face on—and her sister was like hitting her with this doll and she wasn't responding to that, like you could just tell she was in shock.

Drawers have been dumped out, papers are scattered, clothes are strewn across the floor, and drug-dog mucus coats their belongings. The two men closest to them—Santiago and his son, Santiagito—are now detained.

The lock on the door is broken. It's getting cold. And Guadalupe still has not picked up Carlitos. She would have to pick him up eventually, at about 11 p.m. And she would have to tell him that ICE had removed yet two more father figures—his uncle and his cousin—from his life.

Chapter 3

The Last Night He Ever Nursed

Leche.

Milk.

That word was repeated so many times, by so many different people, as they detailed the damage wrought by the immigration enforcement actions of that Thursday in November of 2013.

Guadalupe asked Santiago to pick up some *leche* for their hungry children, but Santiago never returned. Graciela, the organizer who sent out a mass text to warn the community about the arrests on Huron Avenue, said that afterward the fear of deportation hung so thickly in the air that no one left their homes: "What if you needed milk? No, don't go get milk. You drink water. You make do with what you have because you are not leaving the house." Hilda, who watched as ICE shackled and detained her husband, shared that the twenty pounds he lost in detention was due to the pitiful meals he received—oatmeal with water, no milk. From behind bars, Santiago lamented the fate of the family he could no longer support: "What I earned, I earned for diapers, milk, food for the house."

And Fernanda's ability to produce palatable breast milk to nourish her infant evaporated after she stared down the barrel of an officer's gun. "*Se me fue la leche,*" she told me. The milk just left me.

Why was everyone continually mentioning *leche*? What did it mean? What did it symbolize? And what can it tell us about the effects of immigration law enforcement?

Public health researchers use multilevel thinking to consider the numerous factors that shape an individual's health. The socioecological model reminds us that individuals are nested in families, which in turn are nested in communities. These communities, then, are shaped by local, state, and federal policies.[1] Factors at any of these levels can not only make you sick but also affect your ability to get—and remain—healthy. I'll give a simple example. To some extent, we choose what foods we put in our bodies, and our genes partially influence how our bodies process those foods. Yet, what we eat is also a function of what our families and communities teach us to eat and what our local stores have available to purchase. Our stores largely stock what makes a profit, which is shaped, at least in part, by government subsidies and regulations. Then, of course, we have to go to the store, either by driving, walking, or taking public transportation, all of which are shaped by the sidewalks, roads, driving regulations, tax policies, and, here in Michigan, snow removal, that make them possible.

So why did community members keep talking about *leche*?

For community members, *leche* seems to have multiple meanings. *Leche*, milk, is nourishment. It's sustenance. It's calorically denser than water and makes basic meals—like oatmeal—more enjoyable, more filling, something we are more likely to sit down and share with our families. In some ways, it is a luxury, though an easily attainable one. Unlike the water that comes from our taps,[2] we have to leave our homes to get this milk, to drive down the street to the store, to pick up a quart or a gallon, and to come back. We have to have a few dollars to pay for it. There are a lucky few—our infants—who have constant access to this milk from their mothers' bodies, mothers who love *dandoles pecho*—giving them their breasts—while they hold them in their arms.

So when participants talked to me about *leche*, they were talking to me about levels, detailing their own multilevel understanding of the effects of an immigration raid by using a word that had individual, familial, and communal meaning. Milk had individual meaning as calories sustaining one's weight. It had familial meaning, first, as the sustenance a father cannot provide to his children and then as a detention system that failed to nourish a man, an error his wife would never have allowed to happen. It had communal meaning, as a resource one must be willing to traverse public space to purchase. When immigration enforcement stripped the community of *leche*, it stripped them of their capacity to remain healthy across numerous levels. Next, I describe the damage of the raid of Santiago's apartment and *taller* across two levels: the individual and the family. In chapter 4, I consider the impacts of the raid at the community level.

"Nos Iban a Matar"

What is it like to be in an apartment when it is raided? What happens psychologically, emotionally, and physically to those who are forcibly arrested or who witness the arrests and removals of their friends and family?

Legal scholars have detailed what a "typical" home raid looks like based on testimonies of the clients who have experienced them.[3] These raids may involve more than twenty ICE agents, sometimes in collaboration with other law enforcement agencies, storming the house of a suspected undocumented immigrant in an attempt to apprehend him. Raids often occur in predawn hours when occupants of the residence in question are still sleeping. Agents, frequently with guns drawn and wearing body armor, surround the house and pound on doors and windows to gain entry.

Because warrants for immigration-related arrests do not permit ICE agents to enter homes, agents must gain consent to enter.[4] Once inside, occupants are corralled in a central location to be interrogated. If the targeted individual of the raid is present, he is apprehended and taken to ICE offices for processing. If other individuals present are suspected of being undocumented, they are taken as collateral arrests, a procedure that often amounts to legalized racial profiling. Documents and other possessions may be requested and sometimes are not returned. Because immigrants rarely live alone, these arrests frequently include witnesses, often children.[5]

Raids are, by design, swift, surprising, and terrifying. Even in the absence of literal violence, such as death or injury, it is the capacity of agents to kill and maim that allows raids to function smoothly. The militarized officers carrying assault rifles and sidearms, faces barely visible under helmets and behind goggles, bodies bulked up by bulletproof vests, are meant to control the scene through intimidation and threat of injury. In short, raids function because of the sudden appearance of officers with the capacity to kill you and the legal right to do so.

Research on the effects of exposures to traumatic events has provided strong evidence of their lasting impacts on health. Following trauma exposure, individuals may develop post-traumatic stress disorder (PTSD), depression, and anxiety or experience a range of physical health repercussions,[6] which may in turn affect their daily lives. Those who develop PTSD after exposure to trauma may experience flashbacks, nightmares, avoidance of triggering stimuli, hyperactive startle responses, angry outbursts, or distorted emotions.[7] These symptoms may in turn detrimentally affect employment outcomes,[8] relationship satisfaction,[9] or quality of life.[10]

Would an immigration home raid count as a traumatic event?[11] Could we expect one's presence in a raided home to predict or contribute to the development of PTSD, anxiety, depression, or other physical illness in the days, months, and years that followed? The *Diagnostic and Statistical Manual of Mental Disorders*,[12] the manual used by practitioners to diagnose mental illness, describes a traumatic event as one in which "the individual is exposed to death, threatened death, actual or threatened serious injury, or actual or threatened sexual violence." As you will see, this description is not far from that shared by community members in the raided building.

When law enforcement agents stormed the apartment, Guadalupe, Fernanda, Santiagito, and Jessica came face-to-face with the agents who had taken away Santiago and multiple other Latino men from the road in front of them and the *taller* below. Agents kicked in the door and entered with guns drawn as they yelled commands in the second language of most of the apartment residents. At least three of the four adults in the raided apartment wondered whether that Thursday would be the last day of their lives: "I thought they were going to kill us at any moment (*que nos iban a matar en ese instante*)," Fernanda said.

Santiagito echoed this sentiment:

William: And [at the moment the agents entered], what were you thinking?

Santiagito: So many things. What is going to happen to us? The fear was that they were going to strike or shoot me (*que pueden a pegar o dispararme*).

Guadalupe similarly wondered whether she would be shot, a penance for her lack of English proficiency: "My nephew's girlfriend [Jessica] was there and she is American and spoke English. If we had not understood what [the officers] told us, would they have thrown us onto the ground, or something like that? Would they have shot us?"

The near-death experience clearly took a toll on Fernanda, and she spent significant time during her interview describing how the raid affected her psychologically and emotionally. She stated that in the moments after the raid, *"mi cabeza estaba como pomposa,"* probably best translated as "My head was about to explode," or "My head/I was a disaster."

When I spoke with her in October 2015, about two years after the raid, she said, "Well, it was horrible what they did in the house. The truth is even now, I sometimes have nightmares about all of this, about what they did." And later she shared, "[The social worker] saw that psychologically this had affected me . . . So much so that I told her that sometimes I wanted to kill myself, because I felt so desperate and alone, without the help of anyone."

The three WICIR urgent responders who entered the apartment also shared observations about the traumatic reactions of those inside. Amalia, born in Canada, spoke very little Spanish and thus did her best to take note of body language and interactions among those in the apartment. When I asked Amalia what these suggested, she said, ". . . it's like the women were in shock . . . You could almost see [them go] from being almost emotionless and stunned, to then the emotion beginning to rise, and there being tears." Ofelia, a social worker and second urgent responder who entered the raided apartment, wrote to the sheriff's office to protest their involvement in the raid. In the letter, she described the women similarly: "[The] mothers were also in a state of shock and deeply affected by the raid."

Traumatic event exposure affects one psychologically and has somatic repercussions, with each potentially exacerbating the other. Years of research on trauma and PTSD have shown that musculoskeletal, gastro-intestinal, and cardiorespiratory health complaints are associated with the disorder.[13] For women, recent research has shown that PTSD affects pregnancy,[14] birth,[15] and likelihood of breastfeeding following birth.[16]

Fernanda directly attributed the changes in her body to the trauma she experienced as her apartment was raided. Twenty-two years old at the time of the raid, Fernanda had two children, Lena, who was 1½ years old, and Ignacio, who was 3 months old.

In her interviews, Fernanda spoke at length about her own reaction to the raid but also discussed ways in which the impacts on her directly affected her relationship to Ignacio.[17]

William: How did your kids react that night after the raid occurred?

Fernanda: Well, the truth was that it was very horrible. My 3-month-old, I would try to nurse him, and me, with this fright (*susto*, also translated as shock or scare)...so elevated right?...He went all night without nursing (*Se la pasó toda la noche sin mamar pecho*).

The night of the raid was the last night Ignacio ever really nursed. He tried to nurse. Fernanda tried to nurse him. But that Thursday in November was the end of Fernanda's role as a breastfeeding mother.

When I heard this story, I knew immediately that what Fernanda had shared—a *susto* that marked the last day her infant ever consumed the *leche* produced by her body—was analytically important and symboli-cally meaningful. *Susto* has a rich anthropological history, interpreted by Latinos as a fright so serious that the soul leaves the body.[18] A study in El Paso found that among Mexican American women, participants listed *susto* as a cause of their diabetes. Most women were even able to pinpoint a specific frightful event, such as a car accident, witnessing a shooting, or the sudden death of a family member that was the source of the *susto*.[19] Thus, Fernanda's narrative had used the concept of *susto* to link bodily health to an act of twenty-first-century immigration enforcement that scared the soul, or more, specifically, the *leche*, right out of her body.

Yet, as a parent of young children at the time, those words—*se la pasó toda la noche sin mamar pecho*—knocked the wind out of me, leaving me unable and unwilling to draw out more of the story. I had watched my daughter nurse for two years, my son for over two-and-a-half, and I had never considered breastfeeding to be part of their mother's citizen privilege. If breastfeeding—and the connection between mother and child that it engenders—can be severed by immigration enforcement, what is safe? What is sacred? Is there anything that immigration enforcement cannot spoil?

Two months later, Fernanda and I spoke again.

William: You told me that [Ignacio] stopped nursing? (*¿Me dijo que [Ignacio] paró de mamar pecho?*)

Fernanda: Yes, and I stopped giving milk to him also...(*Si, le dejé de dar también*)

William: Mm-hmm.

Fernanda: Yes, and I couldn't give him/could no longer produce milk. Because of the shock, the milk just left my body. My son threw up all the milk. (*Aja, a él ya no le pude dar por el, por el susto se me fue la leche. Este, el niño vomitaba toda la leche.*)

William: Okay, so he was throwing up the milk you said?

Fernanda: I couldn't produce good milk for my son because of the fright (*susto*). But that's what happens when ICE comes in the house right? (*El niño ya no le hizo bien ya la leche de, del susto, como fue que entró el ICE a la casa, ¿verdad?*)

Over a staticky phone line, with concepts that didn't easily translate into English, and as a father who observed his children breastfeeding for more than four years among them, I was unsure that I had heard everything correctly and attempted to confirm:

William: Okay, let me see if I am following. So the raid happened, and after, your son, who was just months old, stopped nursing, and you started to use formula?...

Fernanda: Yes, okay since then [inaudible] I stopped breastfeeding him because, my breast, the milk didn't work anymore...(*Aja, ok ya desde ahí empezaba* [inaudible] *le quité el pecho porque mi pecho lo, mi formula ya, mi leche verdad ya no servía...*)

Fernanda had summarized that, because of the raid, the breast milk her body produced became intolerable to Ignacio, and she thus had to switch to formula—manufactured milk—because he would vomit whenever he tried to nurse. She attributed the spoiled milk production to the fright, the *susto*, she sustained from the raid, noting that her milk just "didn't work anymore" (*"no servía"*), and thus, she had to "take her breast away from him" (*"le quité el pecho"*).

The effects of a violent, armored, military, hypermasculine insertion by force into Fernanda's life had also inserted itself into Fernanda's body, infiltrated her breasts, and soured the milk she used to nourish her son. She then watched her son throw up the milk that had formerly sustained him. The *leche* Fernanda's body produced—the benefits of which included a longer, healthier life for her child[20]—became more collateral in the search for Santiago.

■ ■ ■

The collective testimony by those in the apartment undoubtedly cast the raid as a near-death experience. And the cluster of symptoms elicited—nightmares, shock, suicidality, and physical changes to the body—provide powerful evidence as to the traumatic potential of an immigration home raid. Further, for Guadalupe and Fernanda, who were in the apartment when it was raided, the trauma of the raid was only the first layer on which many more layers of trauma would accumulate. Much research has shown that exposure to one traumatic event increases the chances of developing PTSD with future exposures, therefore increasing the reach of ICE from Guadalupe and Fernanda's apartment into the women's futures.[21]

In addition, however, the health of one community member is intimately linked to the health of others to whom they are connected. For Fernanda and many others, this meant that the effects of the raid impacted their lives and then extended immediately to the family units of which they were a part.

"If You Hold My Hand, No One Will Be Able to Take You Away from Me"

The community members with whom I spoke all belonged to family units[22] that varied in size and composition. Most of these families included children, who ranged in age at the time of the raid from Guadalupe's 2-month-old daughter, Fatima, to Hilda and Arturo's 9-year-old son, Sebastián.[23]

During interviews, community members often spent more time discussing the effects of the raid on their children than discussing these effects on themselves. They would then link the stress the raid caused on children to their own well-being. Similar to the adults described in the previous section, the enforcement actions particularly affected the children who were in the apartment when the raid occurred. All three WICIR urgent responders took note of the behaviors of the children they observed. Ofelia, a social worker, described the scene in a letter to the sheriff's office:

> During our [the urgent responders'] conversation [with Fernanda and Guadalupe], we noted that both women had two small children under the age of 6 months and two toddlers between the ages of 1 and 2. For the majority of the discussion the older child appeared to be disoriented and withdrew into the living room while we spoke with her mother. The smaller toddler displayed aggressive behavior and was trying to get the attention from the adults in the room.

When Ofelia spoke with me later, she added, "One of the toddlers, the older one, she... was just walking around kind of like with a shocked face on and just her sister was like hitting her with this doll. And she wasn't responding to that. Like you could just tell she was in shock."

Elena Maria, also a social worker, noted similar behaviors in the case notes she shared with WICIR: "One child in the home was extremely traumatized by the events. She was laying on the couch stunned, the baby. Was frozen, I thought she may have had a disability—it was complete trauma."

Guadalupe and Fernanda were certain that the trauma of the raid weighed on each of their children, even those who were too young to verbalize any specific effects. Researchers would agree with them. Some work has shown that children exposed to violence and trauma show higher rates of a variety of poor health outcomes, including asthma, the flu, and gastrointestinal illness.[24] Collectively, Guadalupe's and Fernanda's children became emotionally distraught, unable to sleep, and fell ill frequently for some time following the raid.

As Guadalupe shared, "[Sofía] was crying for like three or four months [after the raid]. She tried to sleep, but she would cry and cry. She did things that she didn't do before."

Of 2-month-old Fatima, she said, "I don't know if it was the cold or what else, but physically, her health deteriorated drastically (*su salud también bajó muchísimo*) after . . . She gets sick all the time. It doesn't matter if it's heat, cold, whatever. Her throat and her lungs."

Fernanda's daughter, Lena, about 18 months at the time of the raid, reacted similarly: "My daughter would not stop crying and would not stop crying at all. Everything that they did in my house left her scared (*Le asustó todo eso que hicieron en mi casa*)."

It is a common misconception that age insulates young children and infants from the effects of trauma, as they presumably will not remember the traumatic event. On the contrary, brain development occurs most rapidly in childhood; thus the effects of early trauma exposure can powerfully shape a child's biological, physical, mental, and emotional development.[25] Caregiver relationships (usually between a mother and the child), can also be affected, predicting challenges in healthy attachment later in life.[26] Indeed, traumatic exposure can elicit a long list of negative health effects in children, including intrusive imagery, hypervigilance, confusion, poor language and communication skills, anxiety, phobias, constricted emotion, nightmares, withdrawal, sadness, survivor's guilt, regressive behaviors, impulsivity, self-abusiveness, somatic complaints, and chemical alterations.[27] Even among infants, witnessing severe interpersonal violence directed at their mothers increases the likelihood of exhibiting trauma symptoms.[28]

Could we expect a child's presence at a raid to elicit any of the litanies of traumatic responses shown in the research? According to the National Center for PTSD, the causes of PTSD among children include having "lived through an event that could have caused them or someone else to be killed or badly hurt."[29] Did 2-year-old Sofía, like her *tía* Fernanda and *hermano* Santiagito, think someone would die that day? Did the children bother to differentiate between the potential for deportation or death for their parents, aunts, and uncles?

■ ■ ■

For children, the enforcement actions reminded them of the fragility of their relationships with their parents who could, at any time, be violently removed from their lives. According to parents, many of the children of detained community members—whether these children were in the raided apartment or not—began to fear whenever their parents left the house that they would never see them again.

Guadalupe's son, Carlitos, who had, a few months before the raid, watched while an ICE agent pointed a gun at the father of his sisters before he was detained and deported, told his mother about this fear.

Guadalupe: [Carlitos] says, "It scares me when you leave the house, when you drive, because I don't want the police to take you like they took my dad." He says, "Or like they took my uncle Santiago."

Arturo was detained for a month and one day following his arrest on Huron Avenue. He returned to Hilda, his wife, and their two children to find his children significantly fearful that he would be detained once again:

Arturo: My kids, both of them, they didn't go to school for the first week I was out [of detention]. They just can't, they're scared that if I drop them to school, they're gonna go back home and I wasn't gonna be there. They sleep with me, one on each side, for the whole two months [after I was released] because they're afraid. They said, "If you hold my hand, no one will be able to take you away from me."

No parent, whether an undocumented immigrant or a citizen, can guarantee to his children that he will return home to them at the end of the day. Car accidents happen. Injuries occur at work that may make the next parental encounter take place at the hospital. However, while we all must cope with the stress of the improbable that could, if we are unlucky, keep us from our children, parents like Arturo, Hilda, Guadalupe, and Fernanda must cope with the reality that their removal—and the separation from their children that it entails—is often the express goal of the US government.

But it was not only parental absence that triggered this intense fear in children. Children of all ages reacted specifically to the sight of law enforcement, becoming angry, frightened, and nervous whenever they saw officers or their vehicles nearby. As Arturo shared, "[My sons'] reaction was completely like another person because they're afraid, they're insecure, they're angry, just for what [officers] did to me."

These reactions did not just occur when children saw ICE or Border Patrol. Instead, children began to fear all law enforcement vehicles and officers equally, viewing them as the people who would take their parents away. When I spoke with Fernanda, she had already returned to Mexico; yet, her daughter, Lena, 1½ at the time of the raid, still feared the sight of officers thousands of miles away:

Fernanda: And my daughter [Lena], well, even now she can't see the police without starting to cry. She thinks that they are going to assault her (*que la van a agredir*).

William: Even there in Mexico? She is scared over there as well when she sees the police cars?

Fernanda: Yes, just the same. She sees them, and she is filled with dread/terror (*pavor*). She can't see them. She thinks they will attack her, like when they came to our house and pointed guns at our faces.

Here, Lena, more than two years after the raid, was terrified that law enforcement officers would brutalize her or her family. Lena's inability to distinguish between ICE officers in the United States and police in Mexico highlights children's profound homogenization of law enforcement officers from all departments. That is, any law enforcement officer can come between a child and her parents. It's simply what law enforcement officers do.

Not only was the removal of father figures psychologically and emotionally traumatizing for children, but the absence of the men who were also financial providers placed an enormous economic burden on the women left behind. Further, when women could not care for their children as they hoped, and fathers could not provide for their families as they planned, their failed gender roles served as additional sources of mental and emotional distress, perpetuating a vicious cycle of trauma, removal, failure, and impending poverty, with each reinforcing the other.[30] The economic consequences of the removal of two primary breadwinners—Santiago and Arturo—rippled throughout their families in myriad ways.

■ ■ ■

Santiago, the original (and allegedly only) target of the law enforcement actions, was the primary source of income for his wife, Fernanda, and their two children; his sister, Guadalupe, and her three children; and Santiagito, Santiago's young adult son from a previous marriage who had arrived from Mexico a few months before. Arturo was the primary breadwinner for Hilda and his two children. The removal of Santiago and Arturo from their families had enormous financial repercussions that affected the multiple mothers and children that relied on them. In *Everyday Illegal*, Joanna Dreby[31] describes "one of the most devastating impacts of deportation is the creation of female-headed single-parent households . . . Women become what I term *suddenly single mothers*, scrambling to be the sole providers for their US-born children with no preparation for single parenthood." Indeed, for Guadalupe, Fernanda, and Hilda, this "suddenly single motherhood" required not only that they deal with day-to-day expenses but also with the enormous financial demands that followed the detentions of Santiago and Arturo.

Consider the costs related to Arturo's detention. While some of the men arrested in the raid voluntarily departed[32] from the United States,

Arturo, whose wife and US-citizen children lived in Michigan, did not. Thus, an immigration judge would decide whether he would ultimately be deported or allowed to remain in the United States and whether he would await his court dates in detention or would be released on bond.[33] Arturo did not want to stay in detention any longer than necessary and decided to pay the bond option he was offered. His wife, Hilda, lamented that between Arturo's bond and legal fees, she had to find $10,000 in four days.

To acquire the money necessary, Hilda had to draw from savings, sell possessions at fractions of their values, or abandon other financial responsibilities altogether. Of course, Hilda's situation was not unique but mirrored that of most everyone who experienced a sudden detention of a family member. Francisco—who was arrested as he drove away from Santiago's *taller*—was never able to pick up his car from the *taller*. In one exchange, Frida, Francisco's girlfriend, described how, in an effort to prepare for the possibility of posting bond for Francisco, she decided to collect money from community members and, in the process, was unable to continue payments on the car:

Frida: It stayed in the mechanic shop and they called the towing. So that was that. And [Francisco's] kids' mother was behind with the payments so it just got repossessed. And we were trying to gather money to get him out in case he was gonna get a bail. So we just decided either a car or him, so it was him.

Like Francisco's car, the other cars in Santiago's *taller* were similarly impounded. Many of Santiago's customers were likely put in the same difficult position in which Frida found herself, as they also needed to find a large sum of money—that increased every day—to recover the car from the impound or abandon it altogether. Given the financial cost of removing one's car, the fact that many of the owners may have been deported, and the numerous challenges to removing one's car from impound without a valid driver's license (as Rodrigo and Yolanda show us in chapter 2), I would speculate that other families who were customers of Santiago lost their cars as well. Others whose cars were not impounded sold them at reduced prices to cover immediate needs. Guadalupe sold her car to financially support Fernanda's return trip to Mexico after Santiago was eventually deported.

Phone calls from detention constituted another significant financial expense. Fernanda (who was called by her husband, Santiago), Arturo (who called his wife Hilda), and Frida (who was called by her boyfriend, Francisco) all lamented the enormous financial burden of making or receiving phone calls from detention. Arturo stated that he spent more than $1,600 in phone calls alone, "...and if you ask me how long do I talk for that month, if I put all the time together, maybe thirty minutes. 'cause you speak for two minutes it's already like seventy bucks. Just to get connected you get twenty [dollars], boom, right off the bat."[34]

Fathers lamented their sudden inabilities to provide for their families, a gender role expectation in which they had formerly taken pride. Indeed, for Arturo and Santiago, their inabilities to provide for their families caused more emotional distress than their own detentions.

Arturo: [My wife Hilda said] "Don't worry about it, we are gonna make it happen." And I was like "But how? How? How [are you] going to find a job, be a housewife, take care of the home, take care of the bills and my kids?" [She would tell me] "Don't worry about it." I'm like, "No, I *do* worry about it, 'cause at least here, detained, I'm eating, I sleep, I rest, but you're not, you're outside." [She would say] "Don't worry about me." "I'm worried about you because I don't know how you manage to pay bills, I don't know how you manage to pretend that everything is okay in front of my kids, even though every night you're just like in tears and crying twenty-four-seven, like yes I'm worried."

Santiago, Arturo, and Francisco all discussed the drastic weight loss they experienced while they were detained. I asked Santiago about the seventy pounds he lost in the course of his four-month detainment:

William: [Did you lose the weight] because you didn't eat? Because of the nerves? What do you think?

Santiago: Yes, I think it was the nerves. Just thinking and thinking. Because they gave me food; they gave me three meals a day. I think it was the nerves, and I got sick. They had to take me to the doctor [for] like two or three months because, thinking about it all, thinking about how little I had done for my children, everything was lost.

The economic losses forced women to search for other sources of steady income. But in order to work, mothers had to find someone else to care for their children. Yet trauma, sick children, and removed caregivers exacerbated one another. Fernanda, for example, was caught in a cycle in which she had to cope with her own suicidality and frustration while homeless, jobless, and trying to prevent the deportation of her husband. Each task required childcare, but finding childcare for children who were unpredictably physically ill proved nearly impossible.

Certainly, individual-level health repercussions—physical and mental—took their toll on community members. Yet individuals in this community were members of families, and their roles in their families—and inabilities to fulfill those roles—further affected their physical and mental health. While the focus on deportation is often on the sheer volume of deportees—400,000 a year under President Obama, or about 2.5 million total[35]—not a single person with whom I spoke ever failed to mention the impact on families.

One has to wonder, what do immigration agents think of their work? Do they think of families, too?

■ ■ ■

I had arranged a lunch with Jaime at one of my favorite Mexican restaurants in my Texas hometown. We agree to meet at 12:30 p.m., but he texts to let me know he would be arriving at 12:45 p.m. I decide to go into the restaurant at 12:30 anyway and gather my thoughts amid the smells of the delicious Tex-Mex foods I sorely miss in Michigan. At 12:45 exactly, Jaime walks into the restaurant, impeccably dressed in a gray suit and wide red tie. As he enters, he looks down at his phone at the same moment my phone chimes. I realize that Jaime has sent me a text to let me know he has arrived at the time he said he would arrive, and I can envision him thriving amid rules, order, and well-pressed uniforms. Our Latina waitress takes our order, and he begins to share his story.

Jaime Sanchez was a 57-year-old Latino man and former agent of the Immigration and Naturalization Service, or INS,[36] where he served in Texas in the 1990s and early 2000s for about a decade. During his time at the INS, Jaime was a member of a fugitive operations unit, a team of immigration agents charged with entering homes to locate, arrest, and detain undocumented immigrants targeted for deportation. While Jaime conducted home raids years before and multiple states away from the raid on Guadalupe's apartment, his role in the INS was largely the same as that of the ICE agents who raided the apartment and detained and deported Santiago.

My uncle introduced me to Jaime. Fellow veterans of the US military, my uncle and Jaime had bonded over shared experiences as soldiers in the Gulf War. Both also spoke at religious retreats about the role that faith played in overcoming psychologically and emotionally challenging moments in their lives. For my uncle, this moment was September 11, 2001, when he was working in the Pentagon as a plane was flown into it. For Jaime, this moment was his participation in an immigration home raid that resulted in the paralysis—and, eleven months later, death—of an undocumented immigrant for which Jaime later spent twenty-three months in prison, away from his wife and two daughters. He now serves as a paralegal to immigration attorneys, defending families in deportation proceedings, a fairly consummate switch from his former occupation.

He describes[37] the home raid that led to his imprisonment:

Jaime: While searching a house for a target, we encountered twenty illegal aliens— and life changed. [Sergio] was in his late forties and the only man we encoun- tered who could be described as "armed"—he had a machete under his mat- tress and a rifle bullet keychain—a puncher, [which you use to cut a hole in a cigar]—in his pocket. We will never know why he didn't follow the instruc- tions of [the other INS agent] to exit the house through the kitchen door with his buddies, or why he tried to push his way past him. He was proba- bly hungover from drinking the night before. Perhaps he was a diabetic and suffering from low blood sugar.

Only God knows why [Sergio] tried to push his way past [the agent] towards the kitchen sink where knives were in plain view; [the agent] had been stabbed through his body armor many years ago and had no intention of allowing a suspect near a bunch of kitchen knives. My partner pushed [Sergio] back to the wall, and with the help of our supervisor, took him down to handcuff him. Two other officers assisted by holding down [Sergio's] legs in order to maintain control of him. Once [Sergio] was handcuffed, we finished clearing the house.

In the takedown, Sergio's spine was fractured, leaving him quadriplegic before his death eleven months later. Jaime had no idea that Sergio had been injured; nor could he have predicted it: "It was a takedown! People don't get paralyzed from takedowns! Nowhere in our takedown training at the Academy had this possibility been addressed—we had received no warning at all that such an injury could occur." Jaime told his supervisor that Sergio claimed he was hurt, but the supervisor determined that Sergio was not injured. No medical personnel were alerted.

So Sergio did not receive medical attention for hours after the injury. Because of this delay, Jaime, along with two other officers, were charged with deliberate indifference to Sergio's medical needs. As he reported to work, Jaime was arrested. He was then tried, convicted, and spent twenty-three months in prisons located in different states than his family.

I listen and eat and Jaime talks and, every now and then, takes a brief pause to methodically cut, fork, and chew his food. I eat fast when I am nervous and quickly order a third taco so Jaime would not have an entirely uneaten meal in front of him while my plate had only the leftover oil that drained from my picadillo taco. He continues his story in between occasional bites.

While Jaime was in prison, he had plenty of time to reflect on his role as an immigration agent and the dehumanizing ways in which raids were conducted. Like most every community member with whom I spoke, Jaime grasped that arrests and deportations did not affect individuals but entire families. At one point in his career, he also saw the potential to separate one from his family as a powerful coercive tool:

Jaime: One night, while working with my team, we talked a man into coming out of his trailer and surrendering himself, instead of having to go into the trailer to arrest him in front of his children. In order to convince his wife into coaxing him out of the trailer, we even told her that, if we had to get a search warrant from a federal judge at 10:00 p.m. on a Saturday night, we would certainly make him so angry that, almost certainly, we would have to arrest her for harboring a fugitive and turn her children over to Child Protective Services—a lie but an effective one. As I stood perimeter by the bedroom window, I could hear the man vomiting inside the trailer; since he had been deported from the US before, he knew that he was facing two to twenty years in federal prison. While I felt sorry for the man, I told myself, "Well, he shouldn't have come back." This is what I did, what I was paid to do. While I may not have loved my job entirely, I saw value in serving my country and in doing my job to the best of my ability.

While he believed himself to be doing his work in service to his country, as he had done in a different uniform in the Gulf and Iraq Wars, eventually, the separation of families began to weigh on him, even before his encounter with Sergio:

Jaime: I took men from their wives and children, and sons from their parents. I referred, as was common practice in the Service, to men whom we were arresting as "bodies," as in, "How many more bodies can you load into your van?" or "I have three bodies in this room! How many are in that room?" during raids. Arresting men individually or by the dozen didn't bother me, but breaking up families could be emotionally challenging.

I can't help but think about Santiago, Arturo, and Santiagito as those anonymous bodies, the bodies whose removal doesn't really bother anyone. This would in turn make Guadalupe, Hilda, and Fernanda the women who were left behind, the "wives from whom their men were taken," and I pray that, others, like Jaime, may see in their stories the other side of the violence of immigration enforcement.

Jaime continues to speak in a measured tone. I try to read his body language, but except for a few sighs and pauses, he does not give me clues about what is going on in his head. I can envision this poker face serving him quite well as an INS agent. He tells me that, in addition to his role as a paralegal, he also serves as an unlicensed counselor to families in deportation proceedings, explaining to these families a deportation machine he knows intimately well from having operated it from the inside for a decade.

Through the whole conversation, he has talked around his transition from an agent of deportation to a man attempting to prevent it, but he has not clearly said why he did this. I ask him for his motivation. "I think it was my purgatory on Earth. My penance... You know, I'm sure somebody is keeping an Excel spreadsheet somewhere. I don't know how many families I've destroyed. I hope at some point I've helped as many families stay together as I've destroyed."

As the conversation goes over an hour, the waitress continues to check on us. Eventually, Jaime stands up to return to work. We shake hands and agree to stay in touch. It won't occur to me until later that this conversation—between two Latino men, both citizens—was allowed to continue for as long as we cared to speak. When I spoke with Arturo at his restaurant, he continually stood and walked behind the register to serve customers. When I sat at Guadalupe's kitchen table, she eventually left to pick up Sofía, leaving me with her cell phone in her empty house to talk to a deported Santiago. Yet, Jaime and I sat, we ate, slowly, methodically, as long as we wanted. As men, and as citizens, the world seems to make exceptions for us.

Chapter 4

Se Rompe la Comunidad

In many ways, we can intuitively understand what it means for individuals and families to be healthy. We know when someone is healthy, and we know when she is sick. We know when our children are hungry, ill, or act, in some way, different from what we expect. And we know or, can at least imagine, the depression, pain, and poverty that result from having a father, a husband, an uncle, or a brother taken away. But what does a healthy community look like? And what does it take to make that community sick?

A healthy community is one in which individuals and families are able to thrive. These communities require at least two ingredients, which, for the sake of simplicity, I divide into *people* and *places*. People are the friends, family, and neighbors to whom we talk when depressed; with whom we celebrate birthdays, baptisms, promotions, or quinciñeras; or from whom we borrow a car when ours breaks down. A substantial body of evidence suggests that these social relationships—variously called social integration, social networks, social support, social ties, and more—are good for your health, as they provide you with the emotional, informational, and instrumental support that makes life easier on a daily basis.[1]

Healthy communities also require places we can go both to nurture these relationships and to obtain other resources that make life easier.[2] We go to clinics and hospitals for the vaccinations and physicals our children need to start school, or we seek the counseling we need to overcome the loss of a loved one. Our churches provide us with a sense of belonging, teach us in our native languages, or come together to fight the deportation of a community member. Our schools and libraries educate us, our grocery stores and farmers markets provide us with food, our police departments (ideally) "serve and protect" us, and our meeting centers, parks, bars, restaurants, and churches provide us the space in which we hold our quinciñeras, celebrate a birth, mourn a death, or plan a visit home. Sometimes, when our incomes falter or we get sick and help from our families and friends is not enough, we visit local government offices to seek additional support, such as cash or supplemental food assistance, free or low-cost medical care, or unemployment benefits.[3]

Healthy communities also require the ability to move from one place to the next, to, for example, drive, walk, or bus to your brother's house or to the local health center. That is, even amid a strong network of people and places to keep the community healthy, if community members cannot move about from one location to the next, these resources may as well not exist.

I now consider the impacts of the raid on the community level. As described previously, the threat of deportation can powerfully shape *los días comúnes y corrientes* of mixed-status community members by reducing their worlds into two choices: compliance or deportation. Later, we began to see why the threat of deportation can maintain its stranglehold on a mixed-status community: deportations—and the arrests that precede them—can be brutal, degrading, terrifying, and expensive, with far-reaching repercussions for individuals and families. This chapter illustrates the ways in which the "grim spectacle"[4] of the raid on Santiago's *taller* affects health both acutely and chronically, altering immediate behaviors, but also changing patterns of behavior that ultimately limit access to the people and places needed by community members to stay healthy.

But health in mixed-status communities cannot be understood without an awareness of how law enforcement seeps into nearly every aspect of community members' lives, controlling the roads on which they drive, the people they are willing to visit, and the resources they are willing to access. The raid on Santiago's *taller* and apartment, and the racial targeting of the arrests that preceded it, concretized an image of law enforcement that was ubiquitous, racist, and collusive. Law enforcement was everywhere. They targeted you because of your brown skin. And they colluded with other organizations to get you. Community members thus changed their day-to-day routines to avoid any possibility of encounters with law enforcement. These behavior changes isolated individuals and families, limiting their freedom to access the people and places they needed to stay healthy. Often, it was citizens and visa holders—many of whom were women—who stepped in to support their undocumented friends, family, and neighbors.

"Andamos Volteando"

Hilda paused our conversation in her front yard many times, switching from speaking in Spanish about the raid that forever changed her life to selling, in English, old clothes, bikes, and housewares to anyone who would stop at her garage sale. At the time of the raid, Hilda was 32 years old and had been in the United States for thirteen years. She had lived in Washtenaw County for about eight years, the entire life of her two US citizen sons who were shooting a plastic bow-and-arrow at a target nearby. On that day, her husband, Arturo, one of the first people to be arrested as he drove away from the *taller,* was doing what he normally did and working one of his multiple jobs to support his family.

Sitting with a mixed-status family with enough money to purchase—and then sell—extra goods in their spacious front yard, it was not lost on me that Hilda and Arturo were the "model" immigrants who contributed to family and community without complaint. They were the "good" undocumented immigrants continually contrasted with the "criminals" who "deserved" to get deported. Nonetheless, Hilda, Arturo, and their two sons were subjected to significant violence and emotional trauma by enforcement actions that also wreaked economic havoc on their lives. In many ways, Hilda and Arturo's situation was quintessential of those in mixed-status communities: you don't have to be a target of immigration enforcement to feel its impact; you simply have to live in the same community as those who are.

After telling Hilda that, yes, I would love to buy my daughter the bicycle that she was selling, but there wasn't any room for it in my house, I returned to the immigration enforcement actions of November of 2013:

William: So, after all this happened, did you all change what you did (*sus comportamientos*; literally, "your behaviors")?

Hilda: So, listen . . . As far as being more cautious, yes. Yes, we were much more cautious. We always walk glancing back over our shoulders, making sure there is not a patrol car nearby (*andamos volteando a ver que no está una patrulla alrededor*). You can imagine the fear we feel that there would be a patrol car (*patrulla*) behind us. Lord God. It's the worst thing that could happen to you. It's impossible to be calm again (*O sea, no vienes tranquillo*), that's for sure.

Of course, on the individual level, it is notable that Hilda attributed a heightened vigilance to the events of that Thursday in November of 2013. The literature is replete with data on the damage that hypervigilance can do to one's body. Chronic hyperarousal changes metabolism,[5] affects one's ability to sleep,[6] and contributes to many other physical health conditions, including hypertension.[7] On the family level, this hypervigilance may even work its way through the mother's body to the infant developing inside her, resulting in lower birth weight.[8] That is, *no venir tranquillo* can literally take its toll on the bodies of you and your children.

But as important as this attribution were the words she used to express it: "*andamos volteando.*" On that fateful Thursday morning, Hilda and Arturo dropped off their children at school and then went to Santiago's *taller* to pick up their second car. When they drove away, Arturo was promptly pulled over, surrounded by law enforcement vehicles, shackled, and detained—the alleged result of a blinker he turned off too soon—as Hilda watched from her own car. Hilda's encounter with law enforcement adds another level of meaning to her words. Hilda had literally *volteado*, had searched her surroundings only to witness the shackling and removal of her husband.

But in her description, Hilda extended her single action to a metaphor that captures how she and other members of her community now live and move about their world on a daily basis. The Spanish word "*andar,*" which means "to walk," is often used to change a verb to a habit or a state of being.[9] "*Andar volteando,*" which translates literally as "to walk turning around," thus suggests not that Hilda turned around once but that Hilda was always turning around, always checking over her shoulder for the surprise law enforcement agent who could appear at any moment to separate her from her family. Notably, Hilda also used the first-person plural form of the phrase, *"andamos volteando."* That is, *we,* my family, or perhaps even *we,* my community, are always turning around, always vigilant, always preparing to watch our loved ones be cuffed and our families dismantled behind us.

Hilda, as did Guadalupe and many others throughout the community, also used the word *"patrulla"* to describe the law enforcement agents she feared. *Patrulla* comes from the Spanish verb *patrullar,* or "to patrol," and is used in reference specifically to law enforcement vehicles, usually the local police.[10] The closest English approximation would likely be "patrol car." At first, the focus on the patrol car may not seem notable. But in the context of mixed-status communities, a patrol car is necessary to engage in the law enforcement activity the community fears most: deportation. "Bodies," as former INS Agent Jaime called them, need somewhere to be stored en route to the detention center that precedes their removal. *Patrullas* are therefore an essential part of the chain of deportation, transporting a brown body from the site of the arrest, to the cell in which it will be housed prior to being placed on a plane in handcuffs.

How do community members avoid these mobile deportation units for which they are perpetually looking over their shoulders? One way is to simply never leave the house.

On Lockdown

Originally from Cuba, Graciela, 59 years old at the time of the raid, had worked with the Latino community in Washtenaw County for about twenty-three years on the day we spoke in her living room. Graciela was referred to as a "maven" of the Latino community by another interviewee and was seen by many others as both a leader and a gatekeeper with a deep historical knowledge of the Washtenaw mixed-status Latino community. When Hilda witnessed Arturo's arrest, she promptly picked up her phone and called Graciela to ask for advice on what to do. Thus, Graciela knew intimately not only about the needs of the Latino community but also about the arrests that began early in the morning on that fateful Thursday. In the following exchange, Graciela describes some of the drastic steps taken by community members to avoid any possibility of an encounter with *las patrullas* on the streets of their neighborhoods:

William: And could you tell the difference in the community [after the raid]?

Graciela: Oh yeah. There were people that did not go to work for several days after that. They did not leave their house, and if you don't go to work, you don't make money and then you can't pay your rent or buy food. But there were lots of people that I know that stayed home for at least four days because they were afraid to leave their house because they thought immigration would be down the street waiting for them. And not just in [the city in which the raid occurred], all the way over here [location of the interview, about fifteen miles away], there were people that weren't leaving their house.

To avoid arrest, community members refused to leave their homes, confining themselves indoors lest they cross paths with law enforcement. Graciela continued to detail the multiple levels of impacts of this confinement.

Graciela: So, it's like the news spread like wildfire, like instantly. So yeah, I mean, so these people besides the terror and the fear, not leaving the house. What if you needed milk? No, don't go get milk. You drink water. You make do with what you have because you are not leaving the house…Um, kids didn't go to school. Who's going to drive them to school if you're on lockdown, you are at home, you are not going anywhere? Kids didn't go to school. Um, if you had doctor's appointments or whatever, you were not going anywhere.

Fabián, a 21-year-old Colombian immigrant with a head of curly hair and knowledge well beyond his years, gave a complementary assessment of the impacts of confinement on the community. Fabián was the Latino outreach coordinator at Sowing Seeds, a program that sought to improve communities through access to healthy foods. He had come to Washtenaw County about five years before and had also worked with researchers from the nearby university. Echoing Graciela's statements, Fabián described the ways in which confinement cut right to the core tenets of public health, limiting community members' abilities to eat well and exercise.

Fabián: You saw many Latinos that didn't want to leave their homes...I know that there were many problems at that time in that people could not access places where there was healthy food, where you could exercise. They couldn't go to a park out of fear, because you had to be vigilant if someone would detain you.

The confinement that Graciela and Fabián detailed has been observed nationally following large-scale work-site raids, such as those of manufacturing plants in Greeley, Colorado; Grand Island, Nebraska; and New Bedford, Massachusetts, that took place in 2006 and 2007 in which more than 900 adults were detained. In interviews following those raids, Capps, Castañeda, Chaudry, and Santos[11] describe a similar terror that resulted in what Graciela called a "lockdown": "There were stories of families who hid in their basements or closets for days at a time. People would leave the house only in small groups on short, focused trips, for instance to buy food." Here, the authors echo this restricted access to the places that could keep community members healthy, noting that they only left the house to purchase necessities, and even then, did so as infrequently as possible. Yet this confinement also eliminated contact with the people in their lives: "They kept their shades drawn and houses darkened. Some would not even open the door for people who came to bring them food or other forms of assistance."[12]

At one time, large-scale work raids were decried by all sides of the political spectrum as excessively violent and a violation of human rights.[13] To use the raid of the meat processing plants in Postville, Iowa, as an example, perhaps it stands to reason that a raid that involved 900 agents, military weaponry, including Black Hawk helicopters, and arrest of about 400 plant employees[14] would result in the confinement of residents to their homes.

Graciela and Fabián describe the same "lockdown" among community members following the enforcement actions of November of 2013. These actions, while perhaps the most notable immigration enforcement actions in the county, did not draw statewide attention. Novak and Martinez-Cardoso[15] suggest that the extreme behavior changes of self-preservation that extend from large-scale work raids may indeed extend from comparatively smaller immigration enforcement actions. Large-scale raids, as well as "everyday Postvilles" that barely make the evening news, change the fabric of community life in mixed-status communities.

Graciela and Fabián's words highlight one of the initial behavior changes that resulted from the raid on Santiago's *taller*. As Hilda described, the ubiquitous presence of law enforcement caused community members to *andar volteando*—to walk with vigilance, always glancing around them—lest the *patrullas* surround a family member and take him out of your life and into the detention system. The most straightforward way to avoid contact with law enforcement is to confine yourself inside your house. This self-protective behavior in turn restricts access to the people and places that keep you and your community healthy.

The arrests prior to the raid also reinforced a long-held belief that is often a staple of minority communities:[16] law enforcement was everywhere, and targeted you specifically for the color of your skin. Earlier, Hilda's, Arturo's, and Yolanda's experiences suggested that, when face-to-face with officers and other institutional representatives, the color of your skin may be the "symbol of deportability"[17] they need to *indagar mas*, to dig a bit more into your immigration status. But now, we see that the color of your skin may not only affect the interaction but also be the reason you are targeted in the first place.

"If You Look Hispanic, That's All You Need"

Customers came and went during Hilda's yard sale as the sun shone through the tall pine trees in her yard. She continued to speak rapidly to me in colloquial Spanish, occasionally peppered with English, and her kids biked and ran around us, enjoying the family being together in the same country. After Arturo was arrested, Hilda followed the car for a few moments, wondering what would happen to her husband, and witnessed a number of other arrests before Graciela had advised her that she was observing a detainment and should leave the area. Hilda described to me what the multiple arrests she witnessed had in common: "So *Hispano que pasaba hispano que detenían."* That is, "a Hispanic[18] who passed by was a Hispanic detained."

Arturo was one of those *hispanos que detenían,* and, a month after I spoke with Hilda, he described what this racial profiling looked like from inside the *patrulla:*

Arturo: I was one of the first one that get picked up, throughout like the next five, six hours, I was in the [ICE] car chasing around other cars. And then the only purpose is if you Hispanic, you will get pulled over that day, at that time. It [was] about five-mile range.

William: Right, so it wasn't even folks who were pulling out of that shop [Santiago's *taller*]. It was anybody who was driving—

Arturo: —anybody who was driving by. Like I said, the only request, if you look Hispanic, that's all you need. That was enough purpose to get pulled over.

Many community members with whom I spoke shared stories of law enforcement officers pulling them over for what they perceived to be nothing more than the color of their skin. That is, not only did their skin color affect the face-to-face interaction that occurred after the officer knocked on their car windows, but it was the very reason they were now face-to-face with an officer to begin with. Of course, an officer cannot state that he pulled you over because of your race, so some sort of reason—some pretext—for the stop is usually given. This means that anytime an officer could have stopped a vehicle for a traffic violation, the actual reason does not matter.[19] In Arturo's case, though his car was searched, his shirt raised to look for tattoos, and his work, immigration, and gang history questioned, the reason he was pulled over was allegedly that he turned his blinker off too soon.

Community activists and lawyers have long noted the use of pretextual stops among Latinos to investigate their immigration statuses. For example, the American Civil Liberties Union of Georgia sued Gwinnet and Cobb Counties "because it is clear that many Latino community members are stopped by police officers on pretextual grounds" that then lead to their detainment.[20] Others have noted the widespread use of race in the "crime suppression sweeps" of former Maricopa County Sheriff

Joe Arpaio, whose department was four to nine times more likely to stop Latinos than other drivers.[21]

Yet research has virtually nothing to say about the situation Arturo, Hilda, and countless others described, which is, essentially, the racial profiling of Latino drivers that officers use to *indagar mas* into their immigration statuses. However, the interaction sounds eerily similar to what reams of research have described as the experience of Black drivers throughout the United States. In *Pulled Over: How Police Stops Define Race and Citizenship*,[22] Epp, Maynard-Moody, and Haider-Markel carefully distinguish "traffic stops" from "investigatory stops." Traffic stops, they say, are stops in which a traffic law is broken, such as driving seventy in a sixty-mile-an-hour zone. Investigatory stops, however, are conducted "not to enforce traffic laws or vehicle codes but to investigate the driver. Is the driver carrying a gun or illegal drugs? What is he up to? Why is he in this neighborhood? Is there a warrant for his arrest?" They continue, "Because officers are not supposed to stop a driver without a legal justification, most investigatory stops are nominally justified by minor violations: a burned-out license-plate light, failing to signal a lane change, driving 2 miles per hour over the speed limit, and the like."[23]

While white and Black drivers were equally as likely to be pulled over for breaking traffic laws, Black drivers were three times as likely to be pulled over for an investigatory stop. That is, officers used black skin color as a cue that this particular driver is much more likely to be selling drugs, a cue rooted in stereotypes of Black people as criminals and drug dealers. Arturo's case suggests a parallel in the Latino community, equally rooted in racial tropes: Latinos are likely to be criminals, too, just of the border-crossing variety.[24]

Why does an experience that seems so fundamental to mixed-status Latino communities escape the investigations of researchers? Much work has highlighted the intersection of immigration enforcement and local policing by focusing on 287(g) and Secure Communities programs.[25] Yet research on the daily interactions of police with communities of color generally focuses on interactions with Black communities,[26] especially the extensive body of literature on racial profiling.[27] Emerging literature that considers day-to-day law enforcement among Latinos often focuses on ICE or Border Patrol.[28] When the racial profiling literature[29] includes Latinos, it often does not consider the interplay between racial profiling, local policing, and citizenship, as highlighted by the continual use of the phrase "Hispanic citizens" to describe Latino study samples.[30] Thus, a pretextual traffic stop can be used to investigate a possible drug offense, but it can also be used to arrest and deport undocumented immigrants. Again we observe a strict division in conceptualizations of Black and brown communities, with police enforcement considered the experience of the former, while immigration enforcement pertains mainly to the latter. The shared experiences of the two communities—as well as the ways in which immigration enforcement intertwines with local law enforcement—is made invisible in this dichotomy.

The racialized arrests that preceded the raid were unique from most other instances of racial profiling in their sheer blatancy. Here were numerous men pulled over and arrested, all of whom were Latino, for multiple hours over a wide geographic area by two different law enforcement organizations. It's not like racialized arrests don't happen. But they usually don't happen over and over on the same day. Community members were therefore able to leverage the visibility of these arrests to force a discussion of racial profiling with the sheriff's office, which collaborated with ICE to conduct the arrests.

At the time of the raid, the sheriff's office organized the Law Enforcement Citizens Advisory Board, or LE-CAB, in which representatives from the community liaised with the sheriff's office to discuss relevant policing issues. While meeting with community members after the raid, the board agreed to bring the issue of racial profiling to the sheriff's office. Minutes from a meeting between LE-CAB and the sheriff's office on December 19, 2013, about a month-and-a-half after the raid, detailed the following question and response:

> [Question by Board posed to Sheriff's Office]: Was there any indication of racial profiling on [the day of the raid]? Presenters to the LE-CAB stated all cars stopped that day were occupied by Latino males.

Response: The suspect was a Latino male. Cars stopped were exiting the target location.

This response was notable for a number of reasons. First, the suspect—Santiago—was one of the first people arrested that day, so it is not clear why the arrests of those who resembled him occurred after he had been taken into custody. Had ICE not informed local officers that Santiago was arrested? What did ICE have to gain by allowing the sheriff's office to continue pulling over Latino men who would later be detained, deported, and added to ICE's monthly deportation quota?

Second, the justification for the arrest of solely Latino males was that they (1) matched "the suspect" and (2) drove away from his *taller*. The implications here for the Latino community were understandably frightening, and it appeared that their suspicions of racial profiling had been confirmed. After all, how does one match a suspect in a way that is visible through a car window? In what ways, besides skin color, can an officer possibly assess a resemblance to an alleged drug dealer?

But the second condition—driving away from the target location—was just as destructive to the community as an admission of racial profiling would have been. How could any community member know which businesses were owned by "suspects"? Were there other Santiagos out there who were fixing your car or patching your roof or making your food that it would behoove you to avoid, lest you be Latino while driving away from the target location in which they worked?

While many Latinos in the community may have gone "on lockdown" to avoid the ambling *patrullas* that lurked around every corner, others changed their behaviors in other ways to avoid encounters with law enforcement. While they could not change the color of their skin, they *could* change where they went. If being near the property of a suspect could result in your own apprehension and deportation, then self-preservation required you to avoid the area, even if this meant abandoning the women and children who needed you.

Marquadas

Unwilling to leave her own apartment and with her economic provider suddenly removed from her life, Guadalupe knew she would have
to rely on her community for food and financial support. But she also
suspected that few individuals in her network—many of whom were
Latino and undocumented—would be willing to approach the property
of an alleged drug dealer, as "leaving the property," while Latino had been
cited by law enforcement as sufficient criteria for arrest.

Guadalupe: The next day, well, it was such a sad day because we were so scared
of leaving the house. We didn't know if [law enforcement] was finished or if
they were still detaining people. And in our lives, my brother [Santiago] was
the one who made the money. How could we go buy food?

If I were to tell someone that we needed something, to lend us money,
something like that, no one wanted to get anywhere near there because of
the raid.

William: No one wanted to get near—

Guadalupe: —my brother's [Santiago's] house.

William: You mean to help you?

Guadalupe: Yes, no one, no one wanted to because they were scared that they
[law enforcement] would take them.

Fabián, the Colombian outreach worker for Sowing Seeds, added
another layer of interpretation to the isolation Guadalupe described.
"In the end, this family was marked (*esa familia quedaba marcada*). Many
families ended up leaving that area because [the family in the raid] was
pointed at and seen in a certain way because of what happened with the
raid (*. . . son señalados y son vistos de una manera que sucede por éstas redadas*)."

Thus, community members were not just avoiding the *taller*, but they
seemed also to be avoiding Guadalupe and Fernanda themselves because
of their association with the location in which the raid took place.

Fabián's interview was the first time I remembered hearing the word
"*marcada*" to describe the impacts of immigration enforcement, and I
was unaware of any immigration research that could explain how two

mothers could move so quickly from valued community members who merited community support to individuals to be avoided at all costs. But what Fabián described did seem to exist in another line of research.

"Stigma" is a term used to describe a "mark" that one bears that may result in the bearer's exclusion from society. As Goffman writes in his foundational book on the subject, a stigma is "an attribute that is deeply discrediting" that transforms the bearer of the stigma "from a whole and usual person to a tainted, discounted one." Stigmas can create the categories of "us" versus "them" and serve as social reminders of who to avoid, exclude, and reject.[31] Historically, those infected with contagious illness have been stigmatized and cast out, their personhood reduced to their capacities to serve as vectors of infectious disease.[32] The literature is replete with examples of the effects stigmatization can have on one's health, including elevated mortality among Black people,[33] poorer mental health among lesbian, gay, bisexual populations,[34] and health care avoidance among a range of communities.[35] Were Guadalupe and Fernanda being stigmatized because of their association with an alleged drug dealer?

I followed up with Fabián to ask him to elaborate on his notion of being *marcada*. In his response, he echoed and expanded on the isolation and avoidance Guadalupe described earlier.

Fabián: So, between families, it became, "If I am not part of [the raid] and my neighbor is, I try to distance myself and not talk to them." So, the community was broken (*se rompe la comunidad*), the well-being of the neighborhood, friendships, they were torn apart.

Many friendships ended because they did not want to be close to someone who was at risk of being deported, of being grabbed and taken away (*ser agarrado*).

It seemed as though Guadalupe and Fernanda had been stigmatized by their own network, cast out and avoided, their association with Santiago akin to a contagious disease. But where had this stigma come from? Guadalupe and Fernanda had not been accused of selling drugs, nor, like so many other community members, had they even been arrested during the law enforcement actions associated with the raid. In fact, they had encountered both the police and ICE on that Thursday, both of whom left them in the apartment. So, despite multiple opportunities to be arrested for drug possession, they were not. What had made the community so fearful of approaching them?

Recent trends in stigma research suggest that these stigmas do not occur organically. Rather, those in power often create stigmas to silence those marked by the stigma. As Link and Phelan explain, "When people have an interest in keeping other people down, in or away, stigma is a resource that allows them to obtain ends they desire."[36] Stigmas may not always emerge naturally, but are sometimes created, given meaning, and exploited for their powerful ability to exclude and shut out. The stigma of association with a drug user resulted in *una comunidad rota*, a community fractured and split apart. But who was it that benefited from the stigma placed on Santiago and, later, his family?

By this point, I hope the answer is clear. Marking Santiago as a drug dealer granted ICE immense power over the entire mixed-status Latino community of Washtenaw County. Once ICE had accused Santiago of trafficking drugs out of his *taller*, ICE was able to collaborate with the sheriff's office to coordinate his arrest. Then, for hours afterward and miles away from the site of his original apprehension, law enforcement could racially profile and arrest anyone who could possibly be associated with Santiago, kick in his door and point weapons at his wife and children, and arrest the Latino men they found on his property. And in the end, Santiago and his look-alikes would be punished because of their immigration statuses—legal infractions that were unrelated to Santiago's original targeting to begin with. Thus, ICE infused the drug-dealing stigma with meaning: those suspected of selling drugs—and those with whom they associated—would be the targets of racialized, swift, militarized, and perfectly legal law enforcement violence.

When the drug-dealing stigma had been passed to Guadalupe and Fernanda—whether by association with Santiago or Santiago's *taller*—community members avoided the potential drug dealers, their property, and the roads around their property lest they be swept up in the racialized military violence. Fabián summarized the result of Guadalupe and Fernanda's isolation. "So,... instead of supporting [the families in the raid], [other families] were trying to throw them out. And I know that one or two of those families, after the raid, the next year, they left [the United States]." In this way, ICE exerted their stranglehold not only on their targets but also on their entire community and on the very roads community members now refused to traverse. By cultivating the stigma of the drug dealer, ICE had made it clear that they were after you, and if you tried to access the people and places in your lives that keep you healthy, they would come for you, too.

"A River of Fear"

Marcadas by ICE, avoided by those whose skin color was the color of the suspect, Guadalupe and Fernanda had a decreasing pool of people in their community to whom they could turn for support. But in the absence of people, could Guadalupe and Fernanda count on the places in their community for help? Guadalupe and Fernanda had five US citizen children between them, all of whom were likely eligible for some type of government support. Would the mothers be able and willing to access the offices that could help them put food on their children's table?

Graciela, a well-respected advocate in the Washtenaw Latino community, knew that Guadalupe, Fernanda, and their children would benefit from the services available to them, but doubted they would attempt to access them. As Graciela explained, "The kids can get food stamps, but the mother is probably terrified... She's probably afraid the minute she walks in there, they'll call immigration."

Graciela continued, emphasizing that the fear felt by those who are undocumented limits the available resources their families are legally entitled to. That is, the immigration status of one can affect the health and well-being of the whole family unit.

Graciela: There are a lot of services they just won't access, they won't even think about it. It's just like [they are thinking], "That's for everyone else, not for me." And that's a shame 'cause the kids are born here. They have a right to eat...It's all fear. There's fear underneath everything. There is just fear. It's just like this river of fear underneath the whole, everything.

This "river of fear" that Graciela described was an apt metaphor to capture what other studies have strongly suggested: that fear of immigration enforcement—of deportation—flows from the immigration system to other government services, limiting the willingness of those in mixed-status families to access resources, even if they, or their family members, are eligible for those services.[37] But, while a large and growing body of work attests to the relationship between fear and avoidance of care,[38] rare has been the description of this fear from those who experience it firsthand.

I later had the opportunity to discuss with Guadalupe how this river of fear flowed. In the interview, Guadalupe seemed to be working through her reasoning at that moment, diverging and sometimes retreating before centering in on the criteria with which she felt comfortable. I began with a question comparing fear of *las patrullas* to the services Guadalupe needed to access:

William: You were talking about how frightened you were from *las patrullas?* Do you feel this same fear when you, for example, go to the clinic or a government office, something like that?

Guadalupe: No, no.

William: Why not?

Guadalupe: I don't know. Maybe it's because in clinics and such I have received that help [before the raid]. For me it's *la policía*. *La policía* are the ones who took away the father of my daughters, the ones who took away my brother. They are the ones who took away my family, who, if they detained me, would separate me from my kids.

Guadalupe seemed to say that she would continue to use social services because her fear of deportation stemmed from encounters with *la policía*, not social service agency representatives.

I was surprised to hear Guadalupe say this, given the general level of acceptance that fear flowed from ICE to social service organizations without much divergence. Did the fact that Guadalupe continued to access services after the raid have to do with which services she accessed? Maybe it had to do with the timing? Would Guadalupe access resources that she had already accessed before the raid, but avoid anything new? I followed up.

William: Okay. So, after the raid you use the same services [as you did before]?

Guadalupe: Yes...I asked when I went to [renew my Washtenaw Health Plan[39] insurance], because of [the raid], if there would be any problems. Because they [ICE] had my name and all that, but they told me no, I shouldn't worry. Nothing will happen.

William: Yes. So, you trusted the person who discussed this with you?

Guadalupe: Well, yes, because I thought that they know more about this than I do. She told me that all the information was confidential and that if I wanted anyone to know something I had to sign first to authorize it.

This distinction made sense. Guadalupe trusted those with whom she had previously worked, who were themselves aware of regulations related to sharing immigration status. Research has shown that interventions culturally and linguistically tailored to Spanish-speaking communities tend to be more successful than interventions that do not take these factors into account.[40] Guadalupe's statement perhaps added an important finding to this literature: for members of mixed-status communities, trustworthy organizations also protect your personal information.

I assumed this was the end of the exchange. But after a pause, Guadalupe refined her answer, catching me off guard:

Guadalupe: The truth is that, in that moment, when they told me [that my name would remain confidential], I thought it was a lie, and I was scared. I had [Diane's (Jessica's mother and a white US citizen)] address so that my bills could go there. I didn't want to give my address, where I was, nothing.

William: So, immediately after the raid, you didn't want to share your address? Not with the Washtenaw Health Plan, not with anyone?

Guadalupe: No, nothing like that. I didn't want to share this information with anyone. Including food stamps for the kids. I didn't want to renew anything because I was so scared of everything.

Guadalupe had taken a meandering few turns to arrive at her conclusion. It almost felt as though she was experimenting with exceptions to her own rules. Did she trust organizations while fearing *la policía*? Did she trust some organizations but not others? Did she trust some people and not others? What about if the administrator knew something about immigration law or spoke Spanish?

In the end, the river of fear, as research suggested, flowed from the law enforcement officers who removed her brother to the services that Guadalupe refused to access. Anyone could be lying. Anyone could be trying to catch her. Guadalupe's words suggest that fear of deportation can fracture relationships with even the most culturally sensitive, appropriate, and prepared social service organizations. Sometimes the potential grimness of deportation is more influential than the life-giving support of the people and places in one's life. Better that her children have no food than no mother.

It seemed highly likely that Guadalupe's children, Carlitos, Sofía, and Fatima, and Fernanda's children, Ignacio and Lena, like many children in the aftermath of immigration enforcement,[41] would be increasingly hungry following the raid that occurred in their community. The different paths that would lead to their hunger illustrate the range of repercussions that extend from immigration enforcement actions—through communities, families, and individual bodies—regardless of immigration status and regardless of whether they were the targets of the actions to begin with. Fernanda, traumatized by the agents who kicked in her door and pointed weapons at her, would no longer be able to produce the breast milk—the *leche*—that would have nourished Ignacio. Meanwhile, the pantries in Guadalupe's apartment that could have been filled with canned goods, vegetables, and dairy, would remain empty, as she was too terrified of her own deportation to access food assistance. A single man was targeted, and multiple other men were caught up in the destruction his arrest caused. Left behind were the women and children locked in their homes, isolated, stigmatized, strategically making themselves and their stories invisible to allow for their own survival.

But not all members of the Latino mixed-status community in Washtenaw County were equally at risk of deportation or racial profiling. Guadalupe and Fernanda would ultimately be supported by some community members who, like them, were deeply affected by immigration enforcement though rarely its target: women.

Groceries

In multiple conversations, community members clearly noted the blatant pattern of arrests that occurred on the day Santiago's *taller* was raided: Santiago, "the suspect," was a Latino man. Everyone arrested throughout the day was also a Latino man. Meanwhile, every woman encountered by law enforcement, both on the road and in the raided apartment, was left behind. While the scale and visibility of the arrests on that day was unlike anything the area had experienced, the pattern—a focused removal of Latino men—represented the way in which arrests and deportations have occurred on the national level.[42] With Latino men most at risk of apprehension and deportation, the burden of support largely fell to women, especially those who were white, citizens, or visa holders.[43]

This gendered pattern of support was evident in the moments after the ICE agents departed from Guadalupe's apartment. As the men in uniform left the apartment with Santiagito in tow, four women entered to support Guadalupe and Fernanda and to bear witness to the violence they had experienced. Between Diane (the mother of Santiagito's girlfriend) and the three urgent responders from WICIR, all four women were US citizens, and three were white.[44] None of the four women who entered the apartment were fearful of deportation, and the three who were white were unlikely to even be questioned about their immigration statuses or that of their families.

I asked Guadalupe who had supported her following the raid. Initially, my naïve and admittedly biased intention was to highlight the bravery of the women who, though they may not be deported, still risked interpersonal violence from either law enforcement officers or others they encountered on the property of the *taller*.

William: There were a number of women who helped you then?

Guadalupe: Yes [laughing]. Many women helped us.

William (*sarcastically*): Where were all the men!?

While my point—that it was courageous of the women in the community to support each other at their own risk—was perhaps accurate, Guadalupe educated me about the enormous risk differential for deportation experienced by men versus women.

Guadalupe: [The men were] scared. Just scared.

William: Why do you think there is a difference between how men and women reacted?...

Guadalupe: Well, I talked about that with Hilda [Arturo's wife]. It's this idea that for women, as some kind of justice or something, there is more understanding [from ICE]. For men, no. For men, they just detain them and take them away...

That is, while undocumented women were at risk of deportation, undocumented men were far more so, as they appeared to be immediately swept up and removed. As former agent Jaime had attested, "Arresting men individually or by the dozen didn't bother me." There was no way that undocumented men were approaching the *taller* or the *familia marcada* who had inhabited it.

The support Frida provided in the aftermath of the immigration enforcement actions illustrates the different risk of deportation between men and women that Guadalupe describes. Frida was the girlfriend of Francisco, who was arrested as he drove away from the *taller* in the hours preceding the raid. A light-skinned immigrant from southeastern Europe who spoke fluent Spanish and English, Frida was outspoken, confident, and disturbed by the "lockdown" that followed the raid. And, unlike her boyfriend, Francisco, or Santiago, Guadalupe, and Fernanda, Frida was also a permanent resident of the United States.

Francisco, likely because he had lived in the United States for twenty-one years and had no criminal record, was eligible to be released from detention on bond shortly after his initial arrest. A bond allows a payment to be made to the ICE office in exchange for the promise that the detainee will oblige by the decision of his later court hearing. ICE agrees that you can stay out of detention in exchange for a few thousand dollars, and then, as long as you attend your court hearings and abide by what the court decides—even if that means turning yourself in for deportation—you get your money back.

However, two requirements for bond payment create extraordinary difficulties for mixed-status communities. First, to pay a bond, one must go to the local ICE office and present a work authorization number, a birth certificate or passport, or a number of other documents that only US citizens or permanent residents generally possess. Undocumented community members are therefore unable to pay bonds, even if they were willing to enter the ICE office to do so. Second, the individual who pays the bond becomes responsible for the person released on bond. This means that the person, in addition to sharing her address with ICE, must make sure the individual attends all court hearings and, if he does not, must turn him into the ICE office in order to get the bond money back. Thus, Francisco, while having the opportunity to leave detention on bond, was initially unable and unwilling to do so, first because much of his network was undocumented and did not have the proper paperwork to pay the bond and, second, because he did not want to ask others in his mixed-status network to share their addresses with ICE.

But Frida did not want Francisco to stay in detention, so she leveraged the protection of her visa and paid the bond herself for both Francisco and another detainee. Speaking about Francisco's bond, she shared: "On his next court, his bail was set to, I think, fifteen hundred dollars, but none of the family members had papers, or his sister was actually in the process of getting her papers and she did not want to post the bail, so I just went ahead and did it."

And that is not where Frida's assistance stopped. Aware of the fear that had spread through the community after the raid, Frida did what she could to address the confinement that resulted.

Frida: Meanwhile, in the community, everybody was going crazy. All the people that I know and do not have papers, they were pretty much hiding. They would not get out of the house. I know a few people; I went, I helped, I took groceries and all. They just—they were scared...

I later asked Frida whether her supportive behaviors had anything to do with being a permanent resident.

William: And you weren't scared because of your immigration status?
Frida: No, I mean I'm a green card holder, so they can—
William (*interrupting*): You were at that time, too?
Frida: Yeah, yeah. I still am. They can take it away at any time, but I don't feel like I did anything wrong, nor they [those in detention] did anything wrong. And if I can help somebody I will, no matter what. I didn't think I was endangering myself by anything, the worst thing they could ask me is okay here's my paperwork, [and I'd say], "Here's this."

Frida's words emphasize that the legal statuses of the members of one's social network can shape the type of support they are able and willing to provide. Here, we see at least three important aspects of identity at play: immigration status, race (or at least racial presentation), and gender. Immigration status likely plays the largest role in shaping who is willing to provide support after immigration enforcement actions: if you can be deported, you stay away. Immigration status then intersects with race and gender, each of which highly influences the likelihood that immigration or police officers will detain and question you. Thus, those who feel most vulnerable and with the most at stake—undocumented Latino men—are more likely to go into hiding, while in the cases discussed, citizens and visa-holding women—often those who could not be racially profiled—were able to provide support. In yet another gendered impact of immigration enforcement, while men are removed, women are left behind. When other men go into hiding, other women must rearrange their lives to support them.

■ ■ ■

To some extent, mixed-status and racial minority communities have always had tenuous relationships with law enforcement. Indeed, the

Washtenaw County Latino community was no different in this regard from communities of color and mixed-status communities throughout the country. Yet the enforcement events of that Thursday in November were notably violent and blatantly apprehended and removed solely Latino men. The enforcement events also illustrated to the community the power of the drug dealer stigma: anyone Latino who was marked as a drug dealer, and any Latino who was associated with him, could be racially profiled, swept up, and, if undocumented, deported. You did not even have to be connected to the alleged drug dealer. Merely marking Santiago as a drug dealer allowed ICE to unleash a range of government-funded and state-sanctioned violence on anyone they encountered.

But the Latino mixed-status community was not the first on which law enforcement had inflicted an extraordinary amount of race-based violence. Parallel to these conversations about immigration enforcement in this mixed-status Latino community, Black communities across the country were coping with and advocating against the killings of unarmed Black men, women, and boys by white police officers. I, a Latino man, was in the curious position of riding in police cars with white officers who openly discussed the killings of Black community members. What I learned while in those cars was simple: Black men are violently killed in much the same way that brown men are violently detained and deported.

The Raid: The Hours and Days After

The Hours After

La policía leave the apartment. About the same time, Elena Maria, Amalia, and Ofelia—the three WICIR urgent responders—walk through the broken door to try to support Guadalupe and Fernanda any way they can. Together, the five women sit around a kitchen table covered with plates half filled with food. "It's like they had been eating and then interrupted," Amalia later describes it. The children are in tears now, or, worse, silent and stoic, and the women take turns holding the infants close to their bodies to try to calm their jittery nerves.

Then they hear footsteps. They look over to see an officer coming back into the room. The officer hands Guadalupe the warrant that allowed them to enter the apartment to gather evidence against Santiago, the man who had been arrested about ten hours before. The officer leaves, and the women return to their Spanish conversation.

But they are promptly interrupted again.

This time, it's not an officer delivering a search warrant, but the man[1] who rents the property to Santiago who enters through the broken door.

"These are good people," the landlord says to no one and everyone at the same time. "They are good tenants. They could never have done anything illegal." The landlord, a large, bald white man with a bag of chips in his hand, cuts a powerful figure in the room as he continues his incantations of the "good immigrant" narrative he is compelled to preach to the immigrants in front of him.

"He had this swagger to him," Elena Maria says. "He had all these necklaces. Like, he looked like some typical out-of-the-movies macho white guy. Like scary. Like a ringleader, you know what I mean?" Others called him a "slumlord" or an "asshole."

He continues to speak into the air that there is no way that such good human beings could have broken the law. Amalia is disgusted by his behavior.

"He was trying to control the narrative," she says. "Oh, it was all about him, and what he was trying to do was make sure that nothing negative would come back on him." Then she continued in the sarcastic and biting tone she leveraged when the injustice in a story became palpable: "If they were here illegally, or if they did anything illegal, he certainly had no knowledge of that! He was saying, 'These were good people! No way would they have guns and drugs! They are peaceful people! They work hard! They are good tenants!'" Thus, between crunches of Cheetos, the landlord had efficiently reduced the layered, multilevel, complicated suffering of the mixed-status family who sat in front of him into a simplified narrative of good and bad, deserving and undeserving immigrants.

The landlord then addresses Guadalupe and Fernanda directly: "Now honeys," he begins, "if they ask you if you live here, you know what to say, right? You never lived here. You were just staying here. You never lived here. You never paid rent here."

Eventually, the landlord leaves.

The women look back and forth at each other, relieved that the man has finally left them alone. Now if only they could find Santiago and the other men who had been removed from the *taller*, the apartment, and the road in front of the property. The urgent responders attempt to counsel the women as best as they can and collect as many details about the raid as possible. About an hour and a half later, the three urgent responders leave as well.

Amalia reflects on the departure: "In saying goodbye, it was really hard, because what do you say other than, 'I am so sorry, I am so utterly sorry that you should be subjected to brutality'?"

Guadalupe and Fernanda would like to sleep somewhere other than the house in which they thought they were going to die, in which they witnessed their door kicked in and their loved ones removed. But night had already fallen. And, as Lisbeth,[2] a cofounder of WICIR who would visit Guadalupe and Fernanda the next day, shared: "Because ICE follows people around, I don't think anybody was real anxious to have [Guadalupe and Fernanda] come to their homes that night." *Marcadas*, Guadalupe and Fernanda block the broken door with a chair and hope that no one breaks in a second time.

The Day After

When morning comes, Fernanda finds that the children, including her son who could no longer nurse without vomiting, need diapers. She and Guadalupe decide to go to the grocery store, the same one that Santiago had attempted to visit the previous day to get milk and vegetables for the stew that they will never eat. To do so, Guadalupe and Fernanda know they will have to cross the road on which Santiago and his look-alikes had been detained the previous day.

They pick up the diapers they need and return safely to the apartment. When they arrive, they find it has been ransacked.

To make matters worse, a flatbed truck now sits in front of their property, and cars are being taken out of the *taller* and towed to a property down the street. The women call Elena Maria, the urgent responder they had met the previous day. Elena Maria then calls Lisbeth of WICIR, who drives over to the apartment to help them manage the ensuing chaos.

The landlord had kicked Guadalupe and Fernanda—the good, innocent, law-abiding immigrants—out of the apartment. In exchange for the rent money that Santiago owed him, he had taken it upon himself to confiscate the clothes, furniture, money, and electronics in the apartment and the tools with which Santiago made his living from the *taller* below.

Guadalupe and Fernanda, whose lives were in economic turmoil after the removal of their primary provider, certainly mourned the loss of every penny they now so clearly needed. But equally painful was the loss of the objects that reminded them of better times, of days when they were all in the same country on the same day. As Lisbeth described it, "So any electronics he took had all the memories from their parties, from their babies' birthday parties...All those memories to be able to show their kids were gone... Like they were kind of feeling, like 'our life is already in shambles right now so we just have our memories. They should have given the respect of that,' you know. But those memories had been taken too."

Lisbeth asks Guadalupe and Fernanda whether they want to call the police and file a report about their missing property. The irony of the question is not lost on Lisbeth, who had herself witnessed her friends detained and removed in a home raid in March 2008. She tells Fernanda and Guadalupe, "We will support you in calling the police, and we will stay here and we will help you with the investigation part. But if you don't want to [call the police], I totally understand, because we are going to be calling the same department that came in with the SWAT team last night."

Guadalupe and Fernanda agree to call the police as long as Lisbeth is able to stay and mediate between them and the officers, so Lisbeth makes the call. She explains that she only wants someone to come out to take a report of a breaking and entering (B&E), irrespective of the previous day's actions. The sheriff's office sends an available deputy.

To prepare for the arrival of the officers, the women try to gather evidence of the B&E: "Do you have any pictures to show of what ICE did yesterday compared to what this looks like now?" Lisbeth asks Guadalupe. Together they puzzle over how to differentiate between the men who legally entered and ransacked their home to take their family members and the men who illegally entered and ransacked their home to take their money.

Elena Maria is there by this time and sees the landlord driving up to the *taller marcado*. She pulls out her phone to film his arrival, a video I am later able to track down. The dark, grainy seven seconds of footage is chilling amid the clean Instagram background. The landlord has on a white-collar shirt with a black sports coat over it. Eyes covered by sunglasses, he begins by pointing his index finger aggressively at Elena Maria from the driver's seat of what appears to be a dark purple sedan. "Get the goddamn hell off my property," he screams at her.

His movements are jerky and combative, and in between shouts, he reaches forward to put the car in park. He swings open the door, which passes about an inch or so from Elena Maria's cell phone camera. It's dark in the sedan, but as he heaves open the heavy door, the interior light turns on, and an enormous brown guard dog can be seen climbing on the passenger seat. The landlord advances toward Elena Maria, and it's unclear whether the dog is going to follow him out of the car. Watching the video, it's nearly incomprehensible to me that Elena Maria is able to remain calm. Her hand does not shake while holding the camera, nor does her voice tremble when she tells him, "Sir, you don't need to get physical."

Elena Maria later tells him that the police are on their way. He yells back, "Fuck the police. Fuck the police."

A deputy arrives before the interaction escalates to violence, and, as promised, Lisbeth mediates between the officer, the landlord, and Guadalupe and Fernanda. The deputy tells Lisbeth that they need receipts or serial numbers of the stolen items to file a police report for the B&E. Lisbeth pushes back, questioning the officer: "Okay, think about the digital camera that you have at home. If it was stolen tonight can you put your hands on a receipt for the digital camera you bought however many years ago?" The officer, of course, cannot confirm that he would have receipts for his own electronics, despite being fully aware of the requirements to report a B&E.

Lisbeth continues, "And besides that, who even knows where [the receipt] is now because I am telling you that place was not like that yesterday. This guy [the landlord] and his little entourage totally ransacked [it]."

The officer seems nervous, as if he doesn't want to get involved in such a complicated and evolving narrative of violence. "Have you gone in?" Lisbeth asks him rhetorically, implying that, once he goes in, the evidence of the B&E will be clear.

"No," he responds. "I am just trying to do my job. Don't make this any harder."

Yesterday, on a Thursday in November of 2013, Guadalupe and Fernanda sat in their apartment with their children as agents kicked in their door to gather evidence against Santiago. That evidence, ultimately, was not needed, as Santiago and his look-alikes got deported anyway. But now, on a Friday in November of 2013, an agent from the same department is hesitant to enter the apartment—despite the invitation to do so—to gather evidence in support of Guadalupe and Fernanda's B&E claim.

The officer attempts to sympathize, or at least to de-escalate the situation: "Well the best I can do is work with [the landlord] to give [Guadalupe and Fernanda] some time to get their stuff out. Can I talk to [the landlord] alone please?" The two men step aside to talk without the women interjecting, and, eventually, Guadalupe and Fernanda are allowed to enter the apartment again. The women take out what they can: two mattresses and some clothes for themselves and their children. However, their money and electronics—and Santiago's tools—are gone. Lisbeth takes Guadalupe and her children to a hotel, while Fernanda and her children leave with a friend.

Chapter 5

I Hate to See Them Die Unnecessarily

It was nearing 3 p.m., and we were all exhausted.

Thirty community members, myself among them, had spent the last six hours with thirty law enforcement officers in order to, as the email said, "set expectations, build trust, impact policy decisions, and ultimately improve our community." All sixty of us started out in the same university ballroom. Then, we split into, as the high-ranking law enforcement officer in charge described it, "the community" and "folks who are sworn to protect and serve." In our separate rooms, we talked about each other—what we hated, what we loved, what we feared, and what could be better—and we answered question prompts that we then summarized on multiple poster boards to be hung on the walls. It was tense in our room, in the absence of police, and I imagined the tension would only ratchet up when the officers returned and saw how we described them.

But I highly doubted that tension in our room was unique to our county. Rather, it likely mirrored a smoldering, burning rage that was beginning to bubble over, an anger that grew from the news stories and continuous stream of grainy videos of Black men, women, and boys being choked and shot by police, or simply starting out in their custody and winding up dead.

In fact, twenty-three days before the event, a 44-year-old Black man, Eric Harris, was shot in the back at point-blank range as he lay face down on the cement when white Reserve Deputy Robert Bates drew his gun—a gun he was not authorized to carry[1]—instead of his Taser in Tulsa, Oklahoma. Then twenty-one days before the event, Walter Scott, a 50-year-old Black man, was shot three times in the back, once in the buttock, and once in the ear as he ran away empty handed from white Officer Michael Slager in Charleston, South Carolina.[2]

Then just six days before the event, a 25-year-old Black man, Freddie Gray Jr., was arrested and placed into the back of a police van alive, only to be removed with a broken spine, unable to breathe. He would die seven days later in the hospital.[3]

These deaths followed the particularly grievous and personal wound experienced by the Washtenaw County community, as, five months before the event, a 40-year-old Black woman, Aura Rosser, was shot, once in the chest and once in the head, by white police officer David Reid.[4] She died in her apartment less than ten miles from where we were sitting.

It's time for lunch and officers walk back into the ballroom. Double doors open wide and in comes an intimidating mass of blue and steel. Posters go up on walls. "What does the badge mean?" one reads. We see the officers' answers: "Emblem of public trust," "Calling to make a difference," "Honor, integrity, and professionalism," "Sacrifice," "Means everything," "High expectations," "Symbol of keeping order in Society," "What is going on? Can I help?" and "Hope to the hopeless." I can't imagine how hard it is to be one of the many Black men in the audience and eat lunch with people armed with the same weapons and dressed in the same uniforms as those who were filmed shooting and killing men who looked just like you and to simultaneously have to witness this heroic self-perception.

Officers continually ask community members to move past the killings and work together and to try and empathize with the numerous challenges of being a cop. But community members are resistant to empathizing, asking instead that officers recognize the enormous imbalance of coercive power wielded by the men and women who chose to come clad in bulletproof vests with firearms holstered to their hips to a community breakfast. Why did they require empathy? You don't need community buy-in to stop killing us. Just stop killing us.

Hours pass, and the officer in charge comes in to wrap up the event. He senses the tension in the room, and, as I have seen him do so many times, he attempts to speak to both parties at the same time, to find a middle ground that will temporarily quell the grievances of everyone in the room.

Yes, there is a power imbalance, he says. Yes, officers have power. Officers have the power to take away that which is valued most in this country: "our freedom."

Our freedom?

It feels as though the community lets out a collective sigh of exasperation, a groan of frustration that those asking for empathy cannot themselves empathize with what it must be like to live under the surveillance of those with the weapons and legal and rhetorical means to kill them without penalty. Do they not realize that it is only the living who can ask for empathy?

Our freedom?

We are not here lamenting the loss of freedom. We already lamented that. We already know racial profiling exists, that driving, walking, or standing in a group while Black or Latino means you are more likely to be stopped, questioned, and cuffed. At that moment, it was not our freedom that concerned us. Sure, Laquan McDonald lost his freedom walking away from white officer Jason Van Dyke when Van Dyke emptied his magazine into him. But we were less concerned with his inability to walk the streets and more concerned with bullet holes in Laquan's back, scalp, shoulders, chest, neck, and arms.[5]

Freedom—unlike our Black and brown bodies—can't be shot in the back. Freedom, unlike Eric Garner, can't be suffocated on a sidewalk with an illegal chokehold. Freedom, unlike Sergio, can't have its spine broken during an immigration raid. Freedom can't have the milk stop flowing from its breasts, can't have its children stare blankly into space as officers leave their apartment, can't be homeless and suicidal.

This isn't about freedom.

It's about violence. It's about trauma. It's about dying. It's about never seeing our families again.

And it's about the people who can make it happen, any time, any day, on the most comúnes y corrientes *of days.*

—Adapted from field notes, April 2015

When I was planning the fieldwork for this project, I had intended to spend time with law enforcement officers throughout the county in order to learn about the ways in which local police departments enforce immigration law. There were a few reasons for this component of the fieldwork. First, the raid on Santiago's *taller* and the enforcement actions of that Thursday in November of 2013 all included police collaboration. While it was ICE that detained and deported the men they encountered, local law enforcement officers pulled many of them over and, ultimately, kicked in Guadalupe's door. When and how do officers collaborate with ICE? And how do they weigh the costs and benefits of doing so?

Second, it is most often the local police who shape the *días comúnes y corrientes* in mixed-status Latino communities in states like Michigan and others throughout the Midwest. Unlike southern border states such as Texas, Arizona, and California, much of the interior of the United States is not patrolled by *la migra*.[6] We don't typically have ICE and CBP checkpoints on our roads, and we don't see the green uniformed men and women on a daily basis. While it is true that everyone deported passes through DHS offices, many end up there because of the actions of local police who arrest them, book them in the county jail, and then hold them for ICE to pick up. Taken together, then, observation of local law enforcement could better illustrate the daily role of police in immigration enforcement in everyday, average, predominantly white cities, towns, and counties much like the one in which Guadalupe, Fernanda, Hilda, and I lived.

However, when I decided to work with law enforcement, Tamir Rice, a 12-year-old Black boy, had not yet been shot in the stomach by white police officer Timothy Loehmann two seconds after he pulled up to Tamir in the park as he played with a pellet gun in Cleveland, Ohio.[7] And Sandra Bland, a 28-year-old Black woman, had not been pulled over and jailed after refusing to put out her cigarette, only to be found dead in her cell three days later in Waller County, Texas.[8] These deaths, along with the others described in the opening vignette, numbered only a few among the string of shootings, chokings, and deaths in custody of Black men, women, and boys[9] by police officers throughout the country.[10] The recordings of these killings—whether from cell phone videos or dashboard, body, and sunglass cameras—circulated widely, adding fuel to the firestorm of protests taking place in cities where Black individuals had been killed by officers, such as Baltimore, Maryland,[11] or Ferguson, Missouri.[12] Washtenaw County had its own share of protests following the killing of Aura Rosser. When the name of Rosser's killer was released, advocates marched on a city council meeting to demand that Officer David Reid be fired.[13]

Following the killing of Trayvon Martin by George Zimmerman, a Latino man—who found the 17-year-old Black boy carrying skittles and a tea bottle while wearing a hoody threatening enough to kill—advocates organized the Black Lives Matter movement[14] to situate these individual deaths within the much larger context of violent Black suppression by a racist police state. As advocates pointed out, these deaths were not unique, singular instances of individual "bad apple" cops with itchy trigger fingers, but the predictable and strategic outcome of state-sanctioned violence against Black individuals that began at the birth of the United States.

So when I finally spent time with law enforcement officers, it was not immigration enforcement they talked about. They instead discussed the Black Lives Matter movement, regardless of whether they called it that. They had reflected on these killings, on their roles in and responsibility for them, and on what it meant to police communities of color amid growing racial tensions. So we talked about it. Where I could, I inquired about it and pushed conversations in that direction. And I learned more about immigration law enforcement than I could have possibly imagined.

Researchers often separate the experiences of Black and Latino communities, casting racial profiling and police violence as challenges faced by Black communities, while Latino communities must deal with immigration enforcement. But the justifications for the police killings of Black men largely parallel the justifications for the immigration enforcement actions that took place on Santiago's property, as well as the detentions and deportations that happen on any given day. By casting men of color as dangerous villains who prey on innocent community members, heroic law enforcement officers are able to leverage extremely violent tactics to exert control over them. The war on drugs significantly increases the potential for this violence, first by infusing law enforcement agencies with the funds to militarize their departments and then by reinforcing the typical view of a world of heroes and villains into which law enforcement have traditionally divided their communities. The results of these tactics are similar: by leveraging undocumented immigration status and the family and community relationships of the undocumented, law enforcement officers have an enormous amount of coercive power over mixed-status community members. Likewise, being outright shot and killed by police reduces the world of many Black community members into similarly binary choices: compliance or death.

Villains

"What does the badge represent?"

Officers' responses to this question—"Emblem of public trust," "Calling to make a difference," "Honor, integrity, and professionalism," "Sacrifice," "Means everything," "High expectations," "Symbol of keeping order in Society," "What is going on? Can I help?" "Hope to the hopeless"—certainly reflected the pride and purpose with which they viewed their roles as police officers. Officers at the community meeting came from a range of departments and ranks, and thus these sentiments likely reflected the beliefs of many law enforcement officers throughout the county.

The sense of purpose and meaning imbued on the police badge voiced by these officers in Washtenaw County is also consistent with research on law enforcement officers throughout the United States. Officers often describe policing as a "calling" in which the officer is viewed as the keeper of social order.[15] Officers organize their view of police work around a system of morality in which actions and actors tend to be classified as good and evil, right and wrong.

Steve Herbert, a leading expert on law enforcement who has conducted extensive ethnographic research with the Los Angeles and Seattle Police Departments, describes police officers as "preeminently focused on those who violate moral-cum-legal codes, and define their actions as part of an attempt to protect the good through expunging the evil."[16] According to Herbert, the "discourse of evil is remarkably common in police discourse."[17] Robert Reiner, whose work investigates the politics involved in policing, wrote: "A central feature of cop culture is a sense of mission. This is the feeling that policing is not just a job but a way of life with a worthwhile purpose...The purpose is conceived of not as a political enterprise but as the preservation of a valued way of life and the protection of the weak against the predatory. The core justification of policing is a victim-centered perspective."[18]

Policing is an honorable profession, rooted in the protection of the vulnerable from some sort of ambient danger or evil that seeks to do them harm. Police officers, then, serve as "the thin blue line between order and chaos."[19]

Much research and my observation argue that officers view their profession not only as an honorable one, but one that itself has an honor code rooted in the prevention of evil that can corrupt an otherwise ordered and stable society. Many times throughout my fieldwork, I observed officers referencing their roles as protectors. This often occurred with a simultaneous reference to an innocent or a helpless person, group, or animal that benefited from their heroism.

Chief Radi, with whom I had lunch at the community event, had invited me and Marcus, a local Black activist, to visit him at his station after the three of us had an escalating argument about the role of people of color in policing. In between bites of our sandwiches, Marcus and I argued that police do not need empathy to halt the meting out of deadly violence, while Radi insisted that we couldn't possibly understand how hard policing actually was. He invited us to come to his station to ride in a police car and see for ourselves what the job entailed. Ten days later, I took him up on his offer and joined him for a ride-along with officers in his department.[20]

When I arrive, Radi greets me warmly, and while most ride-alongs require that the individual complete paperwork prior to their arrival and conform to a certain dress code, Radi invites me to complete the paperwork when I arrive and welcomes me into the police station despite my out-of-dress-code jeans. This would be one of many instances in which I felt I received special treatment for being a non-Black racial minority, an educated Latino to whom officers could advertise their commitment to communities of color. This warm embrace I received from many officers caused quite a bit of internal discomfort, as I had thought myself a vocal critic of law enforcement violence. But as I continued to learn, one's criticism of ICE was viewed as entirely unrelated to his perception of local police: they were simply two separate departments with no underlying ethos or worldview in common. That is, a Latino criticizing the violent tactics of ICE presumably revealed nothing about his views on police.

Shortly after my paperwork is completed, I accompany Chief Radi into his office, where he enthusiastically invites me to try on a bulletproof vest from the department's new supply. Then he begins to describe the general work of the police officers under him, who police a 95 percent white city with approximately 5,000 residents who are mostly older adults. He recounts a story of a World War II veteran whose coin collection was stolen, after which the police successfully intervened. It was a telling example, as it created the image of the vulnerable elderly adult who was protected by the police from a nonspecific danger that had the nerve to steal from a member of the greatest generation.

Chief Radi then asks Officer Logan Stephens, a tall, lanky, and athletic white man about 30 years old, to allow me into his car for part of his shift. Logan first walks me through the station's garage and shows me what he describes as his favorite part of the station. In the four-car garage, the back third served as a dog kennel so that, as Logan tells me, "If we find a stray dog, we can take it someplace." Similar to the story told by his chief, Logan's story similarly presented an image of innocence and helplessness (a dog without an owner, wandering the busy city streets) that the police protect from some vague notion of danger.

I later ask Logan if his adrenaline rushes every time he receives a call about a potential crime. He tells me that, no, potential crimes do not get his heart racing. What gets his heart racing are calls like when a child gets hit by a car or other calls in which a child is involved. Not long after, Logan and I drive by a local high school. As we slow down to look around the area, Logan tells me he has no problem with concealed pistol licenses,[21] implying that he found it acceptable for those on high school campuses to carry firearms when licensed to do so. His comment catches me off guard, as I assume that, if there were ever a time to advocate for gun control, it would be when meandering through a local high school, where images of the killing of students—like the twelve students and one teacher shot and killed in Columbine, Colorado, in 1999 or the twenty children and six staff members shot and killed at Sandy Hook Elementary in Newtown, Connecticut, in 2012[22]—cannot help but replay in your head. But these school shootings were precisely the reason that Logan supported concealed carry licenses, as these hidden handguns could be used to protect children from the predators who would harm them.

Herbert noted stories similar to those recounted by Chief Radi and Officer Stephens in his work with officers at the LAPD: "Officers are particularly concerned about those they consider most vulnerable to 'predators'—children and the elderly."[23] And Westley notes, "To the policeman, the child is the approving innocent who is to be guided and taught."[24] In this organization of the world, then, the officer's job was a simple matter of protecting the innocent.

But while these scenarios—as well as other examples used throughout research[25]—gestured toward some general ambient danger, some unnamed "chaos," or "evil," that could cause unspecified harm to defenseless victims, other times, officers were needed to rescue someone from a specific source of danger. Detective Lieutenant Clif Edwards, a former Michigan State Police officer, summarized this law enforcement worldview well and added a bit of Michigan[26] braggadocio in the process.[27] His book *Paths Crossed: Villains-Victims-Victors; Lessons Learned in the Line of Duty* adds another category to the "hope" versus "hopeless" dichotomy of the world described by one officer at the community event. That is, heroes (victors) were needed to rescue the innocent (victims) from danger. But sometimes this danger was not ambient and unnamed. Sometimes it was a concrete source of danger embodied by one person or type of person (that is, a villain).

Sometimes, this person was Black. Other times, he was an immigrant.

Black Men Dying Necessarily

Around the mid-1960s, a spike in media coverage of police brutality and corruption led to a proliferation of writing and research on "police culture."[28] While police culture may be described differently among various authors, it is largely considered to be the "values, norms, perspectives, and craft rules" that shape the everyday habits of the average police officer.[29] Police culture, like all cultures, evolves and changes over time, notably with the gradual rise in female and gay and lesbian recruits.[30] Yet research suggests that much of police culture appears to be stable historically and worldwide, owing to the similar stresses and demands of the profession no matter where the policing is taking place.[31]

In addition to the concept of police morality described in the previous section, much research suggests that officers across the country perceive their jobs to be "laden with danger or the risk of danger."[32] Paoline writes that officers have been described as being "'preoccupied' with the danger and violence that surrounds them, always anticipating both."[33] As Chan describes, many norms of police behavior are "seen to be functional to the survival of police officers in an occupation considered to be dangerous, unpredictable, and alienating."[34]

Thus, the threat of violence powerfully shapes the day-to-day actions of police officers, as officers develop behaviors to mitigate this risk by focusing attention on its potential source as quickly as possible.[35] To survive, you have to find what can kill you, and you have to find it fast. Sometimes you have to use "shortcuts" to help you decide where to look for this danger.[36] But what do these shortcuts look like?

Jerome Skolnick, a former president of the American Society on Criminology and author of the book *Justice without Trial*, describes the way in which law enforcement officers have developed the image of a "symbolic assailant," or a collection of the characteristics that officers believe represent the threat of violence. As Skolnick puts it, "The policeman, because his work requires him to be occupied continually with potential violence, develops a perceptual shorthand to identify certain types of people as symbolic assailants, that is, as persons who use gesture, language, and attire, that the policeman has come to recognize as a prelude to violence."[37]

In modern-day US culture, skin color cannot be separated from the image of the symbolic assailant. As Skolnick highlights in follow-up writing, the "symbolic assailant was most often young, black, and male."[38] As Jones-Brown describes, "policing in the United States is Pavlovian in nature. That is, the police are conditioned to suspect blacks, and black males in particular, of wrong-doing even in the absence of actual criminality."[39]

The interpretation of black skin as criminal cannot be understood outside of the historic role of the police in the United States. The first publicly funded police forces in the South existed largely to preserve the slave economy, and patrols composed of white men began to walk the streets in search of runaway slaves.[40] Even after the end of the Civil War, police units searched for Blacks in the post-antebellum South who had violated Jim Crow regulations and then enforced those regulations, often through violence.[41] For decades, policing institutions saw black skin as a sign of lawbreaking, because, indeed, it was lawbreaking, at least inasmuch as the law allowed white men to own Africans and forced Blacks into separate spaces than whites.[42]

So where does the Black man, whose skin marks him as an out-of-place criminal, fit into the policing narrative? To use Edwards's separation of the policing world, can the Black man be a victor or a victim, or must he always be a villain? And what does this, in turn, tell us about a post-9/11 Santiago? Must he be a villain, too?

■ ■ ■

After Logan and I return to the station, Chief Radi invites me to ride with another white officer, Officer Robert Lee. Robert differs from Logan quite a bit. Whereas Logan is enthusiastic and conversational, Robert is stoic and seems much more interested in talking at me than engaging in any sort of back-and-forth. I imagine him to be more than ten years older than Logan and to be a man who had both grown up and learned how to be an officer before the influx of social media and customer-service-oriented policing.[43] Robert lets me ride with him nonetheless, though I sense he is simply following orders and would much rather be in the car alone.

Shortly after we pull out of the station, Robert segues into his thoughts on many of the killings of Black men that formed the crux of the Black Lives Matter movement. He begins by talking to me about the killing of 18-year-old Michael Brown in Ferguson, Missouri, by white officer Darren Wilson. On August 2014, Wilson pulled up next to Brown, who was walking in the street instead of the sidewalk. Seeing that Brown fit the description of someone who had robbed a convenience store, Officer Wilson confronted him. Wilson reported that Brown reached into the window of Wilson's cruiser, where the pair struggled to gain control of Wilson's gun. Eventually, Brown ran away and was shot by Officer Wilson.[44]

This is where witness testimonies differ, with some saying that Brown's hands were in the air when he was shot, and others, including Wilson, saying that Brown turned around and ran toward him. Ultimately, Wilson fired twelve shots at Brown, hitting him in the arm, hand, forehead, and top of his head.[45] Brown died on the scene. After a grand jury did not agree to indict Wilson, protests erupted; the governor called in the National Guard, who fired rubber bullets and tear gas at protestors, and chants of "hands up, don't shoot," which were meant to call to mind the way in which Brown had allegedly been shot, spread throughout the United States.[46]

Officer Lee reminds me that Officer Wilson—who killed Michael Brown—was found innocent of wrongdoing by not one but two juries.[47] Without making eye contact with me, Officer Lee laments that Wilson's "life is ruined" because he had a run-in with Brown, who he described as "not a good person." Darren Wilson lost his job, Robert tells me, "basically for just being a cop." Again, I can't fathom Officer Lee telling this to a Black man, and as I settle into my racial invisibility, I decide not to refute him but to listen to whatever he is willing to share with me.

Officer Lee then begins to comment on Freddie Gray Jr.'s death, saying that we still don't know what happened in the back of the van in which Gray's spine was severed in Baltimore, Maryland. Gray was 25 years old when, in violation of police policy, he was put into the back of a van without a restraint.[48] It was notable to hear it argued that we don't know what happened in the back of a van, as if Gray could possibly have decided to sever his own spine.

I continue the interaction drawing from field notes:

We drive through a fairly wooded part of town, and it begins to drizzle lightly, as it has on and off all day. As we drive down a hill on a two-lane road, Robert pauses to look behind him and asks me if I noticed whatever it was that he so clearly noticed. I didn't. He tells me there is a turtle on the side of the road.

It's silent in the car for a moment, and I find it challenging to interpret the situation, as it feels as if Robert is waiting for my confirmation that we should indeed go rescue the turtle. I say something vaguely positive to encourage him to do so.

Robert turns the car around and we park on the grass next to the road. The turtle is on the other side, so there are two lanes of traffic between the turtle and us. He tells me it's a snapping turtle, and I tell him we used to have those in the backyard at my grandma's house. He says there are alligator snapping turtles, which are even bigger.

At this point, the many cars that see his patrulla *parked on the grass begin to slow down. Drivers are very clearly unsure of whether or how to proceed. The drizzling continues.*

The city boy that I have become asks Robert what he is going to use to pick up the turtle. He plans to use his bare hands, he says. He opens the door, crosses the two lanes of street, and approaches the turtle. I follow behind him. He picks up the turtle, and we walk it over to this little pond where he plans to set the turtle free.

He puts the turtle in the pond, and we get back in the car and drive on.

I wondered about his motivation: why was he willing to turn his car around, drive the other way, stop two lanes of traffic, and pick up the turtle—with his bare hands—and walk it back to the pond? I ask him.

He tells me he hates to see them "die unnecessarily."

—Adapted from field notes, May 2015

I hate to see them die unnecessarily. Of course, at face value, these words make sense. Who wouldn't want to rescue the helpless turtle from unnecessary death? But it gave me pause—to put it lightly[49]—to hear these words uttered directly following the remorseless conclusions that Brown had brought about his own killing and that Gray's death in the back of a police van was still some sort of inexplicable mystery. Clearly, Officer Lee's moral system had this category for unnecessary death. Why, then, had it not applied to Michael Brown or Freddie Gray Jr.? If their deaths could not be categorized as "unnecessary," did this make them *necessary*? If so, why were they necessary?

But Officer Lee's discussion of the innocence of the turtle and the warranted killing of Michael Brown and the mysterious death of Freddie Gray Jr. fit perfectly well in the villain, victim, victor organization of the world. The turtle, unable to cross two lanes of traffic to get back to the safety of its pond, was just like the stray dogs, the elderly veterans, and the children hit by cars: helpless and in need of rescue, a victim of a force outside of its control that would do it harm. The officer, then, was clearly the victor, the hero, the one whose profession was rooted in the rescue of the innocent and would stop lanes of traffic to do exactly that.

But Michael Brown was neither a victim nor a victor. Instead, he was "not a good person"—or, as another officer later called him, a "bully"—and had come to embody the villain whose dispatch was necessary to maintain the moral order. Thus, Officer Wilson was just "being a cop" when he shot and killed him.

Steve Herbert[50] noted the impact that a moralistic division of the world into good and evil—or to use Edwards's words, villains, victims, and victors—can have on policing behavior: "Over time, officers' ability to discriminate between those who represent actual threats to public safety and those who do not may weaken, and thus all who reside in a given neighborhood may be too easily painted alike as evil."[51] Black men, whose skin has historically been seen by officers as a marker of criminality, simply cannot be victors or victims, and are therefore moralized as villains to be controlled through violence for the sake of the social order.

Other examples of Black men killed during the Black Lives Matter movement support Herbert's proposal, with many of these men viewed as sources of danger even in the absence of evidence. For example, on September 16, 2016, a 40-year-old Black man, Terrance Crutcher, was shot and killed by white officer Betty Shelby in Tulsa, Oklahoma, after his car had broken down in the middle of the road. Video footage taken by two helicopter pilots who circled overhead during the encounter was later released, with one pilot commenting that Crutcher, in a white shirt and khaki pants walking away from police with his hands clearly raised, "looks like a bad dude, too, could be on something."[52] On August 28, 2016, 18-year-old Black man Paul O'Neal was shot and killed after a chase through a residential neighborhood following attempts to escape in a stolen car. Body cam footage from one officer shows O'Neal lying on the cement after he was shot; other officers push his face into the ground and cuff his arms behind his back as blood seeps out of the bullet hole and onto his shirt. One officer attempts to justify their shooting, yelling out, "Bitch ass motherfucker, fucking shoot at us,"[53] even though the only shots fired were from the police (and were notably fired in violation of departmental policy, given they were shot into a moving vehicle in a residential neighborhood[54]).

In yet another example, 32-year-old Black man Philando Castile was pulled over for a broken taillight on July 6, 2016, in Minneapolis, Minnesota. As he sat in the driver's seat with his girlfriend and her 4-year-old daughter also in the car,[55] Latino officer Jeronimo Yanez can be heard asking Philando through the driver's side window for his license and insurance. Philando replies calmly, "Sir, I have to tell you that I do have a firearm on me." As Philando follows the orders of the officer and reaches for his wallet, Yanez pulls out his weapon and fires seven times at Philando, hitting him five[56] and killing him in front of his girlfriend and her daughter. Here, Philando's admission that he possessed a firearm, and his obedience to the officer's request to grab his wallet, were still viewed as deadly enough to require the officer to kill him.

But does the moralistic division of the world into victors, villains, and victims—used frequently among those policing in Black communities—have anything to teach us about immigrant men like Santiago?

■ ■ ■

Nine months into my fieldwork, I attended a meeting of the Law Enforcement Citizens Advisory Board. LE-CAB was established by the sheriff's office to provide a forum for community members to share their opinions on the activities of the sheriff's office, to engender community involvement, and to make recommendations to the office. Any interested member of the county could apply to be on the board.

Many of the members who were on LE-CAB when I attended the meeting in 2015 had been on the board at the end of 2013, when Guadalupe's apartment was raided, and I knew some individuals from other advocacy roles as well. While the purpose of attending this initial meeting was largely to observe, when I brought up the topic of the raid (as I had been invited to do), it was clear that most members of the board had strong opinions to share. They then invited me to attend a separate meeting at which we would engage in a structured reflection of the LE-CAB's role following the raid.

The next month, I arrived at the beginning of the LE-CAB meeting and asked board members a few questions, largely encouraging them to discuss freely their thoughts on the raid and the role they played in its aftermath while I recorded the session. It seemed as though everyone wanted the opportunity to explain their story, as well as defend their efforts, declare their good intentions, and, whether implicitly or not, share how deeply sorry they were that the raid unfolded in the way it did. Collectively, the board professed a feeling of helplessness, caught between a community who wanted answers about the violence and racial profiling they had just experienced and a law enforcement office that did not want to (or could not) share information about an "ongoing investigation." I have every reason to believe everyone on the board was genuinely pained by the way in which the events unfolded.

Indeed, the mood was dark and regretful, and I could feel a deep sadness emanating from many board members. But amid this empathy and pain came a refrain from a high-ranking representative of a local law enforcement department that echoed the previous descriptions of the officer-as-protector:

> I think the [reason] emotions got so strong, on both sides, was this totally different perspective. You know, [the lead officer of the department] was like, "We were protecting folks... Why are you attacking us for trying to protect you?"... [T]he immigrant community is often victimized because they are scared to report, so from [the officer's] perspective he was doing his job to serve and protect [the Latino community] from this person that was a really, really bad guy. And yet, here were people that he worked with and friends attacking him.

These words, spoken about the arrest of a Latino man, seemed to match step-for-step the justification for law enforcement violence perpetrated against Black men. Here was this immigrant community, helpless, fearful, and victimized by this "bad guy," this villain, Santiago. With the victim and villain already cast, only one role remained unfilled: that of the heroic victor. Law enforcement officers, then—regardless of the methods used to enforce the law—filled the remaining role.

What happens when law enforcement interactions with communities of color are reduced to this moralistic model? As we have seen, when men of color are uncritically cast as villains, law enforcement officers are able to leverage extraordinary levels of violence against them. This violence is then justified by the threat officers perceive to exist, the inherent threat presented by the villain of color. Herbert (1996) summarized it well: "Not all who dress, walk, and talk in an apparently threatening way are in fact a danger, but many moralistic officers are unable to appreciate that fact. Thus, they approach those they label as bad in a harsh and imperturbable fashion and needlessly antagonize many who merit a lighter hand."[57] Santiago was dangerous. Brown was dangerous. Castile was dangerous. So doors were kicked in, guns were drawn and fired into cars, and no attempts were made to de-escalate, as the play had already been cast.

But the deaths of Black men at the hands of police and the raid on Santiago's *taller* illustrate at least one more common aspect of law enforcement in communities of color. In addition to the rhetoric of good and evil, of protector and those in need of protection, drugs—selling them, buying them, using them—frequently appear in the narratives of law enforcement violence. Often, the presence of drugs makes the villain that much more villainous by casting him either as inhumanly strong and physically durable or a dealer bent on destruction of an otherwise pure community. This, in turn, justifies the violence used against him. With even a basic description of the war on drugs, we can understand how Guadalupe's, Fernanda's, and Hilda's experiences are a product of the same law enforcement machine that killed Brown, Gray Jr., Rosser, Castile, Gardner, Bland, and other Black community members throughout the United States.

A Broken Tag Light

In a radio broadcast in the winter of 1982, President Ronald Reagan announced a "planned, concerted campaign" against drugs, "hard, soft, or otherwise."[58] In addition to efforts to sensationalize the dangers of crack cocaine in the inner city, Reagan and his ilk also allocated large sums of money to addressing drug use,[59] with some of this funding going to the US Immigration and Naturalization Service (the precursor to ICE).[60] Antidrug allocations to the Department of Defense increased from $8 million to $33 million from 1980 to 1984.[61] This money, in turn, resulted in increases in the militarized equipment used to surveil, arrest, jail, and deport the alleged drug offenders.[62]

Changes in drug sentencing laws during this time also had an enormous impact on patterns of both incarceration and deportation. Briefly, the Anti-Drug Abuse Act of 1986 instituted mandatory minimum sentences of at least five years for drug possession, including marijuana. The racist undertones of these mandatory minimum sentencing regulations were quite clear, as 5 grams of crack, associated with Black, urban communities, received the same penalty as 500 grams of cocaine powder, which was more likely to be used by white people.[63] Deportation norms and policies were also impacted. As prisons became massively overcrowded, the 1986 Anti-Drug Abuse Act expanded the deportation of any noncitizens who were charged with drug-related offenses.[64] The Anti-Drug Abuse Act also authorized the use of detainers—in which ICE requests that local law enforcement departments hold an arrestee in their custody until ICE can detain them—for drug-related offenses[65] (as discussed earlier, local police departments holding arrestees so that ICE can pick them up is one major way in which violation of laws unrelated to immigration status can result in deportation). These detainers have since evolved, with the range of offenses for which ICE can request detainers expanding drastically.[66] Undocumented immigrants with drug convictions also faced lifetime bans on returning to the United States after deportation and were no longer eligible to apply for asylum in the United States if their drug conviction included the sale of drugs.[67]

As many researchers have noted, this focused effort to address the drug epidemic that plagued the United States was largely constructed for political gain, as drug use had not, in fact, increased during the period leading up to Reagan's declaration of war. Rather, the war on drugs allowed politicians to appear "tough on crime," with each politician,

Democrat or Republican, upping the ante with harsher sentences and increased funding to police departments across the country.[68]

Police departments, now flooded with massive amounts of money earmarked to combat the flow of drugs through their communities, needed something on which to spend these funds. SWAT units provided the perfect solution.[69] SWAT units—modeled after and armed like elite military units—were originally designed to address situations of kidnapping or terrorism and, for the bulk of the year, were unused by police departments during day-to-day operations. However, these SWAT units began directing their militarized training and weaponry toward stopping the drug use that threatened the fabric of the United States.

By the late 1990s, about 90 percent of police departments that served populations of over 50,000 and 80 percent of departments that served smaller populations had their own SWAT units. Peter Kraska,[70] who has studied the militarization of police for decades, estimates about 45,000 SWAT deployments occur per year, most of which are proactive, no-knock drug raids, like the one on Santiago, Guadalupe, and Fernanda's apartment.

Yet it was not only the influx of funding that changed the face of law enforcement in the United States. Indeed, the public campaign and antidrug rhetoric created to vilify drugs also—by design—criminalized Black and Latino people who were presumed to be the buyers, sellers, and users of those drugs. As Nunn[71] describes, "As the metaphor of war might suggest, the War on Drugs required both weapons and enemies. A punitive law enforcement policy of prohibition and interdiction provided the weapons and, while the professed enemies of the War on Drugs were drug cartels in drug source countries, those most affected were people of color in inner city neighborhoods, chiefly African Americans and Hispanics."[72]

The war on drugs was therefore able to create a Black and brown villainous drug user, a character who slid easily into the narrative of heroic policing.

But perhaps equally as important as creating a villain, the war on drugs also concretized a perpetually innocent and vulnerable victim. As

Tonry describes, the drug war was motivated "to show that the Bush and Reagan administrations were concerned about public safety, crime prevention, and the *needs of victims*."[73] The Black and brown drug pushers and purchasers were poised not just to destroy their own communities but also to infiltrate white neighborhoods and destabilize their way of life.[74]

The vilification of drugs and drug users established during the war on drugs appeared numerous times to retroactively justify the killings of Black men during the Black Lives Matter movement. For example, when Philando Castile bled out in front of his girlfriend and her child, the officer who fired five shots into his body at point-blank range justified his fear of Philando by referencing his marijuana use. As Officer Yanez shared in his testimony, "If he has...the guts and audacity to smoke marijuana in front of the 5-year-old and risk her lungs and risk her life by giving her secondhand smoke and the front seat passenger doing the same thing then what, what care does he give about me."[75] When Reserve Deputy Robert Charles Bates shot Eric Harris from a few feet away—drawing his gun instead of his Taser—as Harris ran by, the defense attorney argued that the cause of Harris's death was not the bullet that pierced his right lung but "heart disease, meth use, and exertion."[76] Bates, who was carrying a gun restricted by his department, and who was not adequately trained to pull his Taser and pulled his gun instead, was not what killed Eric Harris. That is, even though Harris was running from the police and then shot by the police,[77] his heart failed because of meth use.

In November 2014, Aura Rosser, a Black woman, was shot and killed by white Ann Arbor Police Department Officer David Reid. Aura's boyfriend called the police to separate them during a domestic dispute. Officers entered their apartment, and when Aura turned and approached Reid and a second officer with a four-inch knife, she was shot by Reid and tased by the second officer.[78] After the Washtenaw County prosecutor decided not to charge Officer Reid, protestors marched through downtown Ann Arbor to a city council meeting where activists asked for funds to support Rosser's funeral.[79] Two bottles of medication used to treat bipolar disorder were found still full in Rosser's home, and an autopsy later revealed cocaine in her bloodstream.[80] Summarizing the event, the mayor of Ann Arbor stated, "The events of that night, of course, were a tragedy, but not a tragedy of racism...The events of Nov. 9 were a tragedy of mental illness untreated and drug use unabated."

When Michael Brown was killed, Fox News commentator Jim Pinkerton said, "Eyewitnesses said that Brown was charging the cops...We'll know more with a blood test. If he was high on some drug, angel dust or PCP or something, it's entirely possible you could take a lot more than six bullets and keep charging."[81] The reference to PCP—or phencyclidine, also called "angel dust," that may cause hallucinations and violent behavior[82]—as the creator of a superhuman Black monster able to sustain the bullets of police echoed the beating of Rodney King in 1991, in which Sergeant Stacey Koon testified, "In my mind, he had exhibited this hulk-like strength which I had come to associate with PCP."[83] Yet neither Brown nor King had any PCP in their systems when they were shot and beaten, respectively. The officers' suspicion that they *might* be using it was enough to justify the violence.

Drug use played a key role in the raid of Santiago's *taller* and apartment as well. Law enforcement officers were quick to remind me frequently that the raid that I was investigating was not an immigration raid but a drug raid. Indeed, the raid of Santiago's *taller* and apartment had many of the hallmarks of a drug raid, most important, the use of the SWAT team to gain entry into their property and dogs to search for drugs and drug paraphernalia. Yet no drugs were found, and there were no other prosecutions outside of those related to immigration. The investigation of drug possession shaped the methods used to raid the apartment and *taller* in notably violent, intrusive ways. One article following the raid summarized thusly:

> A release from the Washtenaw Interfaith Coalition for Immigrant Rights paints a different picture: "This drug investigation and search warrant empowered law enforcement entities to collaborate with each other and use especially brutal tactics which have resulted in more separations and trauma to immi-

grant families, including women and very young children, and the detention of eight men by immigration officials, who have been identified and reported to WICIR," the release states.

During fieldwork, I observed officers anchor their enforcement decisions in war-on-drugs rhetoric numerous times. While riding with Officer Lisa Flynn (Lisa is the officer who requested ID of the man who called 911), I inquired about her perceptions of sex work that took place in an area another informant had discussed with me. Lisa had worked with women who had experienced domestic violence, and I noticed in the visor of her police cruiser the phone numbers for domestic violence centers. I thus assumed she would be aware of—and have a strong opinion on—legal issues that primarily affected women. Lisa drove me over to the parking lot in front of a hotel where she told me that johns frequently brought women to pay for sex. Generally, Lisa says, she is uninterested in enforcing prostitution laws. When drugs are involved in sex work, she becomes more concerned, as women's drug use creates an imbalance of power that exposes them to violence from johns who may use their drug addiction against them. It was the presence of drugs that changed a behavior—sex work—from something that could be ignored to a broken law that had to be addressed in order to protect vulnerable women from the men who would take advantage of them. This is not to say that Lisa is incorrect. Drug use may engender situations of vulnerability and increase the risk of exposure to violence among individuals trading sex (though myriad other factors also influence these outcomes[84]). Nonetheless, the addition of drugs into the narrative instantly created both a villain and an innocent victim.

In one situation I witnessed during a ride-along, the officer's interaction with community members he pulled over exemplified the racial profiling, drug prioritization, and heroic officer narratives discussed so far.

I am in a patrol car with Officer Luke Lancaster at around midnight when Luke pulls over a Chevy Malibu with a Black driver and a white passenger, both of whom are teenagers. The passenger had caught Luke's attention when he slumped down in the seat, presumably after noticing the police car, a behavior that Luke believed to be suspicious. I continue the story drawing from field notes I took as I observed the interaction unfolding:

> *Luke steps out of his car to approach the Black driver and white passenger of a Chevy Malibu. He tells the driver that he has a crack in the windshield and broken tag light, telling them, "Now is your chance to be honest" and then asking if there is weed in the car. I do not know if they respond. The tall Black driver of the car steps out, and Luke handcuffs him, brings him to the police car, and sits him in the seat directly behind me.*
>
> *About then, another police car pulls up, and a tall and muscular Black officer exits. The white teen, who remains uncuffed, sits on the curb next to the Black officer.*
>
> *Luke begins to search the driver's seat of the Malibu before moving to the rear driver's side seat. He finds a grinder [used to make marijuana cigarettes]. Luke then searches the front passenger side, then the rear passenger side, and eventually the trunk of the car, where he pulls out a tuxedo.*
>
> *The Black teen handcuffed in the seat behind me starts to talk to me. He tells me that the tuxedo is for their upcoming prom. He continues: "You know what he is doing is wrong. We both know that he wasn't allowed to pull me out of that car. Me or my friend. It's not the first time he did this to me. It's alright though, I'm chillin'."*
>
> *Luke comes back to the car and gives the Black driver a ticket for the cracked windshield and broken tag light before letting them both go.*
>
> *—Adapted from field notes, May 2015*

I am not sure how to interpret the situation outside of blatantly racially differential treatment, so I try to prompt Luke to describe his reasoning for the enforcement choices I just observed. To summarize, these included (1) pulling over a car for the "suspicious" behavior of slumping in the passenger seat, (2) cuffing and placing a Black teen in the *patrulla* while the white teen—who was originally the target of suspicion—sat on the curb with his hands uncuffed, (3) implicitly coercing the occupants of the car to admit to drug use with no evidence that any drug use had occurred, (4) searching the car for drugs and finally finding drug paraphernalia, and (5) only choosing to ticket for a broken tag light and cracked windshield.

Luke is not concerned with small amounts of weed, he tells me, but is interested in removing large amounts of drugs and weapons from the street. Further, he says, had he ticketed the teen for possession of drug paraphernalia, (1) it could have resulted in a drug-related misdemeanor, which would have made it difficult for the teen to find future employment, and (2) had he taken the teen into the police station, Luke would have had to remain in the office doing paperwork, leaving other officers in the area without backup should they find themselves in dangerous situations. Luke uses each rhetorical justification described in this chapter, casting himself as the protector who gets drugs and weapons off the street, underscoring his concern for the innocent teens who would be looking for jobs in the future, and testifying to the vague and ambient threat officers face every day that could materialize at any moment to harm other officers should they be left without backup.

What of the racially differentiated treatment? Luke explains that as well. Because he was busy searching the car, Luke couldn't have kept track of what the Black teen was doing. Another officer was already watching over the white teen, however, so there was no need to cuff him or put him in the car.[85] Shortly after this explanation, Luke adds that the white teen had been on YouTube talking about a firearm he owned. Thus, Luke knew that the white teen owned a gun and had still only cuffed the Black teen and placed him in the police car.

Throughout the entire explanation, Luke remained uncritical of any element of the stop and had no problem with the fact that the end result of the stop—a citation for a cracked windshield and broken tag light—was not in itself necessary anyway, but merely a cover to pull over and search a car whose only evidence of drug use was a passenger slouching in his seat. Similarly, he didn't seem to recognize the tension inherent in the racially preferential treatment, not just to a white teen, but to a white teen *who had been seen with a weapon.*

Black *Dias Comúnes y Corrientes*

Officer Luke Lancaster is really enthusiastic to be a cop and really enthusiastic to have me in his car: maybe I'll get to see him do a "foot chase," he says numerous times.

Shortly after the ride-along begins, we drive over to a corner store that sits about three miles from Santiago's taller. Luke says drug sales occur here often. It looks, at least to me, like any given corner store on any given street in this 20% Black, 5% Latino town of about 20,000. As we pass by, we see two huddles of men out in front of the store. The men in one huddle are white. The men in the other huddle are Black. A man in baggy jean shorts and a white T-shirt breaks from the huddle and walks down the street. Luke decides that he needs to "go talk to him."

Because the downtown area is a maze of one-way streets, "go talk to him" turns out to be sharp turns and rapid acceleration and deceleration until Luke finds the man walking in the street—next to the curb—a few blocks away from where he originally saw him. Luke stops the cop car awkwardly in the middle of the road and hops out to talk to the Black man.

Nonchalantly, Luke asks him where he's been and where he's going. The man responds, saying something about coming from or going to a relative's house. He doesn't mention being at the corner store where we just saw him a few moments before.

Luke keeps prompting, trying to get it out of him, but the Black man never mentions it. So Luke tells him to step in front of the police car. He complies.

From the passenger seat of the car, I watch the interaction unfold a few feet in front of me. I roll down the window slightly so I can hear the exchange.

Luke asks to check the man's pockets. The man again complies.

At this point, another white cop shows up. I am not sure if Luke alerted him or if he just happened to be driving by. This officer is nothing like Luke. A bit shorter at maybe 5'9" or so, he's much more muscular, tattooed, and intimidating. He gets out of the car and stands with his arms folded over his vested chest and stares at the Black man with a poker face that betrays no emotion. Luke continues to talk jovially to the man he followed, and I can see the good cop/bad cop scenario preparing to unfold.

Luke asks for the man's identification. Again, the man complies. Luke brings the license to the car to see if the man has any warrants and talks to me a bit while he looks up his information. When he sees that there is no clear reason to arrest the man, he returns to him and hands his license back, asking if he knows why Luke stopped him. The man does not know why he was stopped. Neither do I.

Luke tells him that he shouldn't have been walking in the street when a sidewalk was clearly present. That's against the law.

As we prepare to leave, the other white cop asks the Black man to open his mouth so he can look inside. The Black man, now for the fourth time, complies, and the officer uses a rubber-gloved hand for a quick oral cavity search on the street. I find out later that the officer was looking for crack or heroin wrapped in a balloon. These balloons, if swallowed, can be passed to be used or sold later.

The man's pockets are empty. His record is clean. And his mouth contains no crack balloon.

Nobody says anything.

Everybody leaves.

—Adapted from field notes, May 2015

Why had the Black man complied, over and over, with the intrusive and groundless requests of the officers who stopped and searched him? Couldn't he have refused? Couldn't he have referenced his Fourth Amendment right to be protected against search and seizure without probable cause? And what about Arturo? Why had he let the agents search his car for drugs and search his body for tattoos? Why do all these Black and brown people keep complying with unreasonable requests from officers that follow unreasonable stops to begin with?

Law enforcement activities—whether performed by ICE or by local police—can be violent, traumatic, and dehumanizing and, ultimately, result in deportation or, as the Black men, women, and boys discussed here attest, death. But it is not necessarily these brutal or deadly acts of law enforcement violence that shape day-to-day life in Black and Latino mixed-status communities. Rather, the *días comúnes y corrientes* in both Black and mixed-status Latino communities are shaped by the *possibility* of intensely traumatic, militarized violence. Everyone has heard of the raid on the apartment. Everyone has seen the video of Eric Garner being choked to death while uttering "I can't breathe" and Alton Sterling being shot in the chest from inches away by the officer who said, "I'm going to kill you, bitch."[86] And everyone, or at least everyone Black and brown, wonders, "Could that be me?"

Black and Latino mixed-status communities do not simply fear that encounters with law enforcement could turn deadly or result in removal. Rather, they fear that any task, any routine, daily activity, could first turn into an interaction with an officer, that, should the officer so choose, could then end in death or removal. Born with skin the color of symbolic assailants and slotted easily into the role of the villain in the war on drugs, Black and brown community members know that, should an officer want to investigate them, there are any number of excuses to permit them to do so, to *indagar más*. Both Sandra Bland[87] and Arturo could not seem to manage their turn signals correctly. Neither this Black man in the street nor Michael Brown could seem to use the clearly visible sidewalks, choosing instead to illegally walk in the street. And no one can seem to get his tag light to operate. For Black and Latino community members, the line between doing what they do every day of the year, dropping kids off at school, going to prom, and being choked, shot, detained, or deported is a thin line indeed.

So the Black man opens his mouth and complies. Arturo bares his tattoo-less torso and complies. And they make no complaint, because they want to see their families again. They want to return to their communities. And they don't want to be killed.

Conclusion

The stories shared throughout this book recount instances that are at once painful, traumatic, violent, and life altering. Yet they are not unique. Rather, they reflect the experiences of thousands of members of mixed-status Latino and Black communities throughout the United States on any given day of the year. What can be done to prevent or mitigate the damage perpetuated by law enforcement to these communities?

Individuals, Families, and Communities: Implications for Advocates and Allies

In November of 2013, a mixed-status community in a small Midwestern town watched as their lives devolved into chaos. Fathers were taken, neighbors were pulled over, cars were left on the side of the road, and no one knew whether or when the arrests would stop. The outcomes of the raid can loosely be organized into three levels—the individual, the family, and the community—to better help us make sense of the aftermath and decide where and how to intervene.

On the individual level, resources were desperately needed by those in the raided facility to cope with the traumatic encounter with ICE and SWAT officers. All of the women in the apartment, as well as all of the children they held in their arms during the raid, would have benefited from mental health counselors trained to address the PTSD that likely resulted from the raid.[1] These counseling efforts would ideally come from culturally and linguistically sensitive counselors who must also be aware of the limits of individuals' self-care practices when they are being surveilled and stalked daily by immigration enforcement agents.

Free or low-cost legal assistance is critical in an immigration system

in which undocumented immigrants are not granted access to court-ap-
pointed attorneys.

Advocates must also bear in mind that immigration enforcement affects a range of life situations unrelated to immigration status. In addition
to mental health and legal assistance, flexible funds are necessary for basic
needs such as food, shelter, diapers, or even infant formula.

Besides food and shelter, the need to care for their children forced
mothers to seek out constant sources of work or, like Fernanda, to return
to Mexico to be with her deported husband. Thus, financial support is
necessary to allow mothers—many of whom may be unable to work
legally—to keep their children fed. Childcare is an essential part of one's
ability to find and maintain employment, and advocates could work to
provide stable care for free or low cost following detention or deportation
of a provider. Further efforts could be made to stabilize children's lives
by providing transportation to and from school and access to school
counselors or tutors.

But the existence of resources does not mean they are accessible.
Most everyone in this book described avoiding government organizations out of fear that their collaboration with ICE or DHS would result in
deportation. Similarly, community members avoided trusted government
organizations when they feared that simply driving could result in racial
profiling and arrest by local police.

Given this fear of walking and driving in public spaces and visiting
social services as described here and by other researchers,[2] organizations
should bring their services into the community or hold meetings and
share resources and information in locations that are (at least comparatively) safe from ICE activity, such as churches or schools. Social service
organizations could also be explicit about the rules and regulations that
govern their interactions with members of mixed-status communities.
All staff members should be aware of the conditions under which they
would ask about immigration status (if at all) and what they would do if
a client disclosed that she is undocumented.

Community members described the constant tension caused by the
unpredictable need to present identification to a range of individuals who

would then arbitrarily decide whether their documents were acceptable. Organizations could reflect on which form of identification they require and the reasons for these requirements. Management who wish to support mixed-status communities must clearly describe their identification policies and hold their staff accountable. Many organizations request driver's licenses reflexively, without considering how this simple request marginalizes undocumented community members who are ineligible for licenses. If a driver's license is not the specific document needed, altering the request to "Do you have any form of identification?" could create a more welcoming environment for members of mixed-status communities.

In the absence of federal or state efforts to provide identification to undocumented individuals, communities could consider creating their own forms of identification. The Washtenaw ID,[3] mentioned periodically throughout this book, is one example. The Washtenaw ID is a form of identification open to all residents of Washtenaw County and was staunchly supported by the Washtenaw County sheriff. These forms of ID can be used to gain access to resources increasingly blocked by ID requirements.[4]

However, these IDs can also play a second and perhaps equally important role: unifying multiple marginalized communities. When advocating for the Washtenaw ID, we purposefully highlighted how ID requirements affected a range of community members, such as transgender individuals whose gender presentation may not match the gender marker noted on their birth certificates, the chronically homeless who do not have stable home addresses, or those who were formerly incarcerated and only have prison IDs (federal identification that is highly stigmatized in day-to-day interactions).

The Washtenaw Coalition for Immigrant Rights' response to the raid offers lessons to other organizations considering urgent response (also referred to as rapid response) to support their communities. Evidence suggests that text messaging on secure systems is useful for rapidly exchanging information about immigration enforcement. However, because the impact and reach of this method of communication is large, it is important to maintain a system for verifying that immigration enforcement is actually occurring. Otherwise, advocates risk unnecessarily confining community members to their homes in their attempts to avoid ICE.

Last, to the extent that this book is impactful, I hope it can serve as a testimony that powerful writing, research, and advocacy can emerge from long-term collaborations between academics, advocates, and local communities.

Implications for Law Enforcement in Mixed-Status Communities

The everyday fear of encountering local law enforcement officers altered the daily routines of members of the mixed-status Latino community, especially in the days following the raid, when many confined themselves to their homes. To support the mixed-status Latino community they have sworn to serve and protect, a local law enforcement department could take a number of simple steps. The practice of requesting identification from every individual with whom an officer comes in contact certainly warrants reflection. While this practice may be, as one officer explained to me, intended to keep officers safe by ascertaining whether the person with whom the officer interacts has a warrant for dangerous crimes, the practice is much more likely to create division between officers and local communities. If individuals fear they and everyone nearby will be asked to show identification every time they interact with an officer, it is unlikely anyone who is undocumented, in the vicinity of others who are undocumented, or unaware of the immigration status of his friend, will contact the police.

This practice can be addressed in two ways. First, law enforcement officers should simply ask for IDs less frequently by not requesting IDs of 911 callers, car passengers, or bystanders in the vicinity of a law enforcement activity. Second, like social service organizations, law enforcement offices can advertise various forms of acceptable identification rather than continually requesting driver's licenses. Acceptable forms of ID could include passports, driver's licenses from other countries, or even expired US driver's licenses, as one's identity does not expire, even if the ID has. Of course, this is both a matter of individual officer discretion as well as departmental policy, and systems must be in place to hold individual officers accountable to departmental policies designed to support mixed-status communities. These suggestions also assume police departments do not *want* to enforce immigration laws or do not purposefully use racial profiling, an assumption I, and many members of mixed-status communities throughout the United States, am not always comfortable making.

As many law enforcement offices have already established,[5] local law enforcement rarely, if ever, benefits from their collaboration with ICE. Instead, collaborative immigration enforcement instills fear in mixed-status Latino community members, who distance themselves from police in any way possible as they worry that any encounter could lead to deportation.[6] In a time of racial tensions augmented by the filmed killings of unarmed Black men, storming homes and traumatizing mothers and their children will only serve to reinforce perceptions of law enforcement as a tool for the violent subjection of communities of color.

To support the health and safety of all residents, local offices should avoid enforcing immigration law whenever possible by, for example, refusing to honor ICE detainers, enforcing traffic laws without enforcing immigration laws (e.g., writing tickets but not detaining), and avoiding collaboration in immigration raids.

ICE has no ties to the communities in which they detain and deport immigrants and no responsibility in dealing with the repercussions their enforcement actions cause. Further, given their need to reach deportation quotas, ICE is incentivized to remove as many community members as possible with no consideration for the damage that results.[7] Local police, however, must continue policing communities after events such as the raiding of *tallers* that leave women and children without providers. There is virtually no way that communities of color will trust police departments that collaborate with ICE and engage in similarly militarized enforcement.

Given their inherent violence and deadly repercussions, I firmly advocate against the use of home raids. However, assuming they will continue, there are ways to mitigate the damage caused by these raids. First, ICE, and any law enforcement departments with whom they collaborate, should take departmental responsibility for the physical damage caused to any raided facility.[8] Guadalupe and Fernanda would not have been homeless had ICE or the law enforcement office repaired the door they had kicked in upon entering the apartment. Should they not be able to fix the door or address the property damage they caused, I advocate that the price of averting homelessness for members of the raided residence be considered in the economic costs of conducting a raid. The hotel in which Guadalupe lived should have been paid for by those who conducted the raid, not donations from the community in which they lived.

Second, the traumatic repercussions following the raid were many. Raids are, by design, startling, confusing, and violent, and the mental and physical health of residents must be a concern every single time one is conducted. Embedded counselors and medical personnel should be available to support those who must cope with the effects of the raid. These resources should be provided regardless of immigration status or criminal history. If counseling and medical personnel cannot speak the language of those in the residence, translators should be readily available. There is no reason law officers cannot bring resources with them to address this damage immediately. I emphasize that I do not support the use of these militarized home raids. But should they continue, no raid should be conducted without careful planning and intentional preparation to address the (predictable) litany of needs that follow.

The Need for Black and Brown Unity against State Violence

This book illustrates the many ways in which police violence in Black communities mirrors immigration enforcement violence in Latino mixed-status communities. While doing this work, I observed as the Black Lives Matter movement gained national, and, later, international, traction and continued to engage in the research and writing that grew from the movement. Black Lives Matter started with the killing of Trayvon Martin in February 2012, about a year before President Obama's second term. It was during this term that deportations began to peak, hitting an all-time high in 2014—the same year Laquan McDonald, Michael Brown, Tamir Rice, Aura Rosser, and Eric Garner were killed. But while the public (or at least certain segments of it) grew increasingly angry about the police shootings and deaths in police custody of Black men, women, and boys, there was less collective anger and organizing to protest the unprecedented rates of deportation.[9] What can Latino advocates learn from those who spearheaded the Black Lives Matter movement? Similarly, do antideportation advocates have insight to share with the Black Lives Matter movement? And to what extent can these movements be unified, thereby joining together to address police and ICE violence as separate arms of the same oppressive state body? I offer three suggestions that developed from the research and advocacy described in this book as well as the collaborative work already occurring among members of these communities.

First, advocates must augment the public's understanding of violence. When I began this work, I envisioned focusing on Santiago, as he had been the target of a viscerally disturbing home raid. Instead, I found myself witnessing the slow unraveling of multiple families amid a toxic and insidious fear that seeped through an entire community. But the slow violence that happened in the aftermath of the raid was simple for the public to overlook, especially as its victims—mostly women—remained hidden and silent for their own self-preservation. To begin to coalesce against immigration law enforcement, Latinos and our allies must expand the public notion of violence. We must work to highlight that illness, hunger, and, ultimately, death, sometimes happen as quickly as the pulling of a trigger or a strangulation on a sidewalk but also happen slowly and chronically, moving from individual to family to community.

Inherently, an expanded notion of violence will also be more inclusive of the experiences of women. In her book *Invisible No More: Police Violence against Women and Women of Color*,[10] Andrea Ritchie shares that she was often told that it simply made more sense to focus on Black men than Black women, as the Black men killed, arrested, and racially profiled far outnumbered Black women. Ritchie responds, "While it is in fact the case that fewer women are killed, brutalized by police, or incarcerated, a focus on police killings and more egregious uses of physical force elides women's more frequent experiences of less lethal violations, like sexual harassment and assault, which go undocumented."[11] That is, our focus on

the hyperviolence of, in some cases, police killings, and in others, deportation, often renders invisible the experiences of women. An expansive
definition of violence will therefore be more inclusive of the experiences
of women in both Black and Latino mixed-status communities.

Further, expanding the concept of violence to include structural or
institutional violence will help to address the range of ways in which
Latino communities are disadvantaged and our life spans shortened.
Indeed, as the Black Lives Matter movement has brilliantly highlighted,
the killings of Black individuals by police are only one manifestation of a
chronically violent, anti-Black system of oppression. Segregation, redlin-
ing, gentrification, and voter disenfranchisement are just a few examples
of structural violence that slowly shortens the lives and diminishes the
quality of life of the community members of color caught in these systems. Chronic, slow violence is violence just the same. As advocates, we
must work to show the public that racist systems damage our health and
shorten our lives on a scale that vastly outpaces the firing of guns and
the kicking in of doors.

Second, Latinos must accept the ways in which we are all impacted by
deportation and anti-immigrant rhetoric. We must refrain from building
walls to segregate our community by immigration status. I would argue
that one of the reasons the Black community rallied around opposition
to police violence was that members throughout the Black community
shared the experience of discrimination, racial profiling, and police ag-
gression. Because Latinos vary in the shades of our skin, some of us do
not have frequent experiences of racial profiling or police violence (as my
warm welcome by police officers perhaps attests). And while members
of Black communities may always be racially profiled, read as a criminal,
and potentially shot, a Latino citizen, for example, who is racially profiled
and pulled over by ICE will ultimately not be deported.

So, should we so choose, Latinos can deny the existence of racist systems and distance ourselves from the violence of deportation. ICE, the
police, and the war on drugs have already provided us with the perfect
rhetoric to create this distance. Those who are deported are reflexively
called "criminals," who, as the popular refrain goes, "should have just

done it the right way." I saw this meritocratic mind-set play out during fieldwork, with some Latinos saying the person who was deported never should have been driving under the influence in the first place without critically assessing why, for some, a DUI means a fee, and for others, it means removal from their families and lives in the United States. Indeed, ICE is thriving off of their ability to divide and conquer, marking only some of us as targets of deportation, and providing rhetorical justification for the rest of us to claim *those* Latinos deserved it but *we* do not. All Latinos, no matter the shades of our skin or the types of documents we carry, must embrace our undocumented community members and advocate for their inclusion and fair and transparent treatment.

Finally, Black and brown movements could benefit from collaborative efforts to address state violence. I want to be clear that unity and collaboration does not mean the erasure of important historical differences. Indeed, Black and Latino communities have experienced vastly different reception and treatment in the United States throughout history, notably beginning with the fact that while many Latinos chose to immigrate to the United States, the ancestors of most Black community members were shackled and brought on ships from Africa to be sold as slaves.

Instead, it is precisely the differences in our communities that provide the most fertile ground for collaboration and mutual progress. Just as Latino citizens stepped in to support the undocumented members of their communities who confined themselves to their homes after the raid, a coherent advocacy movement must leverage the privileges of everyone involved while acknowledging the differential level of risks that exist in our own communities. This may mean that, for light-skinned Latinos like me, we are able to move about in spaces that would be dangerous for our darker-skinned friends, whether Latino or Black. Similarly, those with citizenship status can and should advocate in places where our undocumented neighbors cannot.

Yet racial minority groups would not have to advocate for our own existence if our lives were deemed valuable and worthy of protection in the first place. If white American citizens largely control the political systems of our country, then the creation of equitable systems that value us as human beings begins with them. This is not to say that Black and Latino community members should not have a say in government policy. Rather, if we were not forced to advocate for our own survival, we would have the luxury to work toward policies that allow us to thrive and to be happy and healthy, instead of just alive and together. White US citizens must reflect on their casual acceptance of extreme violence meted out on Black and brown community members for the most minor of legal infractions or, often, no legal infractions at all.

■ ■ ■

Writing this book was difficult. While Guadalupe, Fernanda, and Hilda draw from a well of resilience whose depths I cannot fathom, the silver linings in a life of systematic persecution and violence can be few and far between. But I was fueled to continue writing largely by the belief that this book would emerge into a much brighter moment in our cultural history. I thought this book—about Obama-era immigration enforcement practices—would be a reflection on a time that had passed, when violence and militarization, when racial profiling and police collaboration, would be remnants of an immigration enforcement system we had left behind. How naïve and, ultimately, incorrect I was.

Instead, immigration enforcement under President Trump has trended drastically toward brutality and disregard for the value of family, all from the party of family values. Under this administration, immigration enforcement activities are justified by stoking a blatantly racist and xenophobic fear of Black and brown community members. These activities are increasingly militarized and well funded. And they are happening more often.

On April 5, 2018, ICE collaborated with multiple other federal organizations, including the Tennessee Highway Patrol, to raid a meatpacking plant in Bean Station, Tennessee. Agents arrested ninety-seven immigrants, most of whom had broken no law besides an initial illegal border crossing.[12] The day after the raid, more than 500 kids missed school.[13]

On January 10, 2018, immigration enforcement agents raided ninety-eight 7-Eleven stores in seventeen states across the United States. Twenty-one undocumented immigrants were arrested in this organized series of predawn raids.[14]

On October 24, 2017, Border Patrol stopped an ambulance transporting 10-year-old Rosa María Hernández to the hospital. Rosa María, who has cerebral palsy, was on her way to emergency gallbladder surgery. After assessing her immigration status, agents followed the ambulance to the hospital and waited outside Rosa's room while she recuperated. As reported by a Border Patrol spokesman, "Per the immigration laws of the United States, once medically cleared she will be processed accordingly."[15]

In our own community, on May 24, 2017, ICE agents raided a local restaurant located a few feet from the University of Michigan. Agents ate breakfast made by kitchen staff. Moments later, these staff were taken into custody for deportation.[16]

And many law enforcement offices have jumped at the opportunity to collaborate with ICE, returning to the 287(g) agreements—in which officers are deputized to enforce aspects of immigration law—left behind during the Obama era.[17] In March 2018, 380 sheriffs sent an open letter to Congress in support of Trump's stepped-up immigration enforcement practices and the construction of a border wall, claiming that "without border security and immigration reform, more Americans will continue to be victims of crime. Now is the time to act!"[18]

Not all government officials have extended ICE's reach so enthusiastically however. One notable point of resistance has taken place in county jails throughout the country, where sheriffs have refused to hold arrestees in jail simply based on requests from ICE.[19]

But ICE appears to have developed a cookie-cutter response[20] to this resistance, as exemplified by the statement given by ICE spokesman Khaalid Walls to the sheriff of Washtenaw County. Walls reminds everyone how dangerous immigrants can be to the safety and order of a community: "When a local law enforcement agency fails to honor an ICE detainer, individuals, who often have significant criminal histories are released into the community, presenting a potential public safety threat" that could "needlessly put ICE personnel and innocent bystanders in harm's way."

But, Walls says, heroic officers will do what is necessary to protect the vulnerable citizenry from the villainous immigrant: "ICE officers then have to locate these criminal aliens in the community, which is highly resource intensive."[21]

In the hours upon hours of interviews I conducted, I never once heard Guadalupe, Fernanda, or Hilda—or anyone in their mixed-status Latino community—use "resource intensive" to describe their experiences on that Thursday in November.

■ ■ ■

We are in a new era of immigration enforcement, an era in which violence, police collaboration, and racial profiling are fundamental aspects of the political fabric of our country. Thus, we, as advocates; as researchers; as friends, family, and allies; perhaps even as members of mixed-status communities or communities of color ourselves; must decide what we will do with the stories of Guadalupe, Fernanda, and Hilda, of Aura Rosser, Laquan McDonald, and Michael Brown, and others like them. Will we share these stories? Will we write, speak, and advocate as if lives depended on it? Or will we, too, participate in the violence by erasing the stories of damaged bodies, shattered families, and broken communities who are systematically dismantled by our government systems?

Epilogue
The Raid: The Months and Years After

The law enforcement office that both collaborated in the raid and, the next day, responded to the B&E call at Guadalupe and Fernanda's apartment, continued to state that the raid had nothing to do with immigration. To summarize the circuitous path that led ICE into Guadalupe and Fernanda's apartment and Santiago's *taller*, ICE conducted a stakeout on Santiago's taller, then tipped off the sheriff's office to the possible presence of guns and drugs. Despite their efforts, advocates were not told what evidence was provided to the sheriff's office, nor the minimum amount of evidence that would justify a raid in which SWAT and ICE would collaborate. The sheriff's office obtained a no-knock warrant that permitted the county's SWAT unit to raid the apartment and *taller* in search of guns and drugs. ICE, which generally uses administrative warrants that require consent to enter a residence, was thus able to follow the SWAT agents into the apartment and *taller* and question and arrest every undocumented Latino man they came across. Meanwhile, the sheriff's office found no drugs and no firearms and filed no charges against anyone they encountered. The daylong act of law enforcement activity resulted only in deportations but was nonetheless labeled a drug raid, even though no drugs were found.

In a meeting in his office in December 2015, the sheriff lamented to me the "trauma" the raid had engendered and the role of the sheriff's office in contributing to it. I believe he was sincere in his regret. Since then, under the guidance of the sheriff, the office has adopted the use of body cameras,[1] modified the protocols of SWAT units engaged in raids, and continued to work closely with the Washtenaw Interfaith Coalition for Immigrant Rights (WICIR), the Washtenaw ID Project, and other immigrant rights organizations. The sheriff has become a statewide leader in efforts to curb law enforcement collaboration with ICE,[2] advocated consistently against racial profiling, instructed officers not to call ICE during traffic stops, and refused to hold those arrested in jail for ICE beyond what is legally necessary without a warrant. His stance has angered ICE officials.[3]

■ ■ ■

The raid also exposed the poor conditions in which Guadalupe, Fernanda, and their families had been living. Heated by a deep fryer and with live electrical wires dangling from the ceiling, the apartment was one of many illegal additions the landlord had made to his industrial property since 2001. The township thus took legal action against him for these violations for the third time,[4] a lawsuit it would eventually win in early 2015. As a result, a judge barred anyone from entering the property unless it was in an effort to bring the buildings back up to code.

These multiple lawsuits by the township against the landlord were not his only interactions with the legal system. He had served prison time for attempted murder after a shooting in 1985 and, in 1995, was convicted of domestic violence and felony stalking. Despite his criminal history, he was never even handcuffed during the course of the raid or the B&E call afterward.

■ ■ ■

Santiago, the target of the raid and the man who operated the *taller,* was detained for four months before he was deported to Mexico. Julio, the man in the car with Santiago when it was pulled over, signed a voluntary departure form and was returned to Mexico. Santiagito, Santiago's 18-year-old son who had arrived in Michigan two months before the raid, was detained for a month and eight days before he was deported to Mexico.

Francisco, who was arrested as he drove away from the *taller,* was detained for a month before he was released. Likely owing to a large show of support from his community organized by his visa-holding girlfriend, Frida, and his extensive ties to Michigan nurtured over his nineteen years in Washtenaw County, his case was administratively closed. This was generally a positive turn of events for Francisco: administrative closure temporarily halts deportation proceedings by removing the proceedings from an immigration judge's calendar and sometimes providing the opportunity for the individual to apply for a work permit and driver's license. However, administratively closed cases can be "recalendared" at any time if requested by an immigration judge. Though Francisco may now have a license to show to the officers who pull him over, he likely approaches his mailbox with trepidation every day, wondering if a judge has decided to consider his case again. While Francisco was detained, the truck that was in the *taller* was towed and eventually repossessed, adding to the expenditure of thousands of dollars in legal fees.

Outcomes were less clear for others involved in the raid. I was unable to ascertain what happened to the man who was in the car with Francisco when it was pulled over and what happened to Roberto, the man who had been in the car with Guadalupe. It is believed that approximately four other men were arrested in the *taller* below the apartment during the raid and were all deported. The lack of certainty about who was detained—and whether they were ultimately deported—is not uncommon. Like raids themselves, their aftermath is often painful, chaotic, and confusing, as community members face deportation or do their best to avoid the people and places that may lead to it.

Hilda and Arturo

Arturo was arrested as he drove out of the *taller* and spent the next few hours watching from the backseat as ICE detained more Santiago look-alikes. At about 8:00 p.m., he was taken to the immigration office in Detroit, before later being transferred to Monroe, Michigan, where he was detained. His wife, Hilda, who was also undocumented, did not attend an initial court hearing because she feared that entering the courthouse would result in her own deportation. Arturo's lawyer later worked with the judge to garner an agreement that Hilda would not be arrested if she went to a second hearing. Trusting in the judge's word, Hilda and about fourteen other citizen community members, including family, friends, and coworkers, testified about Arturo's contribution to the community and quality as a father. Ultimately, Arturo was detained for a month and one day before posting a $9,000 bond. Given his time in the United States, his strong connection to his community, and his role as a father and provider, his case, like Francisco's, was likely administratively closed, though I was not able to confirm. He has since applied for and received a work permit and a driver's license.

Fernanda

Fernanda was about 22 years old when her door was kicked in. For Fernanda, the raid engendered a deep cycle of pain and economic struggle, as it had impacted her and her children emotionally and psychologically, thwarted her ability to nurse Ignacio, and left them homeless, hungry, and poor. She could not find care for her children, whose health, after the raid, had become burdensomely unpredictable, and the care she could find she could not afford because of the deportation of the family's economic provider. Alone, frustrated, and suicidal, Fernanda took a bus with her children to McAllen, Texas, before walking across the border to Reynosa, Mexico, with Lena next to her and Ignacio in her arms. Santiago recalled, "[After I was deported], she stayed about fifteen more days... No, not very long, because she didn't even have money to buy milk for the kids."

Guadalupe

The hotel room that WICIR rented for Guadalupe helped her stave off homelessness, and eventually, she was able to find an apartment. A coworker familiar with Guadalupe's situation assisted her in locating childcare and employment. In the absence of Santiago's income, Guadalupe picked up a second job, and, at the time of the interviews in 2015, worked from 8:00 a.m. to 4:30 p.m., six days a week, cleaning rooms, and from 5:00 p.m. to about 12:00 a.m., three or four days a week, doing laundry in a hotel.

When Guadalupe's boyfriend (Carlitos's father) assaulted her outside of a Wendy's parking lot as she left work in 2008, she became eligible to apply for a U visa, a visa given to individuals who are victims of crimes and thereafter cooperate with the police. But applying for the visa required the police record of the domestic violence, a record Guadalupe did not have. Though the record could have been attained with a simple Freedom of Information Act (FOIA) request through the police department webpage, no one in Guadalupe's network was familiar with the procedure (with the exception of a lawyer she knew, who offered to file the FOIA request for $1,500). Guadalupe's family also discouraged her from applying for a U visa, as they feared that sharing her information with the police could lead to her deportation. Pregnant with Carlitos, Guadalupe did not want to risk deportation, even for the possibility of a U visa that could grant her protection in the future.

Then, shortly after the raid but years after the initial abuse, WICIR put Guadalupe in contact with a lawyer the organization trusted who had connections to the Mexican Consulate. The consulate agreed to financially support Guadalupe's U visa application, and I submitted a FOIA request for the police record of the domestic violence. Eventually, in 2015, about eight years after she was beaten by the father of her son, Guadalupe applied for a U visa.

As part of the application process, I drove Guadalupe to the US Citizenship and Immigration Services office in Detroit on a Wednesday in the spring of 2017, where she disappeared into a back room to have her thumbprints scanned and records checked for criminal activity. There is currently a wait of about three years to receive approval or denial of a U visa from USCIS. During this three-year period, Guadalupe is slightly more protected from deportation, as the Department of Homeland Security generally does not remove applicants while they await the judge's decision on U visa applications.[5] If Guadalupe's U visa application were approved, she would join about 80,000 other U visa applicants and wait another eight years for her visa to become available. She would finally be able to work and drive legally during these eight years. Three years after the reception of the U visa, Guadalupe could apply to be a permanent resident of the United States.

In the car on the way to her house, Guadalupe shares with me that she told a relative in Mexico about this book. The relative said that her eventual U visa approval and the US residency it would include would be the perfect climax to the story you are reading now. Guadalupe and I both shake our heads in agreement and smile, and we momentarily allow ourselves to imagine that such light could possibly emerge from such darkness. Then, we momentarily allow ourselves to ignore that Guadalupe had to be beaten by a man and cooperate with the men who kicked in her door for it to happen.

■ ■ ■

It's December. My daughter and I drive to Guadalupe's apartment to chat and deliver a few gifts to her children. Her apartment—the same one she moved into after living in a hotel—is small, but there is enough space in the living room for a Christmas tree covered in lights and decorated with red ornaments. Under the tree lie multiple presents wrapped in sparkling paper, waiting to be opened by excited children on Christmas morning. The hallway wall leading to the tree is lined with family photos, some of people who are here, some of people who are not. Mixed among the photos are certificates from Carlitos's elementary school, notifying his mother that she is the parent of a Star Student.

This time, when Carlitos sees me, he doesn't stand in front of me and detail the father figures he has had forcibly removed by death and deportation. Instead, he and my daughter immediately sit criss-cross applesauce on the threadbare rug and break out their Pokémon card game. Sofía and Fatima are too young to play, though they are just old enough to hover around the pair of card players and interrupt their shuffling.

Guadalupe and I catch up. We eat the doughnut holes I brought them. She yells at her kids not to open their presents until December 25. And they carry on with their day, with their Christmas vacation, with their life. As I sit on Guadalupe's couch with our children buzzing around us, I realize that on this day, *un día común y corriente*, I am in the presence of one of the most courageous women in the world.

Acknowledgments

Writing this book ranks among the single greatest honors of my life. To be trusted not only to hear these stories but also to bring them into a world that prefers they remain untold, is a privilege I do not deserve. I'm spellbound and honored that I was invited to do so. I have a village to thank for the support that made it all possible.

My partner, Katie, and my children, Mia and Miguel, not only encouraged me to do the work but actively stood beside me the whole time. They painted their faces like skeletons at a "Death to Deportation" rally. They skipped dinner to stand in front of a middle school to protest the detention and deportation of a student and her mother. They salsa danced with me at English as a Second Language parties. And they accepted my absence during the busy times of this writing with a grace I can't explain. They are my reason for living and my reason for fighting for those whose families are separated by immigration enforcement.

Thank you to the many members of the Washtenaw Interfaith Coalition for Immigrant Rights, including Margaret and Melanie Harner, Laura Sanders, Ramiro Martinez, and Mary Anne Peronne, who tirelessly answered my questions about what happened on that Thursday in November of 2013. Melanie and Ramiro were essential in carrying out the fieldwork and conducting the interviews in this study. Without them, it simply would not have happened.

I owe a great deal to those from the Detroit Youth Passages project, where I first came to appreciate the anthropological and participatory methods that I used throughout this book. Thanks to Mark Padilla, Armando Matiz, and Caitlin Reardon, with whom I spent many late Saturday nights that turned into early Sunday mornings. Thanks to Angie Reyes from the Detroit Hispanic Development Corporation and Laura Hughes from the Ruth Ellis Center for being such role models of tireless, on-the-ground work. I'd especially like to thank Louis Graham, my mentor and best friend. Louis taught me that, as people of color with letters after our names, we don't have the luxury of bad writing. We write for the communities that depend on us. We write to save lives. I miss you Louis.

When it comes to advocacy, I have truly learned from the best. Thank you to Maria Ibarra-Frayre, Aleck Stephens, Anna Lemler, Julie Quiroz, Laura Sonday,

Kerry Martin, Amy Ketner, Amber Hughson, and many others who taught me that community organizing takes bravery, resilience, patience, and the courage to envision—and strive toward—a world we want to create. I have also been fortunate to learn from academics who never separated advocacy from research, including Amelia Frank-Vitale and John Doering-White.

Writing and interviewing across languages is challenging. Thanks to Raúl Gámez and Carlos Robles, who could answer the most convoluted grammatical and cultural questions within the span of a text conversation but are also, themselves, the type of activists we should aspire to be.

This work was done during the growth of the #BlackLivesMatter movement. Writing about immigration enforcement and police violence while being respectful of the experiences of both Black and Latino communities was challenging, to say the least. Thank you, Amber Williams, for your insight and guidance.

I cannot begin to thank the number of authors who have guided me through the writing process in ways big and small: Heide Castañeda, Ruth Gomberg-Muñoz, Sarah Horton, Nolan Kline, Joanna Dreby, and, especially, Ruth Behar and Jason De León. I often couldn't tell if you were teaching me about advocacy or about writing. I'm pretty sure that's how you want it.

To *mis cómplices* and colleagues Alana Lebrón and Nicole Novak. You have taught me to move bravely toward a public health of empathy, sacrifice, creativity, and daring. I'm honored to work with you.

Thanks to the best freelance editor anyone could ask for, Jessica Yen, who read countless drafts of this work through every possible iteration, and Robin W. Coleman, Kathryn Marguy, Andre Barnett, and the folks at Johns Hopkins University Press for their support, organization, and steadfast belief in the value of this project.

There are many people I have met along the course of this work who have enriched the writing and my life, among them Felipe Riaño and his family; Nayelly Mena-Martinez and her family; Glenda, Armando, and their children; Keta Cowan and the amazing folks with the Washtenaw ID Project; Susan Reed and the folks of the Michigan Immigrant Rights Center; Sarah Yore-Van Oosterhout, Aaron Yore-Van Oosterhout, and the team at Lighthouse Immigrant Advocates; Charo Ledón, Adreanne Waller, Mikel Llanes, and Dan Kruger from the *Encuesta Buenos Vecinos*; Paul Fleming and the Health Inequities and Immigration Research Team; Dalila Reynosa and Julio Salazar, who embody the next generation of this work; Carrie Amber Rheingans, Kate Murphy Guzman, Brad Thomson, Martha Valadez, Jenn Felix, and Heather Branton were and continue to be incredible advocates for immigrant communities and shared generously of their time and energy to inform this work; Jonah Siegel, Lee Roosevelt, Nick Espitia, Richard Nunn, Elizabeth Mosley, and Aleck Kulick continue to keep me grounded and centered; Julia Porth, Vicenta Vargas, Patrick Mullen, and all the stellar students I have had the joy of teaching and mentoring over the years; and Woody Neighbors, Amy Schulz, Barbara Israel, Jorge Delva, Patrick Kruger, Julia Seng, and the many other wonderful professors who taught me how to do public health right.

I owe a debt of gratitude to a number of law enforcement personnel who allowed me into their work and the former Immigration and Naturalization Service agent who shared a meal with me. Derrick Jackson, Kathy Wyatt, and Sheriff Jerry Clayton at the Washtenaw County Sheriff's Office were helpful and cooperative at all times, and I have come to appreciate how they do their work. Their belief in transparency is steadfast and an example to be followed by other departments.

This book was written during a post-doctoral fellowship at the National Center for Institutional Diversity. Thank you to Tabbye Chavous, Marie Ting, John Burkhardt, and Laura Sánchez-Parkinson for creating a wonderful space to be a writer of color.

Every book requires a soundtrack, so thanks to Lin-Manuel Miranda for providing the music that fueled my writing. I had never heard anyone explain my college experience as clearly as Nina did from the top of the fire escape, and when you used "oversensitive" and "relentless" in the same verse I wondered if you stole my journal. Your music showed me that writing with power and writing with vulnerability could coexist. Here's to writing our way out.

My parents-in-law, Bill and Linda; my brother, Ben; and my sisters-in-law, Celena and Ellen: in addition to the moral support, thank you for all the ways you kept the family healthy during the demanding parts of this work. I never doubted that the kiddos were in the best of hands whenever they were with you. Thanks also to my Texas family for the support and love you sent northward and wonderful welcome you extended to us whenever we returned to San Antonio.

To my father, James, and my mother, Maria, thank you for the years of unending support as I went down a path that none of us really understood. It wasn't long into my academic career that I stopped looking for academic role models and realized that I had all the role models I needed back at home. You crossed borders for me, whether those borders were literal or circumstantial. I'm starting to get it now: we cross these borders so our children don't have to. May this book be one less border your grandkids have to cross.

But mostly I'd like to thank Guadalupe, Fernanda, and Hilda, three of the mothers at the center of this raid. Some life experiences cannot be un-felt, cannot be untwined from who we are as people nor separated from the lens through which we will forever interpret the world. I carry with me Guadalupe's story, Fernanda's story, and Hilda's story. I carry with me not only their trauma, but their courage, their *rabia*, their *ganas de vivir*. Let's agree to keep telling their stories, until no one has to live them ever again.

Notes

Introduction

1. Quesada, "Special Issue Part II."
2. Geertz, "Thick Description."
3. Sanders et al., "Grassroots Responsiveness to Human Rights Abuse."
4. De León, *The Land of Open Graves.*
5. LE-CAB later changed its name to "CABLE," or the Community Advisory Board to Law Enforcement, in order to be inclusive of the noncitizens in Washtenaw County. I use LE-CAB here, as that was the name of the board around the time of the raid.
6. See, e.g., Christensen and Crank, "Police Work and Culture in a Nonurban Setting," for an in-depth look at police culture.
7. https://blacklivesmatter.com/about/herstory/.
8. Pearson and Botelho, "5 Things to Know about the Zimmerman-Martin Saga."
9. Horwitz and McCrummen, "Trayvon Martin Documents Reveal New Details."
10. Sanchez and Prokupecz, "Protests after N.Y. Cop Not Indicted."
11. Palmer, "The Crossroads."
12. Nencel, "Situating Reflexivity"; Carney, *The Unending Hunger*; Watkins and Gioia, *Mixed Methods Research*; Behar, *The Vulnerable Observer.*
13. Boehm, *Intimate Migrations.*
14. Boehm, *Intimate Migrations*, 23.
15. De León, *The Land of Open Graves.*
16. Of course, what I am describing at this point is something more akin to "friendship." Ellis, "Telling Secrets, Revealing Lives"; Behar, *Translated Woman.*
17. Kanuha, "'Being' Native versus 'Going Native'"; Narayan, "How Native Is a 'Native' Anthropologist?"

Chapter 1. Guadalupe, Fernanda, and Hilda

1. All names are pseudonyms.
2. Passel and Cohn, "Overall Number of U.S. Unauthorized Immigrants Holds Steady."
3. "Estimated Unauthorized Immigrant Population, by State, 2016."

4. Passel, "Demography of Immigrant Youth."

5. Schueths and Lawston, *Living Together, Living Apart*.

6. Simanski, *Immigration Enforcement Actions: 2013*.

7. Dreby, "US Immigration Policy and Family Separation."

8. Dreby, *Everyday Illegal*.

9. Castañeda, "Mixed-Status Families in the Rio Grande Valley of Texas"; Castañeda, *Borders of Belonging*.

10. Boehm, *Returned*.

11. Lopez et al., "Traumatogenic Potential of Law Enforcement Home Raids."

12. Alexander, *New Jim Crow*.

13. Kraska, "Militarization and Policing."

14. American Civil Liberties Union, *War Comes Home*.

15. Ngai, *Impossible Subjects*; Chavez, *The Latino Threat*.

16. National Commission on Terrorist Attacks upon the United States, *9/11 Commission Report*.

17. Department of Homeland Security, "Organizational Chart."

18. Department of Homeland Security, "Overview: ICE."

19. Department of Homeland Security, "About CBP."

20. De Genova, "Migrant 'Illegality' and Deportability."

21. Kanstroom, *Aftermath*; Stumpf, "The Crimmigration Crisis"; Golash-Boza and Hondagneu-Sotelo, "Latino Immigrant Men."

22. Golash-Boza and Hondagneu-Sotelo, "Latino Immigrant Men," 273.

23. Golash-Boza, "The Department of Homeland Security."

24. Golash-Boza and Hondagneu-Sotelo, "Latino Immigrant Men"; Department of Homeland Security, 2014.

25. Golash-Boza and Hondagneu-Sotelo, "Latino Immigrant Men."

26. Guelespe, "From Driving to Deportation."

27. Leuchter, "The Response of Government."

28. Lopez et al., "Raising Children amid the Threat of Deportation."

29. Golash-Boza and Hondagneu-Sotelo, "Latino Immigrant Men."

30. Passel and Cohn, "Overall Number of U.S. Unauthorized Immigrants Holds Steady."

31. Gouveia and Saenz, "Global Forces and Latino Population Growth."

32. Evans, "The ICE Storm in U.S. Homes."

33. Sinha, "Arbitrary Detention?"

34. Chiu et al., *Constitution on ICE*.

35. Mendelson, Strom, and Wishnie, *Collateral Damage*.

The Raid: Before

1. As noted in the introduction, the words and phrases spoken by law enforcement officers are based on interviews of those arrested, not from officers themselves.

Chapter 2. *Un Día Común y Corriente*

1. Lebrón, "Racialization of Latinos following September 11th."

2. American Immigration Council, "Immigration Detainers."

3. Department of Homeland Security, "Secure Driver's Licenses."

4. State IDs were also impacted by this restriction. Yet while both driver's licenses and state IDs are important forms of identification and both were affected by the REAL ID Act, I focus only on driver's licenses because of their influence on one's ability to drive legally.

5. Gonzales, "Learning to Be Illegal."

6. Stuesse and Coleman, "Automobility, Immobility, Altermobility."

7. For example, WICIR collaborated with the sheriff's office to make sure that officers were aware that it was legal to drive with foreign driver's licenses in the first place and that drivers did not need to be imprisoned or even ticketed for driving with their foreign licenses. Many police departments in the area continued to ticket drivers, even though they were driving legally, and those ticketed had little recourse, as they feared that going to court to complain about their unjust ticketing could result in their deportation.

8. Notably, while drivers are required to know and obey traffic laws, officers can be ignorant of the law and enforce them incorrectly, as long as the officer's "mistaken understanding of the law [is] reasonable." See Heien v. North Carolina, 574 U.S. ___ (2014).

9. Gomberg-Muñoz, *Becoming Legal*; Jordan, "Tattoo Checks Trip Up Visas."

10. There was no way of knowing how many individuals were arrested that morning leaving Santiago's *taller* and how many had been detained within the weeks and months prior. Undoubtedly, not all of the individuals detained were arrested in connection to Santiago.

11. An officer can certainly racially profile a Latino driver, assume he is undocumented, pull him over, and ask for a driver's license. Alternatively, an officer could racially profile a Latino driver, run the car's license plate, and, if the officer sees that the car is registered to someone without a license, he can pull the car over from there. Either way, the first step is the racial profiling.

12. IDLService.Com.

13. Even though both documents are required, officers can, at their discretion, accept a foreign driver's license from a treaty country even without a translation.

14. "Washtenaw ID Project."

15. LeBrón et al., "Restrictive ID Policies."

16. Indeed, the entire interaction felt extremely gendered, as the male cops appeared to be waiting for the female cop to arrive to calm the emotions of the women in distress.

17. Admittedly, this entire interaction, especially in light of others de-

scribed in this book and seen in the media at the time, deserves analysis through a racial lens. Would Lisa have entered the house had the man been Black? How much of her willingness to let the man control the flow of the conversation was because he was white? These are important questions that I attempt to answer, at least in part, in chapter 5.

18. Was Lisa within her rights to request these IDs? Generally speaking, officers may request identification at their discretion, though those from whom they request identification are not necessarily legally compelled to provide it. While drivers must show their licenses and registration upon request, for passengers as well as others who may come into casual contact with officers, they are only required to show their IDs if the officer has a "reasonable and articulable suspicion" that the individual is involved in criminal activity. See Hiibel v. Sixth Judicial District Court of Nevada, 542, U.S. 177 (2004). Thus, Lisa's habit of asking for IDs from everyone was probably acceptable, and I did not witness anyone test her legal rights by refusing to provide her with identification.

19. Theodore, *Insecure Communities*.

20. Barrick, "Latino Confidence in the Police."

21. While I focus here on mixed-status Latino communities, asking for an ID discourages many individuals from interacting with officers. For example, those with outstanding warrants for unpaid traffic tickets may similarly avoid contact with police.

22. There is some sort of hypocritical irony that undocumented Latinos can use proof that they are contributing to the US economy (by working illegally) to avoid immigration enforcement.

23. De Genova, "Spectacles of Migrant 'Illegality,'" 14.

The Raid

1. Anger, rage, or indignation over some sort of injustice.

Chapter 3. The Last Night He Ever Nursed

1. There is, of course, an extensive range of "levels" that would be useful for analysis here and elsewhere. However, I do not aim to advance the theory of the socioecological model but to use the divisions most intuitively relatable to the average reader. I also hope to illustrate that even the simplest of socioecological models—in this case, the individual, the family, and the community—does an excellent job of highlighting the problems inherent in any analysis focused purely on the individual.

2. An early reader of this chapter appropriately pointed out the irony of this statement being uttered in Washtenaw County, MI, while those in Flint, MI, a few miles away, still do not have clean running water.

3. Evans, "The ICE Storm in U.S. Homes."

4. However, a number of documents testify to the use of coercive or

deceptive tactics to gain such "consent." See Evans "The ICE Storm in U.S. Homes" for a detailed discussion.

5. Golash-Boza, "The Department of Homeland Security"; Evans, "The ICE Storm in U.S. Homes"; Adler, "'But They Claimed to Be Police'"; Sanders et al., "Grassroots Responsiveness to Human Rights Abuse"; Kanstroom, *Aftermath*; Treadwell, "Fugitive Operations and the Fourth Amendment"; Bernstein, "Hunts for 'Fugitive Aliens'"; Mendelson, Strom, and Wishnie, *Collateral Damage*; Capps et al., *Paying the Price*; Allen, Cisneros, and Tellez, "The Children Left Behind"; Satinsky et al., *Family Unity, Family Health*.

6. US Department of Veterans Affairs, "Common Reactions after Trauma."

7. National Insitute of Mental Health, "Post-Traumatic Stress Disorder."

8. Smith, Schnurr, and Rosenheck, "Employment Outcomes and PTSD Symptom Severity."

9. Taft et al., "Posttraumatic Stress Disorder and Intimate Relationship Problems."

10. Rapaport et al., "Quality-of-Life Impairment in Depressive Disorders."

11. Of course, there is an inherent problem of what "counts" as trauma and who gets to define it. For the moment, I mean only to use the diagnostic concept of "trauma" to encourage advocates to consider the myriad responses we can reasonably expect to occur following these raids. For feminist perspectives on trauma and violence in marginalized communities, see Webster and Dunn, "Feminist Perspectives on Trauma."

12. *Diagnostic and Statistical Manual of Mental Disorders*, 5th ed., or *DSM-5*.

13. Pacella, Hruska, and Delahanty, "Physical Health Consequences of PTSD."

14. Morland et al., "Posttraumatic Stress Disorder and Pregnancy Health."

15. Choi and Seng, "Predisposing Factors for Dissociation."

16. Eagen-Torkko et al., "Prevalence of Breastfeeding after Childhood Abuse."

17. Because the Spanish words and phrases to describe breastfeeding do not always have clear English equivalents, I maintain much of the Spanish in the conversation.

18. Weller et al., "Regional Variation in Latino Descriptions of Susto"; Rubel, "Epidemiology of a Folk Illness."

19. Poss and Jezewski, "Role and Meaning of Susto."

20. World Health Organization, *Global Strategy for Infant and Young Child Feeding*.

21. Breslau et al., "Posttraumatic Stress Disorder in the Community."

22. I say "family" units whether there is a blood or a legal relationship. Nonmarried significant others are included in this category.

23. Francisco had two children who stayed with an ex-wife. While he spoke about them, I did not record their ages.

24. Graham-Bermann and Seng, "Violence Exposure."

25. Barnett and Hambien, "Trauma, PTSD in Infants and Young Children."

26. Barnett and Hambien, "Trauma, PTSD in Infants and Young Children."

27. Armsworth and Holaday, "Effects of Psychological Trauma on Children and Adolescents."

28. Bogat et al., "Trauma among Infants Exposed to Intimate Partner Violence."

29. US Department of Veterans Affairs, "PTSD in Children and Teens."

30. Lopez et al., "Raising Children amid the Threat of Deportation."

31. Dreby, *Everyday Illegal*, 31.

32. When an undocumented individual is detained, he is often offered the opportunity to "voluntarily depart" from the United States, also referred to as "signing a voluntary departure." When an individual voluntarily departs from the United States, he generally does not proceed to a court hearing nor receive a bar placed on seeking reentry into the United States, as there is following a deportation (US Citizenship and Immigration Services, "U.S. Citizenship and Immigration Services Glossary"). The issue of voluntary departure deserves more attention than I give it here. Like much of the repercussions of deportation, the decision to voluntarily depart is shaped by many factors, including the strength and location of one's family and social network, finances, and ability and desire to come back to the United States. Because the chances of returning to the United States legally (e.g., through marriage) are, at least in theory, higher if one voluntarily departs, it is also used as a tool to coerce immigrants to leave as soon as possible (see the August 2014 ACLU suit in Isadora Lopez-Venegas et al. v. Jeh Johnson et al., American Civil Liberties Union, "ACLU Achieves Class Action Lawsuit Settlement"). In the current case, Arturo's refusal to sign a voluntary deportation order was likely based on both his family and his knowledge of his rights, a decision that likely frustrated the agents.

33. Generally speaking, an immigration judge may not find it necessary for a detained individual to remain in custody, if, among other factors, the individual is (1) not a flight risk, (2) not a danger to the community, and (3) not a national security concern. In this case, the detained individual will be released on bond if someone out of detention, usually a family member of friend, can deliver the funds to the ICE office. If the individual released on bond attends all court-mandated sessions, attends the removal hearing, and, if deported, leaves the country, the individual who paid the bond will get her funds returned. Those who are not released on bond, or those who do not have the funds to pay the bond, remain in detention until their removal hearings, which may be months after the initial arrest. Associated Press, "Immigrants Face Long Detention, Few Rights"; Gavett, "What Are Immigration Detainees' Legal Rights?"

34. This is not unique to Latino communities, nor to interactions with the

detention system. Other literature focused on incarcerated individuals in Black communities has echoed the damaging effects of the price of prison phone calls on family connectedness. Grinstead et al., "Financial Cost of Relationships with Incarcerated African American Men"; Naser and Visher, "Family Members' Experiences with Incarceration."

35. US Immigration and Customs Enforcement, "ICE Enforcement and Removal Operations Report: Fiscal Year 2015."

36. Following the attacks on September 11, 2001, the functions of the INS were transferred to three departments—US Citizen and Immigration Services, Immigration and Customs Enforcement, and Customs and Border Patrol—within the newly formed Department of Homeland Security, as discussed in chapter 1. See dhs.gov/history for an overview of transition from INS to DHS.

37. While I recorded and transcribed Jaime's interview, he also shared with me a copy of a speech he has given at religious retreats. I use both the transcript and this speech for the following story, as both focused on the same events in his life.

Chapter 4. *Se Rompe la Comunidad*

1. Heaney and Israel, "Social Networks and Social Support"; House, Landis, and Umberson, "Social Relationships and Health"; Holt-Lunstad, Smith, and Layton, "Social Relationships and Mortality Risk."

2. Robert Wood Johnson, Healthy Communities.

3. Sherman, Trisi, and Parrott, *Various Supports for Low-Income Families Reduce Poverty*.

4. De Genova, "Spectacles of Migrant 'Illegality.' "

5. Rosmond, "Stress in Pathogenesis of the Metabolic Syndrome."

6. Hicken et al., " 'Every Shut Eye, Ain't Sleep.' "

7. Hicken et al., "Racial/Ethnic Disparities in Hypertension Prevalence."

8. Novak, Geronimus, and Martinez-Cardoso, "Birth Outcomes to Latina Mothers after a Raid."

9. For example, *"andar triste"* and *"andar trabajando"* literally mean "to walk sad" and "to walk working" but are used colloquially to mean "to be sad" or "to be working."

10. While I am confident in my description of *patrulla* here, I imagine there to be regional variation, largely rooted in who is most likely to enforce immigration law. In the Midwest, you are more likely to see a police car than an ICE vehicle.

11. Capps et al., *Paying the Price*, 4.

12. Capps et al., *Paying the Price*, 4.

13. Krogstad, "Iowa Raid Helps Shape Immigration Debate."

14. Novak et al., "Birth Outcomes to Latina Mothers after a Raid"; Camayd-Freixas, "Interpreting after the Largest ICE Raid in US History."

15. Novak and Martinez-Cardoso, "How a Major Immigration Raid Affected Infant Health."

16. Weitzer and Tuch, "Perceptions of Racial Profiling."

17. Lebrón, "Racialization of Latinos following September 11th."

18. As discussed earlier, the words "Hispanic" and "Latino" were often used interchangeably. Though many in the academic community use either the gender inclusive "Latina/o" or, in some circles, "Latinx," I rarely heard or saw these used. "Latina," the feminine, was generally only used when a woman was identifying herself. "Latino" was used when referring to the community broadly. Reference to home countries was also used to define homogeneous groups, e.g., "los Hondureños." Hilda's use of "*hispano*" in this instance was clearly meant to be inclusive of Latinos throughout her community, specifically to note the experiences derived from our shared skin color.

19. Lundman and Kaufman, "Driving While Black"; Harris, "'Driving While Black.'"

20. Shahshahani, "Put an End to Racial Profiling in Georgia."

21. "Ortega Melendres, et al. v. Arpaio, et al.," ACLU.org, September 13, 2017, https://www.aclu.org/cases/ortega-melendres-et-al-v-arpaio-et-al.

22. Epp, Maynard-Moody, and Haider-Markel, *Pulled Over*.

23. Epp, Maynard-Moody, and Haider-Markel, *Pulled Over*, 8.

24. But what do local officers have to gain by pulling over Latinos only for them to later be detained for their lack of licenses? One study, as well as our own experience in the county, suggests that financial gain may be at least one motivating factor. Each traffic ticket generates money for the county, and each detainment in the local jail provides the opportunity to make even more through the request of a bond (Stuesse and Coleman, "Automobility, Immobility, Altermobility"). In Arturo's situation, the local police were likely instructed by ICE to pull him over for some ostensible traffic violation. I would also suggest that the motivation is often simply racism.

25. Jones-Correa and de Graauw, "Looking Back to See Ahead"; Garcia and Keyes, *Life as an Undocumented Immigrant*; Castañeda and Melo, "Health Care Access for Latino Mixed-Status Families"; Theodore, *Insecure Communities*; Doering-White et al., "Testimonial Engagement"; Chaudry et al., *Facing Our Future*.

26. Marks, "Researching Police Transformation"; Christensen and Crank, "Police Work in a Nonurban Setting"; Reitzel, Rice, and Piquero, "Lines and Shadows"; Skolnick, *Justice without Trial*; Lundman and Kaufman, "Driving While Black"; Westley, *Violence and the Police*.

27. Gumbhir, *But Is It Racial Profiling*; Rojek, Rosenfeld, and Decker, "Policing Race"; Skolnick, "Racial Profiling"; Harris, "'Driving While Black.'"

28. Maril, *Patrolling Chaos*; Slack and Whiteford, "Violence on the Arizona-Sonora Border"; Adler, "'But They Claimed to Be Police'"; Slack et al., *In the Shadow of the Wall*.

29. Weitzer and Tuch, "Perceptions of Racial Profiling"; Lundman and Kaufman, "Driving While Black"; Reitzel et al., "Lines and Shadows"; Rice, Reitzel, and Piquero, "Shades of Brown"; Cheurprakobkit, "Police-Citizen Contact and Police Performance."

30. The state of racial profiling literature largely highlights the disconnect between research on Black and brown communities. In *Pulled Over* by Epp et al., for example, the authors extrapolate their findings on Black and white disparities to "illegal immigrants," saying, "As new laws encourage police to hunt for illegal immigrants and the use of investigatory stops expands to target Latinos, these unjust and antidemocratic patterns, unless deliberately checked, are likely to only become more widespread." An accurate assessment, yet an unfortunate use of "illegal immigrant."

31. Link and Phelan, "Conceptualizing Stigma," 3.

32. Keusch, Wilentz, and Kleinman, "Stigma and Global Health."

33. Krieger, "Scientific Study of Discrmination and Health."

34. Hatzenbuehler, Keyes, and Hasin, "Psychiatric Morbidity in Lesbian, Gay, and Bisexual Populations."

35. Corrigan, "How Stigma Interferes with Mental Health Care"; Drury, Aramburu, and Louis, "Body Weight and Health Care Avoidance"; Pietzak et al., "Perceived Stigma and Barriers among OEF-OIF Veterans."

36. Link and Phelan, "Conceptualizing Stigma," 24.

37. Vargas, Sanchez, and Juárez, "Fear by Association"; Vargas, "Immigration Enforcement and Mixed-Status Families"; Castañeda and Melo, "Health Care Access for Latino Mixed-Status Families."

38. Hacker et al., "Barriers to Health Care for Undocumented Immigrants"; Asch, Leake, and Gelberg, "Does Fear of Immigration Deter Tuberculosis Patients?"; Berk and Schur, "Effect of Fear on Access to Care"; Chavez, "Undocumented Immigrants"; Maldonado et al., "Fear of Discovery"; Blewett et al., "Health Care Needs of Latino Population in Rural America."

39. The Washtenaw Health Plan provides health insurance to all members of Washtenaw County, regardless of immigration status.

40. Ockene et al., "Latino Community-Based Intervention for Diabetes"; Rogler et al., "What Do Culturally Sensitive Mental Health Services Mean?"; Abad, Ramos, and Boyce, "Delivery of Mental Health Services to Spanish-Speaking Minorities."

41. Carney, *The Unending Hunger*.

42. Golash-Boza and Hondagneu-Sotelo, "Latino Immigrant Men and the Deportation Crisis."

43. Visa holders are still at risk of deportation, albeit less so. Crimes that can lead to the deportation of a visa holder include marriage fraud, child abuse, and other violent crimes.

44. One of the women was a Canadian immigrant, who identified herself as "white/anglo" and was visibly so. She was a naturalized US citizen.

The Raid: The Hours and Days After

1. I did not speak with the landlord. His quotes are taken from descriptions of the raid on other recorded interviews and conversations.

2. Lisbeth took me to the raid site and allowed me to record her description of what had occurred. Dialogue attributed to the landlord and the officer is taken from her recording in addition to other interviews.

Chapter 5. I Hate to See Them Die Unnecessarily

1. Goforth and Branstetter, "Experts Disagree on Bullet or Bad Heart."

2. Schmidt and Apuzzo, "Officer Charged with Murder of Walter Scott."

3. Barajas, "Freddie Gray's Death Ruled a Homicide."

4. Counts, "Ann Arbor Police Officer Identified."

5. Gorner and Meisner, "Teen Shot 16 Times by Chicago Cop."

6. Importantly, however, Detroit has CBP and ICE offices, and thus there are patrol cars driving casually through the streets. Further, the entire state of Michigan lies within one hundred miles of an international border, an area the ACLU calls the "Constitution free zone" due to Border Patrol's willingness to ignore Fourth Amendment protections against unlawful searches and seizures. American Civil Liberties Union, "Know Your Rights."

7. Fortin and Bromwich, "Police Officer Who Shot Tamir Rice Is Fired."

8. Philip, "Trooper Arrested Sandra Bland."

9. I say "boys" as Tamir Rice was 12 years old when he was killed (Fortin and Bromwich, "Cleveland Police Officer Fired"), and Laquan McDonald was 17 years old (Husain, "Laquan McDonald Timeline").

10. Moore, Robinson, and Adedoyin, "Special Issue on Police Shooting of Unarmed African American Males."

11. Marquez and Almasy, "Freddie Gray Death."

12. Cobbina, Owusu-Bempah, and Bender, "Race, Crime, and Policing among Ferguson Protesters."

13. Abbey-Lambertz, "Protester on Police Shooting of Aura Rosser."

14. Garza, Tometi, and Cullors, "Herstory."

15. Herbert, "Morality in Law Enforcement"; Reiner, *Politics of the Police*.

16. Herbert, "Morality in Law Enforcement," 800.

17. Herbert, "Morality in Law Enforcement," 802.

18. Reiner, *Politics of the Police*, 119.

19. Loftus, "Police Occupational Culture."

20. When I went into his office, we began to discuss the community event, including what Marcus had said. Radi told me, with an air of dismissal in his voice, that he had "looked him [Marcus] up" and that he had pictures posted with "eff the police" on them. My guess was that, if Marcus had been looked up, that I had been looked up too, and being a pretty liberal-leaning Facebook and Twitter user, that I had posted photos similar to Marcus. While my Face-

book posts, unlike Marcus's, were only visible to my Facebook friends, with any sort of diligence it was obvious that I had shared a picture directly from Marcus's page that said mockingly, "Maryland Police have killed 111 people since 2010 but they only declare a state of emergency when people throw rocks." What would Radi have done had Marcus took him up on his offer to join him for a ride-along?

21. Not all officers would agree with Logan, as many think saturating the public with more weapons makes their job more dangerous. Robertson and Williams, "As States Expand Gun Rights, the Police Object."

22. As well as many more since that time, including the fifteen students and teachers shot at Marjory Stoneman Douglas High School in Florida while this chapter was being written. Grinberg Levenson, "At Least 17 Dead in Florida School Shooting."

23. Herbert, "Morality in Law Enforcement," 803.

24. Westley, *Violence and the Police*, 96.

25. Reiner, *Politics of the Police*; Herbert, "Morality in Law Enforcement"; Loftus, "Police Occupational Culture."

26. "The Victors" is the University of Michigan fight song, and it's hard to go anywhere in Ann Arbor without seeing the word emblazoned in blue on a wall, business, card, or building.

27. Edwards, *Paths Crossed*.

28. Prenzler, "Is There a Police Culture?"

29. Reiner, *Politics of the Police*, 43.

30. Loftus, "Police Occupational Culture."

31. Terpstra and Schaap, "Police Culture, Stress Conditions."

32. Paoline, "Taking Stock." How risky is it to be a police officer? As of 2016, law enforcement was not among the top ten most dangerous jobs in the United States. Johnson, "Top 10 Most Dangerous Jobs in America."

33. Paoline, "Taking Stock," 201.

34. Chan, "Changing Police Culture," 111.

35. Prenzler, "Is There a Police Culture?"; Paoline, "Taking Stock"; Chan, "Changing Police Culture."

36. Chan, "Changing Police Culture."

37. Skolnick, *Justice without Trial*, 45.

38. Skolnick, "Racial Profiling—Then and Now," 65.

39. Jones-Brown, "Forever the Symbolic Assailant," 103.

40. Moore et al., "Hands Up—Don't Shoot"; Waxman, "How the U.S. Got Its Police Force."

41. Bass, "Policing Space, Policing Race."

42. Jones-Brown, "Forever the Symbolic Assailant."

43. Loftus, "Police Occupational Culture."

44. US Department of Justice, *Report regarding the Shooting Death of Michael Brown*.

45. Buchanan et al., "What Happened in Ferguson?"

46. Swaine, "Protests Met with Rubber Bullets and Teargas."

47. This is not technically correct. Shortly after the shooting, a state grand jury declined to bring charges against Wilson (Buchanan et al., "What Happened in Ferguson?"), and a federal investigation later cleared Wilson of civil rights violations (Eckholm and Apuzzo, "Darren Wilson Is Cleared of Rights Violations"). Thus, Wilson was "not indicted" twice is more accurate than "found innocent," but admittedly this is functionally the same. Wilson resigned on November 29, 2014, saying in his resignation letter: "I'm not willing to let someone else get hurt because of me" after his department allegedly received threats of violence (Byers, "Wilson Resigns from Ferguson Police").

48. Peralta, "Timeline."

49. Among all the fieldwork I have ever done, this is one of the moments that impacted me most. My brain replayed the conversation for months after.

50. Herbert, "Morality in Law Enforcement."

51. Herbert, "Morality in Law Enforcement," 811.

52. Stack, "Video Released in Terence Crutcher's Killing."

53. Gorner and Meisner, "Two Chicago Cops Recommended for Firing."

54. Gorner and Meisner, "Two Chicago Cops Recommended for Firing."

55. Croft, "Philando Castile Shooting."

56. Croft, "Philando Castile Shooting."

57. Herbert, "Morality in Law Enforcement," 811.

58. "Reagan, in Radio Talk, Vows Drive against Drugs."

59. Alexander, *New Jim Crow*.

60. Gomberg-Muñoz, "Inquality in a 'Postracial' Era."

61. Beckett, *Making Crime Pay*.

62. Alexander, *New Jim Crow*.

63. Alexander, *New Jim Crow*; Nunn, "Race and the Pool of Surplus Criminality."

64. Macías-Rojas, *From Deportation to Prison*.

65. Meng, *A Price Too High*.

66. Preston, "Sheriffs Limit Detention of Immigrants."

67. Meng, *A Price Too High*.

68. Nunn, "Race and the Pool of Surplus Criminality"; Alexander, *New Jim Crow*.

69. Alexander, *New Jim Crow*.

70. Kraska, "Militarization and Policing."

71. Nunn, "Race and the Pool of Surplus Criminality."

72. Nunn, "Race and the Pool of Surplus Criminality," 391.

73. Tonry, *Malign Neglect*, 82; italics added.

74. Nunn, "Race and the Pool of Surplus Criminality"; Alexander, *New Jim Crow*.

75. Croft, "Philando Castile Shooting."

76. Pickard, "Robert Bates Trial."

77. From a public health perspective, even had Harris died of heart disease and not the bullet through his chest, as a Black man, his death likely still would have been influenced by his experiences of racism. Clark et al., "Racism as a Stressor for African Americans."

78. Counts, "Read Memo on Fatal Police Shooting of Aura Rosser."

79. Abbey-Lambertz, "No Charges for Officer Who Killed Mentally Ill Woman."

80. Counts, "Read Memo on Fatal Police Shooting of Aura Rosser."

81. Sullum, "Shooting of Michael Brown."

82. Bush, *Emergency Department Visits.*

83. "Sergeant Says King Appeared to Be on Drugs." Officer Darren Wilson also used the word "hulk" to describe Michael Brown before he shot him: "I tried to hold his right arm and use my left hand to get out to have some type of control and not be trapped in my car any more. And when I grabbed him, the only way I can describe it is I felt like a five-year-old holding on to Hulk Hogan." Glenza, "'I Felt Like a Five-Year-Old.'"

84. Romero-Daza, Weeks, and Singer, "'Nobody Gives a Damn If I Live or Die.'"

85. While this is of course true at face value, the one-to-one cop-to-teen ratio strikes me as arbitrarily created in the moment, and I can easily imagine the large and intimidating Black cop who stood watch over the white teen as perfectly able to watch the white and Black teen simultaneously. The single cop who had forced my brother and his two friends to kneel down on the pavement with their hands on their heads for half an hour after someone had thrown a glass bottle off the stairs at a movie theater had at least a three-to-one cop-to-teen ratio.

86. Almasy et al., "No Federal Charges in Alton Sterling Death."

87. Almasy and Friedman, "Trooper Indicted on Perjury Charge."

Conclusion

1. Lopez et al., "Traumatogenic Potential of Home Raids."

2. Hacker et al., "Impact of Enforcement on Immigrant Health"; Hardy et al., "Research on Impact of Immigration Policies on Public Health."

3. "Washtenaw ID Project."

4. LeBrón et al., "Restrictive ID Policies."

5. Khashu, *Role of Local Police.*

6. Quesada et al., "'As Good as It Gets.'"

7. Hsu and Becker, "ICE Officials Set Quotas."

8. During one ride-along with an officer, we stopped for a reported breaking and entering at a doctor's house in a wealthy neighborhood. The window

on the front door was shattered, and it was clear anyone could reach through the window and unlock the door if they wanted to enter. Another officer and I paced around the house, fingerprinting the doorknobs, while a second officer (four were on the scene) spent about twenty minutes on what appeared to be his personal cell phone, sharing with the owner of the house his recommendations for locksmiths. The effort to prevent a second B&E at the doctor's house and the lack of effort to prevent Guadalupe and Fernanda from being homeless provided a stark and unsettling contrast.

9. There are many legitimate reasons that account for the differences in advocacy between Latino and Black movements. A full discussion of these reasons is beyond the scope of this book, but it is appropriate to mention that advocating while undocumented brings with it a visibility that many fear could lead to deportation.

10. Ritchie, *Invisible No More*.

11. Ritchie, *Invisible No More*, 234.

12. Sacchetti, "ICE Raids Meatpacking Plant."

13. Shoichett, "ICE Raided a Meatpacking Plant."

14. Gomez, "ICE Raids Showcase New Strategy."

15. Dart, "Texas Girl with Cerebral Palsy Faces Deportation."

16. Haynes, "Restaurant Says ICE Agents Detained 3 Workers."

17. Rosenberg and Levinson, "Police Aid Immigration Officials in Crackdown."

18. Da Silva, "Trump's Border Wall Must Be Built."

19. Echenique, "Which Are Receiving the Most ICE Detention Requests?"

20. See, for example, remarks by Attorney General Jeff Sessions after the mayor of Oakland warned her community of immigration raids (Veklerov, Gutierrez, and Tucker, "Attorney General Blasts Oakland Mayor") or the statements by DHS representatives about Mario Granados-Alvarado ("ICE Arrests Public Safety Threat"), Andres Flores Lopez ("ICE Arrests Registered Sex Offender"), or Elder Antonio Quintero Rodriquez and Rolando Herrera Saavedra (McCarthy, "ICE Arrests 2 Undocumented Immigrants").

21. Hunter, "Feds Blast Washtenaw Co. for Not Detaining Immigrant."

Epilogue

1. Freed, "Deputies Will Begin Using Body-Worn Cameras."

2. Stanton, "'We Don't Enforce Immigration Law.'"

3. Moran, "Sheriff Says He Didn't Ignore ICE Request." It is impossible to tell what pro-immigrant advancements the sheriff's office would have made had the raid not occurred and advocates spoken out in its aftermath, though I confidently suggest that the raid contributed to some of these practices that developed in the months and years that followed.

4. Other articles refer to this instance as the "fourth or fifth" time the township took legal action against him.

5. See memo "Guidance Regarding U Nonimmigrant Status (U visa) Applicants in Removal Proceedings or with Final Orders of Deportation," for more information on the visa process, https://www.ice.gov/doclib/foia/dro_policy _memos/vincent_memo.pdf.

Works Cited

Abad, V., J. Ramos, and E. Boyce. "A Model for Delivery of Mental Health Services to Spanish-Speaking Minorities." *American Journal of Orthopsychiatry*
44, no. 4 (1974): 584–95.

Abbey-Lambertz, Kate. "No Charges for Officer Who Killed Mentally Ill
Woman Who 'Confronted' Police with a Knife." *Huffington Post*, February
3, 2015.

———. "Protester on Police Shooting of Aura Rosser: 'We Can't Be Silent When
It Happens to a Woman.'" *Huffington Post*, December 6, 2017.

Adler, R. H. "'But They Claimed to Be Police, Not La Migra!': The Interaction
of Residency Status, Class, and Ethnicity in a (Post-PATRIOT Act) New
Jersey Neighborhood." *American Behavioral Scientist* 50, no. 1 (2006): 48–69.
https://doi.org/10.1177/0002764206289654.

Alexander, Michelle. *The New Jim Crow: Mass Incarceration in the Age of Color-
blindness*. New York: New Press, 2012.

Allen, Brian, Erica M. Cisneros, and Alexandra Tellez. "The Children Left
Behind: The Impact of Parental Deportation on Mental Health." *Journal of
Child and Family Studies* 24 (2015): 386. https://doi.org/10.1007/s10826-013
-9848-5.

Almasy, S., H. Yan, J. Lynch, and E. Levenson. "No Federal Charges against
Officers in Alton Sterling Death." CNN, June 27, 2017.

Almasy, Steve, and Chandler Friedman. "Trooper Who Arrested Sandra Bland
Indicted on Perjury Charge." CNN.com, January 6, 2016. http://www.cnn
.com/2016/01/06/us/sandra-bland-trooper-brian-encinia-indicted/.

American Civil Liberties Union. "ACLU Achieves Class Action Lawsuit Settlement That Ends Deceitful Immigration Practices." ACLU of Southern
California, August 27, 2014. https://www.aclusocal.org/en/press-releases
/aclu-achieves-class-action-lawsuit-settlement-ends-deceitful-immigra
tion-practices.

———. "Know Your Rights: In the 100-Mile Border Zone." Accessed March 17,
2019. https://www.aclu.org/know-your-rights-100-mile-border-zone.

———. *War Comes Home: The Excessive Militarization of American Policing*. New
York: ACLU Foundation, 2014.

American Immigration Council. "Immigration Detainers: An Overview." Fact

sheet, March 21, 2017. https://www.americanimmigrationcouncil.org/re
search/immigration-detainers-overview.

Armsworth, Mary W., and Margot Holaday. "The Effects of Psychological
Trauma on Children and Adolescents." *Journal of Counseling & Development*
72, no. 1 (1993): 49–56. https://doi.org/10.1002/j.1556-6676.1993.tb02276.x.

Asch, S., B. Leake, and L. Gelberg. "Does Fear of Immigration Authorities Deter Tuberculosis Patients from Seeking Care?" *Western Journal of Medicine*
161, no. 4 (1994): 373–76. http://www.pubmedcentral.nih.gov/articlerender
.fcgi?artid=1022616&tool=pmcentrez&rendertype=abstract.

Associated Press. "Immigrants Face Long Detention, Few Rights." NBC News
.com, March 2009.

Barajas, Joshua. "Freddie Gray's Death Ruled a Homicide." *PBS Newshour: The
Rundown*, May 1, 2015. http://www.pbs.org/newshour/rundown/freddie
-grays-death-ruled-homicide/.

Barnett, E. R., and J. Hambien. "Trauma, PTSD, and Attachment in Infants
and Young Children." PTSD: National Center for PTSD, February 23, 2016.
http://www.ptsd.va.gov/professional/treatment/children/trauma_ptsd_at
tachment.asp.

Barrick, Kelle. "Latino Confidence in the Police: The Role of Immigration
Enforcement, Assimilation, and Immigration Status." *Journal of Ethnicity in
Criminal Justice* 12, no. 4 (2014): 289–307. https://doi.org/10.1080/15377938
.2014.893218.

Bass, Sandra. "Policing Space, Policing Race: Social Control Imperatives and
Police Discretionary Decisions." *Social Justice* 28, no. 1 (2001): 156–77.

Beckett, Katherine. *Making Crime Pay: Law and Order in Contemporary American
Politics*. New York: Oxford University Press, 1999.

Behar, Ruth. *Translated Woman: Crossing the Border with Esperanza's Story*. Boston: Beacon Press, 1993.

———. *The Vulnerable Observer: Anthropology That Breaks Your Heart*. Boston:
Beacon Press, 1996.

Berk, M. L., and C. L. Schur. "The Effect of Fear on Access to Care among Undocumented Latino Immigrants." *Journal of Immigrant Health* 3, no. 3 (2001):
151–56. https://doi.org/10.1023/A:1011389105821.

Bernstein, N. "Hunts for 'Fugitive Aliens' Lead to Collateral Arrests." *New York
Times*, July 23, 2007. http://www.nytimes.com/2007/07/23/nyregion
/23operation.html?_r=0&gwh=9D09D1F0CA4D27E7E1880BFC368FDC
B4&gwt=pay.

Blewett, Lynn A., Sally A. Smaida, Claudia Fuentes, and Ellie Ulrich Zuehlke.
"Health Care Needs of the Growing Latino Population in Rural America:
Focus Group Findings in One Midwestern State." *Journal of Rural Health* 19,
no. 1 (2003): 33–41. http://www.ncbi.nlm.nih.gov/pubmed/12585772.

Boehm, Deborah A. *Intimate Migrations: Gender, Family, and Illegality among Transnational Mexicans.* New York: New York University Press, 2012.

———. *Returned: Going and Coming in an Age of Deportation.* Oakland: University of California Press, 2016.

Bogat, G. Anne, Erika DeJonghe, Alytia A. Levendosky, William S. Davidson, and Alexander Von Eye. "Trauma Symptoms among Infants Exposed to Intimate Partner Violence." *Child Abuse and Neglect* 30, no. 2 (2006): 109–25. https://doi.org/10.1016/j.chiabu.2005.09.002.

Breslau, N., R. C. Kessler, H. D. Chilcoat, L. R. Schultz, G. C. Davis, and P. Andreski. "Trauma and Posttraumatic Stress Disorder in the Community: The 1996 Detroit Area Survey of Trauma." *Archives of General Psychiatry* 55, no. 7 (1998): 626–32. http://www.ncbi.nlm.nih.gov/pubmed/9672053.

Buchanan, L., F. Fessenden, K. K. R. Lai, Haeyoun Park, A. Parlapiano, A. Tse, T. Wallace, D. Watkins, and K. Yourish. "What Happened in Ferguson?" *New York Times*, August 10, 2015.

Bush, D. M. *Emergency Department Visits Involving Phencyclidine (PCP).* Rockville, MD: Center for Behavioral Health Statistics and Quality, Substance Abuse and Mental Health Services Administration, 2013. https://www.ncbi.nlm.nih.gov/pubmed/27656747.

Byers, Christine. "Darren Wilson Resigns from Ferguson Police Department." *St. Louis Post-Dispatch*, November 30, 2014.

Camayd-Freixas, Erik. "Interpreting after the Largest ICE Raid in US History: A Personal Account." *New York Times*, June 13, 2008. http://graphics8.nytimes.com/images/2008/07/14/opinion/14ed-camayd.pdf.

Capps, R., R. M. Castañeda, Ajay Chaudry, and R. Santos. *Paying the Price: The Impact of Immigration Raids on America's Children.* Washington, DC: National Council of La Raza, 2007. http://www.urban.org/publications/411566.html.

Carney, Megan A. *The Unending Hunger: Tracing Women and Food Insecurity across Borders.* Oakland: University of California Press, 2015.

Castañeda, Heide. *Borders of Belonging: Struggle and Solidarity in Mixed-Status Immigrant Families.* Redwood City, CA: Stanford University Press, 2018.

———. "Mixed-Status Families in the Rio Grande Valley of Texas: Health Disparities along the US-Mexico Border." In Schueths and Lawson, *Living Together, Living Apart.*

Castañeda, Heide, and Milena Andrea Melo. "Health Care Access for Latino Mixed-Status Families: Barriers, Strategies, and Implications for Reform." *American Behavioral Scientist* 58, no. 14 (2014): 1891–1909. https://doi.org/10.1177/0002764214550290.

Chan, Janet. "Changing Police Culture." *British Journal of Criminology* 36, no. 1 (1996): 109–34. https://doi.org/10.1017/CBO9780511518195.

Chaudry, Ajay, R. Capps, Juan Manuel Pedroza, R. M. Castañeda, R. Santos, and M. M. Scott. *Facing Our Future: Children in the Aftermath of Immigration Enforcement.* Washington, DC: Urban Institute, 2010. https://doi.org /10.1037/e726272011-001.

Chavez, Leo R. *The Latino Threat: Constructing Immigrants, Citizens, and the Nation.* 2nd ed. Palo Alto, CA: Stanford University Press, 2013.

———. "Undocumented Immigrants and Their Use of Medical Services in Orange County, California." *Social Science & Medicine* 74, no. 6 (2012): 887–93. https://doi.org/10.1016/j.socscimed.2011.05.023.

Cheurprakobkit, Sutham. "Police-Citizen Contact and Police Performance: Attitudinal Differences between Hispanics and Non-Hispanics." *Journal of Criminal Justice* 28, no. 4 (2000): 325–36. https://doi.org/10.1016/S0047-2352 (00)00042-8.

Chiu, B., L. Egyes, P. L. Markowitz, and J. Vasandani. *Constitution on Ice: A Report on Immigration Home Raid Operations.* New York: Cardozo Immigration Justice Clinic, 2009.

Choi, Kristen R., and Julia S. Seng. "Predisposing and Precipitating Factors for Dissociation during Labor in a Cohort Study of Posttraumatic Stress Disorder and Childbearing Outcomes." *Journal of Midwifery and Women's Health* 61, no. 1 (2016): 68–76. https://doi.org/10.1111/jmwh.12364.

Christensen, Wendy, and John P. Crank. "Police Work and Culture in a Nonurban Setting: An Ethnographic Analysis." *Police Quarterly* 4, no. 1 (2001): 69–98. https://doi.org/0803973233.

Clark, R., N. B. Anderson, V. R. Clark, and David R. Williams. "Racism as a Stressor for African Americans." *American Psychologist* 54, no. 10 (1999): 805–16.

Cobbina, Jennifer E., Akwasi Owusu-Bempah, and Kimberly Bender. "Perceptions of Race, Crime, and Policing among Ferguson Protesters." *Journal of Crime and Justice* 39, no. 1 (2016): 210–29. https://doi.org/10.1080/0735648X .2015.1119950.

Corrigan, Patrick. "How Stigma Interferes with Mental Health Care." *American Psychologist* 59, no. 7 (2004): 614–25.

Counts, John. "40-Year-Old Woman Fatally Shot by Ann Arbor Police Officer Identified." MLive, November 2014. https://www.mlive.com/news/ann -arbor/2014/11/ann_arbor_police_shooting_name.html.

———. "Read Prosecutor's 12-Page Memo on Fatal Ann Arbor Police Shooting of Aura Rosser." MLive, January 30, 2015.

Croft, J. "Philando Castile Shooting: Dashcam Video Shows Rapid Event." CNN.com, June 21, 2017.

Dart, Tom. "Texas Girl, 10, with Cerebral Palsy Faces Deportation after Trip to Hospital." *The Guardian*, October 25, 2017.

De Genova, Nicholas P. "Migrant 'Illegality' and Deportability in Everyday

Life." *Annual Review of Anthropology* 31, no. 1 (2002): 419–47. https://doi
.org/10.1146/annurev.anthro.31.040402.085432.

De Genova, Nicholas P. "Spectacles of Migrant 'Illegality': The Scene of Exclusion, the Obscene of Inclusion." *Ethnic and Racial Studies* 36, no. 7 (July
2013): 1180–98. https://doi.org/10.1080/01419870.2013.783710.

De León, Jason. *The Land of Open Graves: Living and Dying on the Migrant Trail.*
Berkeley: University of California Press, 2016.

Department of Homeland Security. "About CBP." Accessed March 17, 2019.
http://www.cbp.gov/about.

———. "Organizational Chart." 2013. http://www.dhs.gov/organizational
-chart.

———. "Overview: ICE." Accessed March 17, 2019. https://www.ice.gov/over
view.

———. "Secure Driver's Licenses." Accessed March 14, 2019. https://www.dhs
.gov/archive/secure-drivers-licenses.

Diagnostic and Statistical Manual of Mental Disorders. 5th ed. Arlington, VA:
American Psychiatric Publishing, 2013.

Doering-White, John, P. Horner, L. Sanders, R. Martinez, William D. Lopez,
and J. Delva. "Testimonial Engagement: Undocumented Latina Mothers
Navigating a Gendered Deportation Regime." *Journal of International
Migration and Integration* 17, no. 2 (2014). https://doi.org/10.1007/s12134-014
-0408-7.

Dreby, J. *Everyday Illegal: When Policies Undermine Immigrant Families.* Oakland:
University of California Press, 2015.

———. "US Immigration Policy and Family Separation: The Consequences for
Children's Well-Being." *Social Science & Medicine* 132 (2015): 245–51.

Drury, A., C. Aramburu, and M. Louis. "Exploring the Association between
Body Weight, Stigma of Obesity, and Health Care Avoidance." *Journal of the
American Association of Nurse Practitioners* 14, no. 12 (2002): 554–61.

Eagen-Torkko, Meghan, Lisa Kane Low, Ruth Zielinski, and Julia S. Seng.
"Prevalence and Predictors of Breastfeeding after Childhood Abuse."
Journal of Obstetric, Gynecologic, & Neonatal Nursing 46, no. 3 (2017): 465–79.
https://doi.org/10.1016/j.jogn.2017.01.002.

Echenique, M. "Which States and Counties Are Receiving the Most ICE Detention Requests?" CityLab.com, September 6, 2017. https://www.citylab
.com/equity/2017/09/which-states-and-counties-are-receiving-the-most-ice
-detention-requests/538749/.

Eckholm, E., and M. Apuzzo. "Darren Wilson Is Cleared of Rights Violations
in Ferguson Shooting." *New York Times*, March 4, 2015.

Edwards, Clif. *Paths Crossed: Villains-Victims-Victors.* Kansas City, MO: ShowMe
Publishing, 2013.

Ellis, C. "Telling Secrets, Revealing Lives: Relational Ethics in Research with

Intimate Others." *Qualitative Inquiry* 13, no. 1 (2007): 3–29. https://doi
.org/10.1177/1077800406294947.

Epp, Charles R., Steven Maynard-Moody, and Donald Haider-Markel. *Pulled Over: How Police Stops Define Race and Citizenship*. Chicago: University of Chicago Press, 2014.

"Estimated Unauthorized Immigrant Population by State, 2016." Pew Research Center: Hispanic Trends, November 3, 2016. http://www.pewhispanic.org /interactives/unauthorized-immigrants/.

Evans, Katherine. "The ICE Storm in U.S. Homes: An Urgent Call for Policy Change." *NYU Review of Law & Social Change* 33 (2009): 561–611.

Fassin, D. *Enforcing Order: An Ethnography of Urban Policing*. New York: Wiley, 2013.

Fortin, J., and J. E. Bromwich. "Cleveland Police Officer Who Shot Tamir Rice Is Fired." *New York Times*, May 30, 2017.

Freed, Ben. "Washtenaw County Sheriff's Deputies Will Begin Using Body-Worn Cameras." MLive, November 21, 2014. http://www.mlive.com/news /ann-arbor/index.ssf/2014/11/washtenaw_county_sheriffs_offi_11.html.

Garcia, A. S., and D. G. Keyes. *Life as an Undocumented Immigrant: How Restrictive Local Immigration Policies Affect Daily Life*. Washington, DC: Center for American Progress, 2012.

Garza, A., O. Tometi, and P. Cullors. "Herstory." Black Lives Matter. Accessed April 27, 2016. blacklivesmatter.com/herstory/.

Gavett, Gretchen. "What Are Immigration Detainees' Legal Rights?" *Frontline*, October 2011. http://www.pbs.org/wgbh/frontline/article/what-are-immi gration-detainees-legal-rights/.

Geertz, C. "Spectacles of Migrant 'Illegality': The Scene of Exclusion, the Obscene of Inclusion." *Ethnic and Racial Studies* 36, no. 7 (2013): 1180–98. https://doi.org/10.1080/01419870.2013.783710.

———. "Thick Description: Toward an Interpretive Theory of Culture." In *The Interpretation of Cultures*, 3–30. New York: Basic Books, 1973.

Glenza, Jessica. "'I Felt Like a Five-Year-Old Holding on to Hulk Hogan': Darren Wilson in His Own Words." *The Guardian*, November 25, 2014.

Goforth, D., and Z. Branstetter. "Experts Disagree on Whether Bates' Bullet or Bad Heart Killed Harris." *The Frontier*, April 26, 2016.

Golash-Boza, T. M. "The Department of Homeland Security and the Immigration Enforcement Regime of the Twenty-First Century." In *Immigration Nation: Raids, Detentions, and Deportations in Post-9/11 America*. Boulder, CO: Paradigm Publishers, 2012.

Golash-Boza, T. M., and Pierrette Hondagneu-Sotelo. "Latino Immigrant Men and the Deportation Crisis: A Gendered Racial Removal Program." *Latino Studies* 11, no. 3 (2013): 271–92. https://doi.org/10.1057/lst.2013.14.

Gomberg-Muñoz, Ruth. *Becoming Legal: Immigration Law and Mixed-Status Families*. Oxford, UK: Oxford University Press, 2017.

———. "Inquality in a 'Postracial' Era: Race, Immigration, and Criminalization of Low-Wage Labor." *Du Bois Review* 2, no. 2012 (2012): 339–53.

Gomez, Alan. "ICE 7-Eleven Raids Showcase New Immigration Strategy." *USA Today*, January 12, 2018.

Gonzales, Roberto G. "Learning to Be Illegal: Undocumented Youth and Shifting Legal Contexts in the Transition to Adulthood." *American Sociological Review* 76, no. 4 (2011): 602–19. https://doi.org/10.1177/0003122411411901.

Gorner, J., and J. Meisner. "FBI Investigating Death of Teen Shot 16 Times by Chicago Cop." *Chicago Tribune*, April 14, 2015.

———. "Two Chicago Cops Recommended for Firing in Fatal Shooting of Teen in 2016." *Chicago Tribune*, January 12, 2018. http://www.chicagotribune.com/news/local/breaking/ct-met-chicago-police-shooting-paul-oneal-2018 0112-story.html.

Gouveia, L., and R. Saenz. "Global Forces and Latino Population Growth in the Midwest: A Regional and Subregional Analysis." *Latino/Latin American Studies Faculty Proceedings & Presentations* Paper 1 (2000): 305–28.

Graham-Bermann, Sandra A., and Julia Seng. "Violence Exposure and Traumatic Stress Symptoms as Additional Predictors of Health Problems in High-Risk Children." *Journal of Pediatrics* 146, no. 3 (2005): 349–54. https://doi.org/10.1016/j.jpeds.2004.10.065.

Grinberg, E., and E. Levenson. "At Least 17 Dead in Florida School Shooting, Law Enforcement Says." CNN, February 14, 2018.

Grinstead, O., B. Faigeles, C. Bancroft, and B. Zack. "The Financial Cost of Maintaining Relationships with Incarcerated African American Men: A Survey of Women Prison Visitors." *Journal of African American Men* 6, no. 1 (2001): 59–70.

Guelespe, Diana M. "From Driving to Deportation: Experiences of Mixed-Status Immigrant Families under 'Secure Communities.'" In Schueths and Lawston, *Living Together, Living Apart*, 198–213.

Gumbhir, Vikas K. *But Is It Racial Profiling? Policing, Pretext Stops, and the Color of Suspicion*. New York: LFB Scholarly Publishing, 2007.

Hacker, Karen, Maria Anies, Barbara L. Folb, and Leah Zallman. "Barriers to Health Care for Undocumented Immigrants: A Literature Review." *Risk Management and Healthcare Policy* 8 (2015): 175–83. https://doi.org/10.2147/RMHP.S70173.

Hacker, Karen, Jocelyn Chu, Carolyn Leung, Robert Marra, Alex Pirie, Mohamed Brahimi, Margaret English, Joshua Beckmann, Dolores Acevedo-Garcia, and Robert P. Marlin. "The Impact of Immigration and Customs Enforcement on Immigrant Health: Perceptions of Immigrants in Everett,

Massachusetts, USA." *Social Science & Medicine* 73, no. 4 (2011): 586–94. https://doi.org/10.1016/j.socscimed.2011.06.007.

Hardy, Lisa J., Christina M. Getrich, Julio C. Quezada, Amanda Guay, Raymond J. Michalowski, and Eric Henley. "A Call for Further Research on the Impact of State-Level Immigration Policies on Public Health." *American Journal of Public Health* 102, no. 7 (2012): 1250–54. https://doi.org/10.2105/AJPH.2011.300541.

Harris, David A. "'Driving While Black' and All Other Traffic Offenses: The Supreme Court and Pretextual Traffic Stops." *Journal of Criminal Law and Criminology* 87, no. 2 (1997): 544–82. https://doi.org/10.2307/1143954.

Hatzenbuehler, Mark L., Katherine M. Keyes, and D. S. Hasin. "State-Level Policies and Psychiatric Morbidity in Lesbian, Gay, and Bisexual Populations." *American Journal of Public Health* 99, no. 12 (2009): 2275–81. https://doi.org/10.2105/AJPH.2008.153510.

Haynes, J. "Ann Arbor Restaurant Says ICE Agents Ate Breakfast, Then Detained 3 Workers." MLive, May 25, 2017.

Heaney, Catherine A., and Barbara A. Israel. "Social Networks and Social Support." In *Health Behavior and Health Education: Theory Research and Practice*, 3rd ed., edited by Karen Glanz, Barbara K. Rimer, and Frances Marcus Lewis, 185–209. Hoboken, NJ: John Wiley & Sons, 2007.

Herbert, Steve. "Morality in Law Enforcement: Chasing 'Bad Guys' with the Los Angeles Police Department." *Law and Society Review* 30, no. 4 (1996): 799–818.

Hicken, M. T., H. Lee, J. Ailshire, S. A. Burgard, and David R. Williams. "'Every Shut Eye, Ain't Sleep': The Role of Racism-Related Vigilance in Racial/Ethnic Disparities in Sleep Difficulty." *Race and Social Problems* 5, no. 2 (2013): 100–112.

Hicken, M. T., H. Lee, J. Morenoff, J. S. House, and D. R. Williams. "Racial/Ethnic Disparities in Hypertension Prevelance: Reconsidering the Role of Chronic Stress." *American Journal of Public Health* 104, no. 1 (2014): 117–23. https://www.ncbi.nlm.nih.gov/pmc/articles/PMC3910029/.

Holt-Lunstad, Julianne, Timothy B. Smith, and J. Bradley Layton. "Social Relationships and Mortality Risk: A Meta-analytic Review." *PLoS Medicine* 7, no. 7 (2010). https://doi.org/10.1371/journal.pmed.1000316.

Horwitz, Sari, and Stephanie McCrummen. "Trayvon Martin Documents Reveal New Details in Case." *Washington Post*, May 17, 2012. https://www.washingtonpost.com/politics/trayvon-martin-autospy-report-indicates-struggle/2012/05/17/gIQAxw6HXU_story.html?utm_term=.169de58837dd.

House, J. S., K. R. Landis, and D. Umberson. "Social Relationships and Health." *Science* 241, no. 4865 (1988): 540–45. http://www.ncbi.nlm.nih.gov/pubmed/3399889.

Hsu, Spencer S., and Andrew Becker. "ICE Officials Set Quotas to Deport

More Illegal Immigrants." *Washington Post*, March 27, 2010. http://www
.washingtonpost.com/wp-dyn/content/article/2010/03/26/AR201003260
4891.html.

Hunter, G. "Feds Blast Washtenaw Co. for Not Detaining Immigrant." *Detroit News*, May 31, 2017.

Husain, Nausheen. "Laquan McDonald Timeline: The Shooting, the Video, and the Fallout." *Chicago Tribune*, June 27, 2017.

"ICE Arrests Public Safety Threat after Detainer Not Honored." ICE.gov, May 8, 2017.

"ICE Arrests Registered Sex Offender Released on an Active Detainer." ICE .gov, May 31, 2017.

IDLService.Com, 2014.

Johnson, D. "The Top 10 Most Dangerous Jobs in America." *Time*, December 22, 2017.

Jones-Brown, Delores. "Forever the Symbolic Assailant: The More Things Change, the More They Remain the Same." *Criminology & Public Policy* 6, no. 1 (2007): 103–21. https://doi.org/10.1111/j.1745-9133.2007.00424.x.

Jones-Correa, Michael, and Els de Graauw. "Looking Back to See Ahead: Unanticipated Changes in Immigraiton from 1986 to the Present and Their Implications for American Politics Today." *Annual Review of Political Science* 16, no. 1 (2013): 209–30. https://doi.org/10.1146/annurev-polisci-051211 -164644.

Jordan, M. "Tattoo Checks Trip Up Visas." *Wall Street Journal*, July 11, 2012. https://www.wsj.com/articles/SB1000142405270230393340457750519226659 87100.

Kanstroom, D. *Aftermath: Deportation Law and the New American Diaspora*. New York: Oxford University Press, 2012.

Kanuha, Valli Kalei. " 'Being' Native versus 'Going Native': Conducting Social Work Research as an Insider." *Social Work* 45, no. 5 (2000): 439–47.

Keusch, Gerald T., Joan Wilentz, and Arthur Kleinman. "Stigma and Global Health: Developing a Research Agenda." *Lancet* 367 (2006): 525–27.

Khashu, Anita. *The Role of Local Police: Striking a Balance between Immigration Enforcement and Civil Liberties*. Washington, DC: National Police Foundation, 2009. https://www.ncjrs.gov/App/Publications/abstract.aspx?ID =250600.

Kraska, Peter B. "Militarization and Policing—Its Relevance to 21st Century Police." *Policing* 1, no. 4 (2007): 501–13. https://doi.org/10.1093/police/pam065.

Krieger, N. "Methods for the Scientific Study of Discrimination and Health: An Ecosocial Approach." *American Journal of Public Health* 102 (2012): 936–44.

Krogstad, J. M. "Iowa Raid Helps Shape Immigration Debate." *USA Today*, May 9, 2013.

Lebrón, Alana M. W. "Racialization of Latinos and Implications for Health following September 11th: Findings from a Northern Border Community" (PhD diss., University of Michigan School of Public Health, 2015). https://deepblue.lib.umich.edu/handle/2027.42/111428.

LeBrón, Alana M. W., William D. Lopez, K. Cowan, N. L. Novak, O. Temrowski, M. Ibarra-Frayre, and J. Delva. "Restrictive ID Policies: Implications for Health Equity." *Journal of Immigrant and Minority Health* 20, no. 2 (2018): 255-260. https://doi.org/10.1007/s10903-017-0579-3.

Leuchter, Ana Stern. "The Response of Government and Organized Civil Society to the Nightmare of US Deportations of Mexican Migrant Women." In *Compassionate Migration and Regional Policy in the Americas*, edited by S. Bender and W. Arrocha. London: Palgrave Macmillan, 2017.

Link, B. G., and J. C. Phelan. "Conceptualizing Stigma." *Review Literature and Arts of the Americas* 27, no. 2001 (2001): 363-85.

Loftus, Bethan. "Police Occupational Culture: Classic Themes, Altered Times." *Policing and Society* 20, no. 1 (2010): 1-20. https://doi.org/10.1080/10439460903281547.

Lopez, William D., Pilar Horner, John Doering-White, Jorge Delva, Laura Sanders, and Ramiro Martinez. "Raising Children amid the Threat of Deportation: Perspectives from Undocumented Latina Mothers." *Journal of Community Practice* 26, no. 2 (2018): 225-35. https://doi.org/10.1080/10705422.2018.1450318.

Lopez, William D., Nicole L. Novak, Melanie Harner, Ramiro Martinez, and Julia S. Seng. "The Traumatogenic Potential of Law Enforcement Home Raids: An Exploratory Report." *Journal of Traumatology* 24, no. 3 (2018): 193-99.

Lundman, Richard J., and Robert L. Kaufman. "Driving While Black: Effects of Race, Ethnicity, and Gender on Citizen Self-Reports of Traffic Stops and Police Actions." *Criminology* 41, no. 1 (2003): 195-220. https://doi.org/10.1111/j.1745-9125.2003.tb00986.x.

Macías-Rojas, Patrisia. *From Deportation to Prison: The Politics of Immigration Enforcement in Post-Civil Rights America*. New York: New York University Press, 2016.

Maldonado, Cynthia Z., Robert M. Rodriguez, Jesus R. Torres, Yvette S. Flores, and Luis M. Lovato. "Fear of Discovery among Latino Immigrants Presenting to the Emergency Department." *Academic Emergency Medicine* 20, no. 2 (2013): 155-61. https://doi.org/10.1111/acem.12079.

Maril, Robert Lee. *Patrolling Chaos: The U.S. Border Patrol in Deep South Texas*. Lubbock: Texas Tech University Press, 2004.

Marks, Monique. "Researching Police Transformation: The Ethnographic Imperative." *British Journal of Criminology* 44, no. 6 (2004): 866-88. https://doi.org/10.1093/bjc/azh049.

Marquez, Miguel, and Steve Almasy. "Freddie Gray Death: Protesters Damage

Cars; 12 Arrested." CNN.com, April 2015. http://www.cnn.com/2015/04/25 /us/baltimore-freddie-gray-protest/index.html.

McCarthy, Craig. "ICE Arrests 2 Undocumented Immigrants Released from N.J. Jail." NJ.com, June 1, 2017. https://www.nj.com/middlesex/2017/06 /ice_says_middlesex_jail_released_2_immigrants_with.html.

Mendelson, Margot, Shayna Strom, and Michael Wishnie. *Collateral Damage: An Examination of ICE's Fugitive Operations Program*. Washington, DC: Migration Policy Institute, 2009.

Meng, G. *A Price Too High: US Families Torn Apart by Deportations for Drug Offenses*. New York: Human Rights Watch, 2015. https://www.hrw.org/report /2015/06/16/price-too-high/us-families-torn-apart-deportations-drug-of fenses.

Moore, Sharon E., Michael A. Robinson, and A. Christson Adedoyin. "Introduction to the Special Issue on Police Shooting of Unarmed African American Males: Implications for the Individual, the Family, and the Community." *Journal of Human Behavior in the Social Environment* 26, nos. 3–4 (2016): 247–50. https://doi.org/10.1080/10911359.2016.1139995.

Moore, Sharon E., Michael A. Robinson, A. Christson Adedoyin, Michael Brooks, Dana K. Harmon, and Daniel Boamah. "Hands Up—Don't Shoot: Police Shooting of Young Black Males; Implications for Social Work and Human Services." *Journal of Human Behavior in the Social Environment* 26, nos. 3–4 (2016): 254–66. https://doi.org/10.1080/10911359.2015.1125202.

Moran, D. "Washtenaw Sheriff Says He Didn't Ignore ICE Request to Hold Immigrant." *Ann Arbor News*, June 1, 2017. http://www.mlive.com/news /ann-arbor/index.ssf/2017/06/sheriff_requests_ice_retract_s.html.

Morland, Leslie, Deborah Goebert, Jane Onoye, Leighann Frattarelli, Chris Derauf, Mark Herbst, Courtenay Matsu, and Matthew Friedman. "Posttraumatic Stress Disorder and Pregnancy Health: Preliminary Update and Implications." *Psychosomatics* 48, no. 4 (2007): 304–8. https://doi.org/10.1176 /appi.psy.48.4.304.

Narayan, K. "How Native Is a 'Native' Anthropologist?" *American Anthropologist* 95, no. 3 (1993): 671–86.

Naser, Rebecca L., and Christy A. Visher. "Family Members' Experiences with Incarceration and Reentry." *Western Criminology Review* 7, no. 2 (2006): 20–31.

National Commission on Terrorist Attacks upon the United States. *The 9/11 Commission Report*. Washington, DC: 9/11 Commission, 2004. http://gov info.library.unt.edu/911/report/index.htm.

National Institute of Mental Health. "Post-Traumatic Stress Disorder." NIMH, February 2016. https://www.nimh.nih.gov/health/topics/post-traumatic -stress-disorder-ptsd/index.shtml.

Nencel, Lorraine. "Situating Reflexivity: Voices, Positionalities and Representations in Feminist Ethnographic Texts." *Women's Studies International Forum* 43 (2014): 75–83. https://doi.org/10.1016/j.wsif.2013.07.018.

Ngai, Mae M. *Impossible Subjects: Illegal Aliens and the Making of Modern America.* Princeton, NJ: Princeton University Press, 2004.

Novak, Nicole L., Arline T. Geronimus, and Aresha M. Martinez-Cardoso. "Change in Birth Outcomes among Infants Born to Latina Mothers after a Major Immigration Raid." *International Journal of Epidemiology* 46, no. 3 (2017): 839–49.

Novak, Nicole L., and Aresha M. Martinez-Cardoso. "How a Major Immigration Raid Affected Infant Health." The Conversation, January 23, 2017. https://theconversation.com/how-a-major-immigration-raid-affected-infant-health-70700.

Nunn, Kenneth B. "Race, Crime, and the Pool of Surplus Criminality: Or Why the 'War on Drugs' Was a 'War on Blacks.'" *Journal of Gender, Race and Justice* 6, no. 1 (2002): 422–27.

Ockene, I. S., T. L. Tellez, M. C. Rosal, G. W. Reed, J. Mordes, P. A. Merriam, B. C. Olendzki, G. Handelman, R. Nicolosi, and Y. Ma. "Outcomes of a Latino Community-Based Intervention for the Prevention of Diabetes: The Lawrence Diabetes Prevention Project." *American Journal of Public Health* 102, no. 2 (2012): 336–42.

Pacella, Maria L., Bryce Hruska, and Douglas L. Delahanty. "The Physical Health Consequences of PTSD and PTSD Symptoms: A Meta-analytic Review." *Journal of Anxiety Disorders* 27, no. 1 (2013): 33–46. https://doi.org/10.1016/j.janxdis.2012.08.004.

Palmer, B. J. "The Crossroads: Being Black, Immigrant, and Undocumented in the Era of #BlackLivesMatter." *Georgetown Journal of Law & Modern Critical Race Perspectives* 9, no. 1 (2017): 99–121.

Paoline, Eugene A. "Taking Stock: Toward a Richer Understanding of Police Culture." *Journal of Criminal Justice* 31, no. 3 (2003): 199–214. https://doi.org/10.1016/S0047-2352(03)00002-3.

Passel, Jeffrey S. "Demography of Immigrant Youth: Past, Present, and Future." *The Future of Children* 21, no. 1 (2011): 19–41.

Passel, Jeffrey S., and D'Vera Cohn. "Overall Number of U.S. Unauthorized Immigrants Holds Steady since 2009." Pew Research Center: Hispanic Trends, September 2016.

Pearson, M., and G. Botelho. "5 Things to Know about the George Zimmerman-Trayvon Martin Saga." CNN, February 26, 2013. https://www.cnn.com/2013/02/25/justice/florida-zimmerman-5-things/index.html.

Peralta, E. "Timeline: What We Know about the Freddie Gray Arrest." NPR, May 1, 2015.

Philip, Abby. "A Trooper Arrested Sandra Bland after She Refused to Put Out a Cigarette: Was It Legal?" *Washington Post*, July 22, 2015. https://www

.washingtonpost.com/news/morning-mix/wp/2015/07/22/a-trooper-arrest
ed-sandra-bland-after-she-refused-to-put-out-a-cigarette-was-it-legal/?nore
direct=on&utm_term=.8dd196f6a4bc.

Pickard, Arianna. "Robert Bates Trial: Forensic Pathologist Maintains Gunshot
Killed Eric Harris." *Tulsa World,* April 23, 2016.

Pietzak, R. H., D. C. Johnson, M. B. Goldstine, J. C. Malley, and S. M. South-
with. "Perceived Stigma and Barriers to Mental Health Care Utilization
among OEF-OIF Veterans." *Psychiatric Services* 60, no. 8 (2009): 1118–22.

Poss, Jane, and Mary Ann Jezewski. "The Role and Meaning of Susto in Mexican Americans' Explanatory Model of Type 2 Diabetes." *Medical Anthropology Quarterly* 16, no. 3 (2002): 360–77. https://doi.org/10.1525/maq.2002.16
.3.360.

Prenzler, Tim. "Is There a Police Culture?" *Australian Journal of Public Administration* 56, no. 4 (1997): 47–56. https://doi.org/10.1111/j.1467-8500.1997.tb0
2488.x.

Preston, Julia. "Sheriffs Limit Detention of Immigrants." *New York Times,* April
19, 2014. https://www.nytimes.com/2014/04/19/us/politics/sheriffs-limit-de
tention-of-immigrants.html.

Quesada, James. "Special Issue Part II: Illegalization and Embodied Vulnerability in Health." *Social Science & Medicine* 74, no. 6 (2012): 894–96. https://doi
.org/10.1016/j.socscimed.2011.10.043.

Quesada, James, Alex Kral, Kurt C. Organista, and Paula Worby. "'As Good as
It Gets': Undocumented Latino Day Laborers Negotiating Discrimination
in San Francisco and Berkeley, California, USA." *City and Society* 26, no. 1
(2014): 29–50. https://doi.org/10.1111/ciso.12033.City.

Rapaport, Mark Hyman, Cathryn Clary, Rana Fayyad, and Jean Endicott.
"Quality-of-Life Impairment in Depressive and Anxiety Disorders." *American Journal of Psychiatry* 162, no. 6 (2005): 1171–78. https://doi.org/10.1176
/appi.ajp.162.6.1171.

"Reagan, in Radio Talk, Vows Drive against Drugs." *New York Times,* October 3,
1982. https://www.nytimes.com/1982/10/03/us/no-headline-194726.html.

Reiner, R. *The Politics of the Police.* New York: Harvester Wheatsheaf, 1992.

Reitzel, John D., Stephen K. Rice, and Alex R. Piquero. "Lines and Shadows:
Perceptions of Racial Profiling and the Hispanic Experience." *Journal of
Criminal Justice* 32, no. 6 (2004): 607–16. https://doi.org/10.1016/j.jcrimjus
.2004.08.011.

Rice, Stephen K., John D. Reitzel, and Alex R. Piquero. "Shades of Brown:
Perceptions of Racial Profiling and the Intra-ethnic Differential." *Journal of
Ethnicity in Criminal Justice* 3, nos. 1–2 (2005): 47–70. https://doi.org/10.1300
/J222v03n01.

Ritchie, Andrea J. *Invisible No More: Police Violence against Black Women and
Women of Color.* Boston: Beacon Press, 2017.

Robertson, C., and T. Williams. "As States Expand Gun Rights, the Police Object." *New York Times*, May 3, 2016.

Robert Woods Johnson. Healthy Communities. Accessed March 16, 2019. https://www.rwjf.org/en/our-focus-areas/focus-areas/healthy-communi ties.html.

Rogler, L. H., R. G. Malgady, G. Costantino, and R. Blumenthal. "What Do Culturally Sensitive Mental Health Services Mean? The Case of Hispanics." *American Psychologist* 42, no. 6 (1987): 565-70.

Rojek, Jeff, Richard Rosenfeld, and Scott Decker. "Policing Race: The Racial Stratification of Searches in Police Traffic Stops." *Criminology* 50, no. 4 (2012): 993-1024. https://doi.org/10.1111/j.1745-9125.2012.00285.x.

Romero-Daza, Nancy, Margaret Weeks, and Merrill Singer. "'Nobody Gives a Damn If I Live or Die': Violence, Drugs, and Street-Level Prostitution in Inner-City Hartford, Connecticut." *Medical Anthropology* 22, no. 3 (2003): 233-59.

Rosenberg, Mica, and R. Levinson. "Police in Trump-Supporting Towns Aid Immigration Officials in Crackdown." Reuters, April 27, 2017.

Rosmond, R. "Role of Stress in Pathogenesis of the Metabolic Syndrome." *Psychoneuroendocrinology* 30, no. 1 (2005): 1-10.

Rubel, J. "The Epidemiology of a Folk Illness: Susto in Hispanic America." *Ethnology* 3, no. 3 (1964): 268-83.

Sacchetti, M. "ICE Raids Meatpacking Plant in Rural Tennessee; 97 Immigrants Arrested." *Washington Post*, April 6, 2018.

Sanchez, Ray, and Shimon Prokupecz. "Protests after N.Y. Cop Not Indicted following Chokehold Death; Feds Reviewing Case." CNN.com, December 4, 2014. http://www.cnn.com/2014/12/03/justice/new-york-grand-jury -chokehold/index.html.

Sanders, L., R. Martinez, M. Harner, M. Harner, P. Horner, and J. Delva. "Grassroots Responsiveness to Human Rights Abuse: History of the Washtenaw Interfaith Coalition for Immigrant Rights." *Social Work* 58, no. 2 (2013): 117-25. https://doi.org/10.1093/sw/swt004.

Satinsky, Sara, Alice Hu, Jonathan Heller, and Lili Farhang. *Family Unity, Family Health: How Family-Focused Immigration Reform Will Mean Better Health for Children and Families*. Oakland, CA: Human Impact Partners, 2013.

Schmidt, Michael S., and M. Apuzzo. "South Carolina Officer Is Charged with Murder of Walter Scott." *New York Times*, April 7, 2015. https://www.ny times.com/2015/04/08/us/south-carolina-officer-is-charged-with-murder -in-black-mans-death.html.

Schueths, April, and Jodie Lawston, eds. *Living Together, Living Apart: Mixed Status Families and US Immigration Policy*. Seattle: University of Washington Press, 2015.

"Sergeant Says King Appeared to Be on Drugs." *New York Times*, March 20,

1992. https://www.nytimes.com/1992/03/20/us/sergeant-says-king-ap
peared-to-be-on-drugs.html.

Shahshahani, Azadeh N. "Time to Put an End to Racial Profiling in Georgia."
ACLU, March 23, 2010. https://www.aclu.org/blog/speakeasy/time-put
-end-racial-profiling-georgia.

Sherman, Arloc, Danilo Trisi, and Sharon Parrott. *Various Supports for Low-
Income Families Reduce Poverty and Have Long-Term Positive Effects on Families and Children.* Washington, DC: Center on Budget and Policy Priorities,
2013. https://www.cbpp.org/sites/default/files/atoms/files/7-30-13pov
.pdf.

Shoichett, Catherine. "ICE Raided a Meatpacking Plant: More Than 500 Kids
Missed School the Next Day." CNN, April 12, 2018.

Silva, Chantal da. "Trump's Border Wall Must Be Built, 380 Sheriffs Tell Congress." *Newsweek*, March 29, 2018. http://www.newsweek.com/trumps
-border-wall-must-be-built-hundreds-sheriffs-40-states-tell-congress-865
813.

Simanski, John F. *Immigration Enforcement Actions: 2013.* Annual Report. Washington, DC: Department of Homeland Security, Office of Immigration
Statistics, 2014.

Sinha, Anita. "Arbitrary Detention? The Immigration Detention Bed Quota."
Duke Journal of Constitutional Law & Public Policy 12, no. 2 (2017): 77–121.

Skolnick, Jerome H. *Justice without Trial.* New York: John Wiley & Sons, 1996.
———. "Racial Profiling—Then and Now." *Criminology & Public Policy* 6, no. 1
(2007): 65–70.

Slack, Jeremy, D. E. Martínez, Scott Whiteford, and Emily Peiffer. *In the
Shadow of the Wall: Family Separation, Immigration Enforcement, and Security.*
Tucson: Center for Latin American Studies, University of Arizona, 2013.

Slack, Jeremy, and Scott Whiteford. "Violence and Migration on the Arizona-Sonora Border." *Human Organization* 70, no. 1 (2011): 11–21.

Smith, Mark W., Paula P. Schnurr, and Robert A. Rosenheck. "Employment
Outcomes and PTSD Symptom Severity." *Mental Health Services Research* 7,
no. 2 (2005): 89–101. https://doi.org/10.1007/s11020-005-3780-2.

Stack, L. "Video Released in Terence Crutcher's Killing by Tulsa Police." *New
York Times,* September 20, 2016. https://www.nytimes.com/2016/09/20/us
/video-released-in-terence-crutchers-killing-by-tulsa-police.html.

Stanton, R. "'We Don't Enforce Immigration Law,' Says Washtenaw County
Sheriff." *Ann Arbor News*, January 30, 2017. http://www.mlive.com/news
/ann-arbor/index.ssf/2017/01/we_dont_enforce_immigration_la.html.

Stuesse, Angela, and Mathew Coleman. "Automobility, Immobility, Altermobility: Surviving and Resisting the Intensification of Immigrant Policing."
City and Society 26, no. 1 (2014): 51–72. https://doi.org/10.1111/ciso.12034.

Stumpf, J. P. "The Crimmigration Crisis: Immigrants, Crime, and Sovereign

Power." *American University Law Review* 56 (2006): 367–419. http://law.be
press.com/expresso/eps/1635/.

Sullum, J. "The Shooting of Michael Brown and the Phantom Menace of Drug-
Crazed Blacks." *Forbes*, August 21, 2014. https://www.forbes.com/sites
/jacobsullum/2014/08/21/the-shooting-of-michael-brown-and-the-phan
tom-menace-of-drug-crazed-blacks/#502e6f2c48c4.

Swaine, Jon. "Michael Brown Protests in Ferguson Met with Rubber Bullets
and Teargas." *The Guardian*, August 14, 2014. https://www.theguardian
.com/world/2014/aug/14/ferguson-police-teargas-rubber-bullets-michael
-brown.

Taft, Casey T., Laura E. Watkins, Jane Stafford, Amy E. Street, and Candice M.
Monson. "Posttraumatic Stress Disorder and Intimate Relationship Problems: A Meta-analysis." *Journal of Consulting and Clinical Psychology* 79, no. 1
(2011): 22–33. https://doi.org/10.1037/a0022196.

Terpstra, J., and D. Schaap. "Police Culture, Stress Conditions and Working
Styles." *European Journal of Criminology* 10, no. 1 (2013): 59–73. https://doi
.org/10.1177/1477370812456343.

Theodore, Nik. *Insecure Communities: Latino Perceptions of Police Involvement in
Immigration Enforcement.* Chicago: University of Illinois at Chicago, 2013.

Tonry, Michael. *Malign Neglect—Race, Crime, and Punishment in America.* New
York: Oxford University Press, 1995.

Treadwell, Nathan. "Fugitive Operations and the Fourth Amendment: Repre-
senting Immigrants Arrested in Warrantless Home Raids." *North Carolina
Law Review* 89 (2011): 507–67.

US Citizenship and Immigration Services. "U.S. Citizenship and Immigration
Services Glossary: Voluntary Departure." Accessed July 21, 2016. https://
www.uscis.gov/tools/glossary/voluntary-departure.

US Department of Justice. *Department of Justice Report regarding the Criminal
Investigation into the Shooting Death of Michael Brown by Ferguson, Missouri
Police Officer Darren Wilson.* Washington, DC: Department of Justice, 2015.
http://www.justice.gov/sites/default/files/opa/press-releases/attachments
/2015/03/04/doj_report_on_shooting_of_michael_brown_1.pdf.

US Department of Veterans Affairs. "Common Reactions after Trauma." PTSD:
National Center for PTSD, August 13, 2015. https://www.ptsd.va.gov/un
derstand/isitptsd/common_reactions.asp.

———. "PTSD in Children and Teens." PTSD: National Center for PTSD, August 13, 2015. https://www.ptsd.va.gov/public/family/ptsd-children-ado
lescents.asp.

US Immigration and Customs Enforcement. *ICE Enforcement and Removal
Operations Report: Fiscal Year 2015.* Washington, DC: Immigration and Customs Enforcement, 2014.

Vargas, E. D. "Immigration Enforcement and Mixed-Status Families: The

Effects of Risk of Deportation on Medicaid Use." *Child and Youth Services Review* 57 (2015): 83-89. https://doi.org/10.1158/2159-8290.CD-16-0307.PD-1.

Vargas, E. D., G. R. Sanchez, and M. Juárez. "Fear by Association: Perceptions of Anti-immigrant Policy and Health Outcomes." *Journal of Health Politics, Policy and Law* 42, no. 3 (2017): 459-83. https://doi.org/10.1215/03616878 -3802940.

Veklerov, K., M. Gutierrez, and J. Tucker. "Attorney General Blasts Oakland Mayor Schaaf, She Fires Back." *San Francisco Chronicle*, March 7, 2018.

"Washtenaw ID Project," 2016. www.washtenawid.com.

Watkins, D. C., and D. Gioia. *Mixed Methods Research*. New York: Oxford University Press, 2015.

Waxman, O. B. "How the U.S. Got Its Police Force." *Time*, May 18, 2017.

Webster, Denise C., and Erin C. Dunn. "Feminist Perspectives on Trauma." *Women & Therapy* 28, nos. 3-4 (2005): 63-92. https://doi.org/10.1300 /J015v28n03.

Weitzer, Ronald, and Steven A. Tuch. "Perceptions of Racial Profiling: Race, Class, and Personal Experience." *Criminology* 40, no. 2 (2002): 435-56. https://doi.org/10.1111/j.1745-9125.2002.tb00962.x.

Weller, Susan C., Roberta D. Baer, Javier Garcia de Alba Garcia, Mark Glazer, Robert Trotter, Lee Pachter, and Robert E. Klein. "Regional Variation in Latino Descriptions of Susto." *Culture, Medicine and Psychiatry* 26 (2002): 449-72. https://doi.org/10.1023/A:1021743405946.

Westley, William A. *Violence and the Police: A Sociological Study of Law, Custom, and Morality*. Cambridge, MA: MIT Press, 1970.

World Health Organization. *Global Strategy for Infant and Young Child Feeding*. Geneva, Switzerland: WHO, 2003.

Index

administration closure, 164-65
advocacy work, 32, 151-54, 186n9. *See also*
  Law Enforcement Citizens Advisory
  Board (LE-CAB); Washtenaw Interfaith
  Coalition for Immigrant Rights (WICIR)
Alejandro, 25, 37, 95, 100. *See also* Hilda
Amalia, 36, 71, 77, 117, 118
American Civil Liberties Union (ACLU),
  101, 178n32, 182n6
andar volteando, as term, 96-97, 100
Anti-Drug Abuse Act of 1986, 140
antidrug campaign, 139-44
Antonio, 18
anxiety, 76, 82, 96. *See also* embodied
  vulnerabilities; emotional impacts of
  arrests and deportations; isolation
Arpaio, Joe, 101-2
Arturo: arrest of, 30-31, 46, 47-50, 101,
  180n24; on children's trauma from
  arrest, 83; description of, 25, 46-47, 165;
  detention of, 85-86, 87, 165-66; family
  and background of, 25-26, 95; on police
  request for identification, 62-63; on voluntary departure, 178n32. *See also* Hilda
author's background and identity, ix-x,
  12-16, 64, 92, 129, 182n20

B&E incidents, 119-21, 185n8
bank accounts, 33
Bates, Robert, 123, 142
bias policing. *See* ethno-racial profiling
birthright citizenship, 14, 20, 25, 37, 67.
  See also citizenship
Black community members: deaths from
  police violence of, 10-11, 123-27, 133-37,
  142-43, 149, 156-58, 185n77; history of
  slavery and, 132-33; and Latino unity
  against police violence, 156-60; police
  morality on, 124, 127-31, 135-37. *See also*
  ethno-racial profiling; racism

Black Lives Matter, 10-11, 126-27, 156-58.
  See also racism
Bland, Sandra, 126, 149
Boehm, Deborah, 13
bond payments and process, 85-86,
  113-14, 178n33
border crossings, 4, 17, 160, 166
breaking and entering, 119-21, 185n8
breastfeeding, 73-75, 78-80, 111, 177n17.
  See also food assistance and support
  services; hunger
Brown, Michael, 133-34, 135, 136, 143, 156,
  185n83
Bush administration, 142

car insurance, access to, 33, 53-59. *See
  also* vehicle abandonment; vehicle
  impoundment
Carlitos: deportation fear of, 83; effects of
  raid on, 19, 111; family and background
  of, 18, 20, 29, 34, 35, 71, 167; home life
  of, 168. *See also* Guadalupe
Casa Latina, 32
Castile, Philando, 137, 142
childcare, 3, 21-22, 88, 152, 166
children of immigrants: breastfeeding
  and *leche* for, 73-75, 78-80, 111, 177n17;
  effects of detention on, 83, 87; effects
  of raids on, 19, 78-85, 111, 151, 160;
  established lives of, 25, 37, 95, 100; food
  and health care access for, 108-11, 117,
  119-20, 152, 181n39; as witness to raid,
  18, 68-71. *See also* family separation; *and
  specific children's names*
citizenship: by birthright, 14, 20, 25,
  37, 67; privileges of, 14-15, 16, 64, 92,
  158-59; racialized scholarship on, 102-3.
  See also visas
cocaine, 32, 140, 143
coercion: effectiveness of, 94; evidence of,